ENGLISH network 2

Gaynor Ramsey
mit
Dieter Kranz und Donald Porsché

Langenscheidt-Longman
ENGLISH LANGUAGE TEACHING

English Network 2

Autoren:
Gaynor Ramsey (Unitteil)
mit
Dr. Dieter Kranz (Grammatikanhang, Homestudy)
Dr. Donald Porsché (Homestudy)
sowie
Prof. Dr. Jürgen Beneke (Andere Länder, andere Sitten)
Michael Rutman (Stories)

Beratende Mitwirkung:
Dr. Dieter Kranz, Silvia Stephan

Projektteam:
Prof. Dr. Jürgen Beneke, Consultant für betrieblichen Fremdsprachenunterricht und Unternehmenskommunikation, Hildesheim
Ingrid Boczkowski, Fachbereichsleiterin, Völklingen
Michele Charlton, Kursleiterin, Genf
Carolyn Kilday Wittmann, Kursleiterin und Lehrbeauftragte, München
Dr. Dieter Kranz, Kursleiter und Akademischer Direktor, Münster
Gerry Montague, Volkshochschulleiter, Burghausen
Dr. Donald Porsché, Programmbereichsleiter, Frankfurt
Gaynor Ramsey, Autorin, Kursleiterin und Lehrerfortbildnerin, Zürich
Michael Rutman, Landesbeauftragter, Zürich
Silvia Stephan, Kursleiterin und Lehrerfortbildnerin, Offenburg

Verlagsredaktion:
John Stevens, Projektleiter;
Doris Michels, Redakteurin

Design:
Sylvia Tate

Illustrationen:
John Fraser
Chris Ryley

Graphik und Layout:
Jürgen Bartz
Frank Fischer

Umschlag:
Zero Grafik & Design GmbH

Umschlagphoto:
Innenstadt von Chester, Cheshire, mit den bekannten Fachwerkhäusern.

Lehrwerkskomponenten:	
Kursbuch	50 398
Textcassetten (2)	57 566
Text-CDs (2)	57 521
Lernercassette 1	57 567
Lernercassette 2	57 568
Lerner-CDs (3)	57 525
Break	50 410
Lehrerhandreichungen	50 399
Einstufungstest	50 392
Lehrwerksbegleitend:	
Network Grammar	50 412
Grammar Workbook 1	50 413

Der Innenteil dieses Buches wurde auf chlorfrei gebleichtem Papier gedruckt.

1. Auflage 1992

Druck: Freiburger Graphische Betriebe, Freiburg i. Br.
ISBN 3-526-50398-2

12 13 14 / 03 02 01

Übrigens: Wenn Sie in den Sommerferien Ihre Kenntnisse festigen möchten, können Sie mit *English Network 2 Break* auf unterhaltsame Weise Grammatik, Wortschatz und Redewendungen aus dem Kursbuch wiederholen. Damit sind Sie für das neue Semester bestens vorbereitet!

Wegweiser

Viele von Ihnen haben sicher schon mit *English Network 1* gearbeitet und kennen daher den Aufbau des Buches. *English Network 2* folgt insgesamt diesem Muster. Doch auch diejenigen von Ihnen, die erst jetzt mit *English Network* beginnen, werden sich mit Hilfe der folgenden Hinweise bestimmt schnell im Buch zurechtfinden. Weitere Informationen ‚speziell für Quereinsteiger' finden Sie in Lerntip 1, auf Seite 69 des *Homestudy*-Teils.

Für wen ist das Buch gedacht?

English Network 2 ist die Fortführung von *English Network 1* und wendet sich an Erwachsene, die bereits über Grundkenntnisse des Englischen verfügen.

Was lerne ich?

In diesem Buch lernen Sie verschiedene Personen aus englischsprachigen Ländern kennen. Sie erleben, wie diese Personen über Hobbies, Urlaub und Freizeit erzählen, sich auf eine Stellenanzeige bewerben und das Vorstellungsgespräch führen, Verabredungen am Telefon treffen, über Gesundheit und Zuhause sprechen, Einkäufe machen und über ihre Pläne für die Zukunft berichten. So lernen Sie die Redewendungen, die Sie benötigen, um über sich selbst, Ihre Arbeit, Interessen und Pläne zu sprechen.
English Network 2 baut auf dem Kenntnisstand von *English Network 1* auf und erweitert diesen. Am Ende der ersten beiden Bände von *English Network* kennen Sie bereits ca. 1000 englische Wörter und verfügen über ausreichende Kenntnisse, die es Ihnen ermöglichen, sich in verschiedenen Alltagssituationen mit Englisch sprechenden Menschen unterhalten zu können.

Wie lerne ich?

Mit *English Network 2* lernen Sie nicht allein, sondern in einer Gruppe mit anderen Kursteilnehmerinnen und -teilnehmern. Im Unterricht hören Sie die Textcassetten (= ■), üben das Sprechen, lesen Dialoge und Texte und schreiben Sätze oder kurze Texte über sich auf. Sie arbeiten mal alle zusammen, mal alleine, mal mit einem anderen Kursmitglied oder einer kleinen Gruppe von Kursmitgliedern zusammen. Ihre Kursleiterin / Ihr Kursleiter steht Ihnen mit Rat und Tat zur Seite. Mit Hilfe der Lernercassetten oder Lerner-CDs (= □) und dem *Homestudy*-Teil können Sie Ihre fremdsprachlichen Fertigkeiten auch alleine vertiefen. Außerdem finden Sie im *Homestudy*-Teil zu jeder Unit eine Seite mit Lerntips, die Ihnen helfen, besser und schneller zu lernen. Anhand der *Test yourself*-Seiten können Sie in regelmäßigen Abständen Ihre Fortschritte und Ihren Lernerfolg selbst überprüfen.

Wie ist das Buch aufgebaut?

Das Buch besteht aus 6 Units, d.h. Lerneinheiten, die verschiedene Themenschwerpunkte haben. Jede Unit ist in drei Steps unterteilt. Im ersten Step einer Unit steht das Sprechen im Vordergrund. Sie erleben dort, wie sich Briten und Amerikaner in verschiedenen Situationen sprachlich verhalten, und üben selbst in Gesprächen mit anderen Kursmitgliedern diese Redewendungen ein. Den Schwerpunkt des zweiten Steps bildet die Grammatik. Hier werden Ihnen systematisch die wesentlichen Grammatikstrukturen vermittelt, die Sie mit Hilfe von lebendigen Aktivitäten einüben. Im dritten Step schließlich hören, lesen, sprechen und schreiben Sie über das Unit-Thema und erfahren Interessantes über verschiedene englischsprachige Länder der Welt. In der Sektion *Panorama* und den *English Gazettes* lesen Sie Texte, in denen bewußt Wörter verwendet werden, die Sie eventuell noch nicht kennen. Lassen Sie sich davon nicht abschrecken. Sie werden erstaunt sein, wieviel Sie bereits aus dem Zusammenhang erschließen können und verstehen.

Die Units bearbeiten Sie mit Ihrer Kursleiterin / Ihrem Kursleiter. Die *Homestudy*-Seiten (Sie erkennen sie an dem blauen Streifen am Rand) mit zusätzlichen Übungen sind für die Nacharbeit zu Hause gedacht. Ausführliche Informationen zum *Homestudy*-Teil finden Sie auf Seite 64.

Im übrigen Anhang des Buches finden Sie Informationen, die Ihnen beim Lernen helfen. Unter der Rubrik *Andere Länder, andere Sitten* erhalten Sie nützliche Tips und Hintergrundinformationen über das Leben in englischsprachigen Ländern. Eine Zusammenstellung der gesamten Grammatik, die in diesem Band auftritt, finden Sie in der Sektion *Grammar*. Auf diese Sektion wird in den Grammatikkästen in Step 2 jeder Unit verwiesen (☞ G ...). Dem Wortschatzlernen und -nachschlagen dienen *Vocabulary* und *Dictionary*, die den gesamten Wortschatz des Buches mit Beispielen und deutscher Übersetzung auflisten. Das *Dictionary* enthält darüber hinaus auch noch die wichtigen Wörter aus *English Network 1*. Neben anderen weiteren Lernhilfen finden Sie außerdem einen *Leitfaden Aussprache* und eine Übersicht der *Übungsanweisungen* zum schnellen Nachschlagen.

Viel Spaß und viel Erfolg beim Lernen
wünschen Ihnen

Autorenteam und Verlag

English around the world

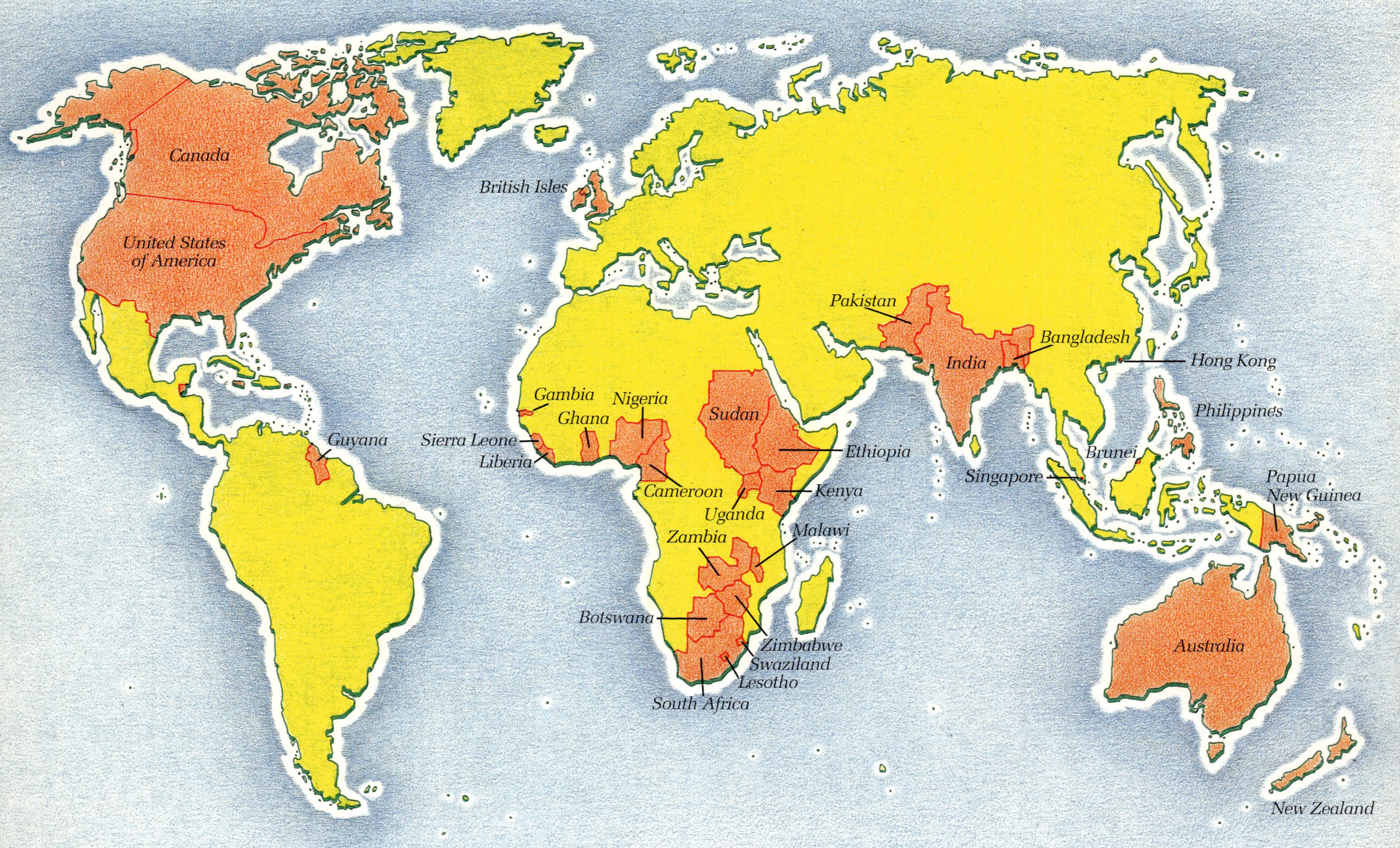

Inhalt

Inhalt

Inhalt

Inhalt

Anhang Unitteil

Anhang Homestudy

Anhang Grammatik und Wortschatz

Texte, Übungen und Lieder mit diesem Symbol finden Sie auf den Textcassetten.

Texte, Übungen und Lieder mit diesem Symbol finden Sie auf den Lernercassetten und den Lerner-CDs.

Unit 1

Free time

When do you have free time?

- [ ] mornings
- [ ] afternoons
- [x] evenings
- [x] weekends
- [ ] irregular times
- [ ] not very often
- [ ] never!

What do you sometimes do in your free time?

STEP 1 *Language in use*

1 A letter from Greece

Here is part of a letter from Sue to her friend Marge. Sue lived in a big city in England for 55 years, and then last year she and her husband sold their house and car and went to live on a Greek island.

We're very happy here on our island. Both John and I work part-time, so we have more free time now. We've both got new hobbies. My hobby is my camera - I enjoy taking photos of the sea and the small villages on the island (the photo is of our village). John took up cooking when we arrived here. He likes cooking Greek food (and I enjoy eating it). Have you ever been to Greece? Would you and the children like to come and visit us next summer? Our house is a bit small, but I'm sure it'll be big enough for us all in the good summer weather.

☞ *Andere Länder, andere Sitten (S. 59)*

1a Vocabulary

- Write in words from Sue's letter:

1 Sue is happy, and John is happy, too. They ...both... like Greece.

2 They don't work every day. They work ...part-time... .

3 Taking photos isn't Sue's job. It's her ...hobby... .

4 John's a good cook. Sue ...enjoys... eating his dinners.

- Find the words in the letter which mean:

5  ...Island...

6  ...camera...

7 time when you don't work ...evening...

8 to start something new ...take up...

1b Comprehension

Listen. Are the sentences about Sue and John true (T) or false (F)? If the text doesn't tell you, write a question mark (?).

1 ...... 2 ...... 3 ...... 4 ...... 5 ...... 6 ...... 7 ...... 8 ......

1c And now you!

What do you enjoy / like / don't like doing?

I love I enjoy I like I don't like I hate	watching going to walking cooking driving	films / football / ... museums / art galleries /... in big cities / in the country /... ...

Folgt *love, enjoy, like* und *hate* ein weiteres Verb, so wird an dieses oft die Endung *-ing* angehängt.

1d How to say it: Invitations

Practise the intonation first.

Would you like to come and visit us next summer?
Can you come and visit us next summer? We'd love to see you.
Why don't you come and visit us next summer?

And here are two possible reactions:

Thanks very much, I'd love to come.
I'd love to, but I'm afraid I can't. (I ...)

Now invite someone in your class to

- come for a drink with you after the lesson.
- come to the cinema with you one day next week.

2 Dialogue: Holiday plans

(M = Marge, TA = travel agent)

M: We've got a friend on the island of Tinos. We'd like to have a week there and a week in a hotel on a bigger island.
TA: Well, why don't you go to Corfu? It's bigger than Tinos. Have you ever been there?
M: No, we've never been to Greece at all.
TA: Look, here's our Greece brochure. And you can see all our Corfu hotels here on page 38. For example, there's the Hotel Paradise. That's very good.
M: What! 620 rooms! We'd prefer a smaller hotel.
TA: Well, there's the Hotel Apollo Beach. That's smaller than the Paradise, but the Paradise is cheaper.
M: Oh dear, I don't know.
TA: Why don't you take your time and read our brochure at home?
M: Yes, that's a good idea. Thanks.

2a Comprehension

What do you know about Tinos? Corfu? The Hotel Paradise? The Hotel Apollo Beach?

2b With your partner!

Before you start this activity, say these numbers:

100	154	253	398	631	754
103	168	300	578	738	999

Partner A, look at this page. B, please look at page 56. Partner A. You want to find out the missing information about these other hotels on the island of Corfu. Ask B questions like this:

How many ...? *How much is ...?*
How far is ...?

Name of hotel	Lido	Palace	Beach
Number of rooms	154	398	300
Km from the airport	14 km	25 km	28 km
Km from the town centre	300m	12km	15
Double room for 2 weeks + flight	£631 per person	£754 per person	£738
Extra cost of a single room	£84	£84	£168

2c How to say it: Making suggestions

Practise the intonation first.

Why don't you ask your friends about Corfu?
Why don't we go there for a week?
Shall we go by car this time?
Let's go to Spain for a month.

Make holiday suggestions with a partner. Here are some possible reactions:

Oh yes, that's a good idea.
Oh yes, let's.
Well, I'd prefer to ...
I don't really want to ...

Before you go on ...

Most people take these eight things on a summer holiday. Match the words to the pictures.

☐ toothbrush ☐ swimming costume ☐ towel
☐ toothpaste ☐ suntan cream ☐ comb
☐ sunglasses ☐ beach shoes

Listen and check your answers. Then repeat the words.
Speaking practice. Listen and do the exercises on the cassette.

STEP 2 *Grammar in action*

Starter: A holiday by the sea

Sit in a circle if possible. You all had a holiday by the sea last summer. What did you take with you?

If your class is too big and the sentence gets too long, make two groups.

1 Grammar: Comparatives and superlatives

Hotel A is	Hotel B is	Hotel C is
near.	**nearer than** Hotel A.	**the nearest.**
big.	**bigger than** Hotel A.	**the biggest.**
nice.	**nicer than** Hotel A.	**the nicest.**
sunny.	**sunnier than** Hotel A.	**the sunniest.**
modern.	**more modern than** Hotel A.	**the most modern.**
expensive.	**more expensive than** Hotel A.	**the most expensive.**
good.	**better than** Hotel A.	**the best.**
bad.	**worse than** Hotel A.	**the worst.**

Hotel A isn't **as big as** Hotel B.
Hotel B isn't **as expensive as** Hotel C.
Hotel C isn't **as far as** Hotel A.

Im Englischen werden kurze Eigenschaftswörter (mit einer Silbe) sowie zweisilbige Wörter, die auf *-y* enden, gesteigert, indem man *-er* oder *-est* an das Wort anhängt. (Achtung: *y* wird dann zu *i*.) Andere Wörter mit zwei und Wörter mit mehr Silben werden mit *more* und *most* gesteigert. *Good* und *bad* haben unregelmäßige Steigerungsformen, die Sie lernen müssen: *good – better than – the best, bad – worse than – the worst.* ☞ G 1

1a Write some sentences.

Write six sentences about the hotels in the grammar table above. Three of your sentences should be true, and three should be false (in mixed order).

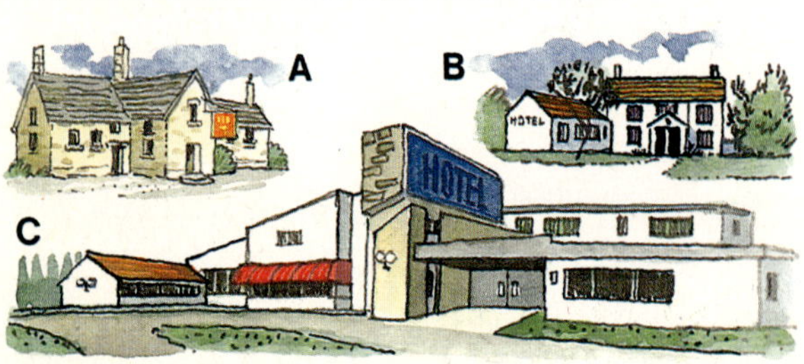

Hotel C is more modern than A. (true)
Hotel B isn't as expensive as A. (false)

Give your sentences to another student, he/she can sort them into true and false.

1b Ask a partner.

Match the two halves of these questions and then ask them to a partner.

1 Which is the nicest	☐ of the week?
2 Who is the best student	☐ in New Zealand?
3 Which is the most expensive	☐ person that you know?
4 Which is the sunniest month	☐ country in the world?
5 How far is the nearest	☐ sport on television?
6 Who is the oldest	☐ month of the year?
7 Which is the worst day	☐ in your class?
8 Which is the most interesting	☐ restaurant from here?

Begin your answers like this: *I think ...*

2 Grammar: The present perfect

Have you ever **been** to London?	Yes, I **have**.	No, I **haven't**.
Has he/she ever **been** to Paris?	Yes, he/she **has**.	No, he/she **hasn't**.
Have they ever **been** to Rome?	Yes, they **have**.	No, they **haven't**.
Have you ever **played** golf?	Yes, I **have**.	No, I **haven't**.
Has he/she ever **worked** there?	Yes, he/she **has**.	No, he/she **hasn't**.
Have they ever **lived** here?	Yes, they **have**.	No, they **haven't**.

Die vollendete Gegenwart wird mit dem Hilfsverb *have* und dem Partizip Perfekt (= Mittelwort der Vergangenheit) gebildet. Oft ist das Partizip Perfekt mit der Vergangenheitsform gleich: *play – played – have played*. Aber es gibt auch unregelmäßige Formen, z.B. *be – was/were – have been*. Eine Liste mit diesen Wörtern finden Sie im Grammatikanhang. ☞ G 7, G 16

2a Ask a partner.

Look at this dialogue.

Have you ever been to Paris?
No, I haven't.
Have you ever been to Rome?
Yes, I have.
When did you go there?
About three years ago.

Now ask your partner questions about these places.

	no	yes	when
America	X		
Spain		X	
Heidelberg		X	
India	X		
...			

Now report one negative and one positive answer (if possible) to the class.

Karin has never been to New York, but she has been to Hamburg. She went there about three years ago.

2b Have you ever ...?

You know the participle *been* – here are some more. Which verbs do they come from?

1 bought	3 drunk	5 met	7 seen
2 driven	4 eaten	6 read	

And you know that some participles are the same as the past. Here are some examples: *lived, travelled, worked, played, walked, watched.*

Now ask the other students in your class some questions. Use the verbs above.

Have you ever driven a French car?
Have you ever met a film star?
Have you ever worked in an office?

If you get a positive answer, ask a second question:

When did you ...? Where did you ...? What ...? Who ...?

Have you ever driven a French car?
Yes, I have.
Where did you drive it?
In the south of France.

Before you go on ...

Match these weather words to the pictures.

- ☐ it's sunny
- ☐ it's raining
- ☐ it's hot
- ☐ it's snowing
- ☐ it's windy
- ☐ it's cloudy
- ☐ it's cold
- ☐ it's foggy

Listen and check your answers. Then repeat the expressions.
Speaking practice. Listen and do the exercises on the cassette.

STEP 3 *Language and life*

Starter: The weather

Which three words do you associate with *sun*, *rain* and *snow*? Write them in the blue circles.

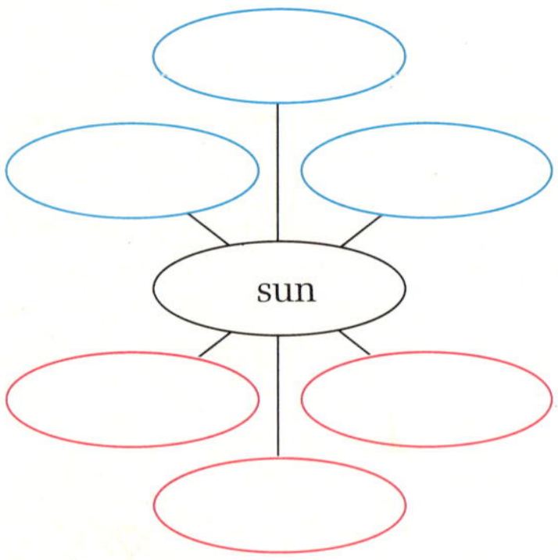

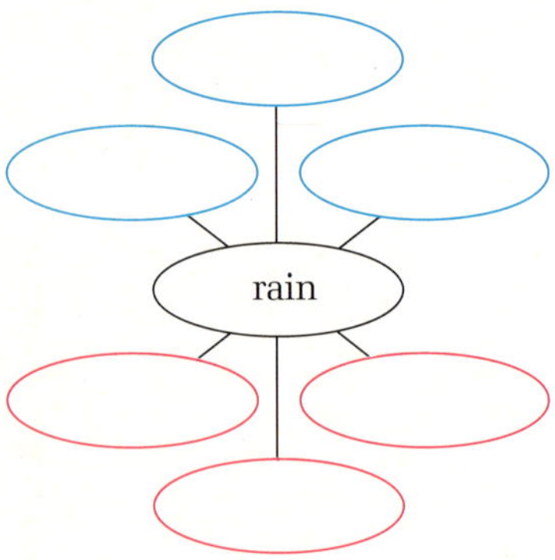

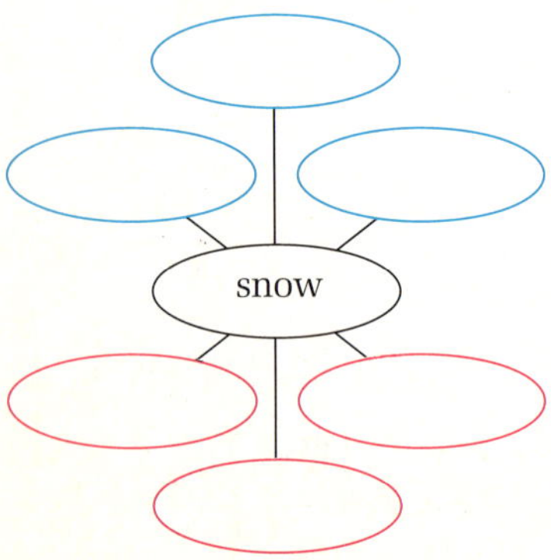

When you've finished, tell another student your words. You can fill your red circles with other words from other students.

☞ *Andere Länder, andere Sitten (S. 59)*

1 A holiday brochure

Do you remember Marge? She went to the travel agent's in Step 1. She wanted to get some information about holidays in Greece. This is what she saw on the last page of the brochure:

This brochure gives you a lot of information about holidays in Greece. Now we'd like some information from you ... please! You can win a holiday for two in Greece!

Our competition:
You did a competition in a newspaper, and you won the first prize.
CONGRATULATIONS!
Your prize is a holiday next June, a holiday in Waizoona. Waizoona? Where's that? You've never heard the name Waizoona before. You would like to know more about Waizoona before you go there. What ten questions would you like to ask?

Why is the travel agent interested in these ten questions?

1a Personal dictionary

You want to write ten questions and to send them to the travel company. (Does the page from the brochure give you any ideas?) What words do you need? You can start your questions like this:

Is/Are there ...? Can ...? Where/How/What etc ...?

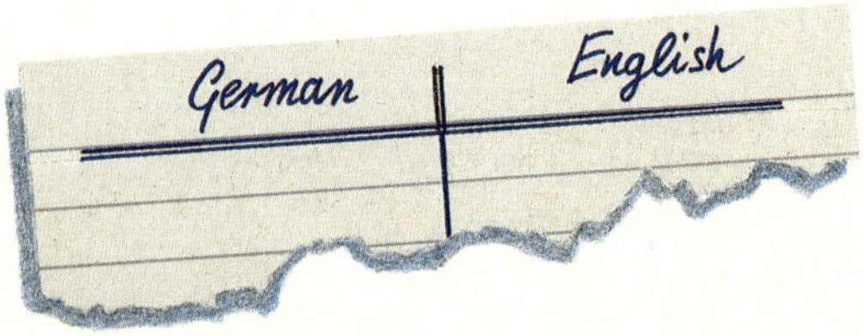

Now write your ten questions.

Work in a group with two other people and compare your questions. How many different questions have you got in your group?

1b A five-minute conversation!

Work in groups of three or four. Tell the others in your group about a past holiday. Tell them:

- where you went
- how you travelled there
- how long you stayed there
- what you saw there
- if the weather was good or bad
- ...

Then ask the others if they've ever been to this place.

Panorama

EVENING COURSES

Marge works in a public library. You can go there and get information about evening courses. Here are some of the courses on offer. Match the sections with the course descriptions.

☐ Art

☐ Commercial and Business Studies

☐ Do-It Yourself

☐ General Education

☐ Modern Languages

☐ Sports

1 Russian Survival Course
A holiday in Russia? A business trip? Would you like to get around Moscow without a guide? Would you like to order a meal without a translator? Then our survival course is for you!
6 weeks/£15.

2 You Too Can Paint!
A beginner's course in painting and drawing for those who think they haven't got any talent.
15 weeks/£38.

3 Get Fit – Stay Well
An enjoyable lively class with various exercise techniques. We work on flexibility, stamina and muscle tone.
20 weeks/£50.

4 Clock Repairing – Beginners
A practical course on how to repair clocks – how to diagnose faults and repair them.
20 weeks/£50.

5 Shorthand (Teeline)
Teeline is a modern form of shorthand, for those who want to return to work in the near future.
34 weeks/£84.

6 Ten English Cathedral Cities
Cathedral Cities are some of the loveliest places to visit in England. The ten will include York, Lincoln and Canterbury.
20 weeks/£50.

Listen to the three evening school students. Which of the six evening courses do they go to?

1 ....

2 ....

3 ....

Would you like to do one of these six courses?
What other course or courses would you like to do apart from your English course?
What would you like to learn?
Where can you do free time courses in or near your home?

UNIT 1 *Revision activities*

Starter: What will you take with you?

Sit in a circle. You have all got a holiday next month. Say what you'll take with you. Follow the alphabet: a, b, c ..., and write down all the things.

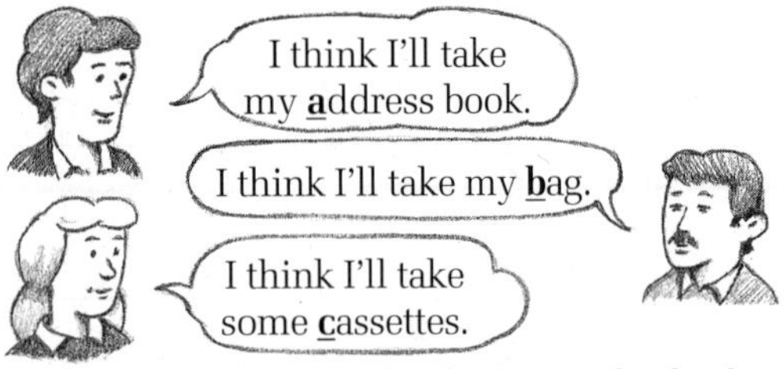

If you come to a letter and nobody can think of a word, write the letter down. When you get to the end of the alphabet, see if your teacher can help you. Don't be too serious!

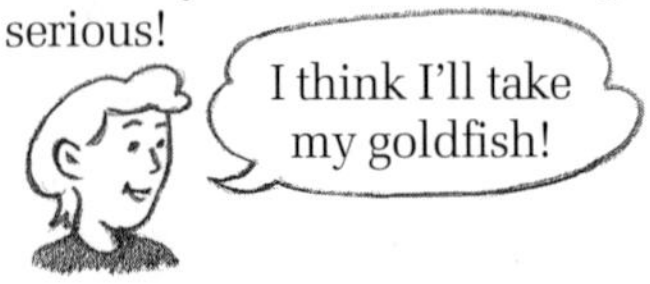

1 Please complete these invitations.

Complete these three invitations with: *can, don't, like to, why, would, you, you, you.*

1 .... come to dinner on Friday?

2 .... come to dinner on Friday?

3 .... come to dinner on Friday?

Then write three possible but different reactions.

Now invite a partner to dinner on Friday. Then invite him/her to something different.

2 With your partner!

Partner A, look at this page. B, please look at page 56. Partner A. Read this list of words to B. Then listen to B's list. Match B's words with your list here.

Munich	New York
Fiat	....
Greece	....
The Rhine	....
English	....

Now work *with* your partner. Write two sentences and compare the things. The two sentences must begin with different words:

Munich is smaller than New York.
New York is more international than Munich.

If you're not very sure, then start with: *We think ... .*

3 Have you ever ...?

Choose three of these topics and write a question with *Have you ever ...?*

another country — Have you ever been to America?

a person — Have you ever met a famous film star?

Ask about:

- another country
- a place in your country
- ways of travelling
- a colour
- a drink
- a person
- a language
- a sport

Now work with the class as one group. One student should ask his/her questions to the others until someone answers with *Yes, I have.*

Have you ever learned Spanish?

Yes, I have.

Then the other students can ask for more information. Don't forget that you change to the past now!

Did you learn it in Spain?	No, I didn't.
Where did you learn it?	I did a VHS course.
How many people were there in your class?	About ten.
Was your teacher Spanish?	No, she wasn't.
Did you like your book?	Yes, I did.
...	

4 Wordfields

Put these words in five word groups with four words in each group. Give each group a name. Here's one group to give you a start.

Places where you can have a holiday:

in the mountains
on an island
in the country
by the sea

in the country	reading	cooking
towel	watching films	beach shoes
in the mountains	playing tennis	foggy
riding a bicycle	on an island	snow
learning English	walking	suntan cream
by the sea	sunny	sunglasses
swimming	rain	

O━ page 62

Unit 2

Work

What's your work situation at the moment?

- [x] I've got a job outside my home.
- [ ] I work at home for my family.
- [ ] I haven't got a job at the moment.
- [ ] I'm a student.
- [ ] I'm an apprentice.
- [ ] I'm retired.

Which of the jobs in the pictures are good?
Which of these jobs would you <u>not</u> like?

STEP 1 *Language in use*

1 A new job

Read the advertisement in the newspaper.

Dialogue: More information, please.

Angela Read saw the advert and decided to telephone Ms Bagley.

(T=telephonist, AR=Angela Read)

T: Mega Magazines, good morning. Can I help you?
AR: Good morning. Can I speak to Christine Bagley, please?
T: Hold on, please – I'll put you through. ...
I'm afraid Ms Bagley's busy at the moment.
Can I give her a message?
AR: Well, I wanted to ask about your ad. The one in the newspaper yesterday.
T: Oh yes. Shall I ask her to call you back?
AR: No. I won't be at home very much today.
I'll try again this afternoon.
T: Yes, okay. But please don't ring before three-thirty. (3)
She'll be out in the early afternoon. (3)
AR: Oh, okay. I'll phone between four and half past.
T: Yes, that's fine. Thank you for calling. Goodbye.
AR: Goodbye.

☞ *Andere Länder, andere Sitten (S. 59)*

1a Vocabulary

- What are the two shorter forms of the word *advertisement*? ....ad.... ....advert....
- Which three other words can you use for *telephone* here?

I'll try to [telephone] you this afternoon.

....call.... ....phone.... ....speak / ring.... to you this afternoon

- Find the words in the dialogue which mean:

1 just a moment 2 I'm sorry (3) after lunch

1b Comprehension

Are these sentences correct? If they aren't, please correct them.

1 The job in the advert is a nine-to-five job.
2 Angela saw the ad in yesterday's newspaper. ✓
3 Christine Bagley can't talk to Angela now. ✓
4 Angela will be at home, near her telephone, all afternoon.
5 Ms Bagley will be there from four o'clock.

1c English on the telephone

The telephonist used these seven expressions in the conversation with Angela. In which order did he say them? Number them 1-7.

[4] I'm afraid she's busy at the moment.
[1] Good morning. Can I help you?
[6] Shall I ask her to call you back?
[7] Thank you for calling.
[5] Can I give her a message?
[3] I'll put you through.
[2] Hold on, please.

1d With your partner!

Partner A, look at this page. B, please look at page 56. Partner A. Write a short telephone conversation with your partner. You are a telephonist in a large company. You must use all the seven expressions in 1c.

A:	give company name / say 'Good ...' / offer to help	→ B:	...
A:	Hold ... / ... put through / busy	→ B:	...
A:	don't know ... / message?	→ B:	...
A:	call back after four?	→ B:	...
A:	fine / thank ...	→ B:	...

2 Dialogue: An interview

Angela spoke to Christine Bagley in the afternoon and arranged an interview for the next morning. She's with her now in her office.

(CB=Christine Bagley, AR=Angela Read)

CB: What did you do when you left school?
AR: I trained as a teacher. Then I worked as an English teacher for four years.
CB: Have you ever done this sort of work before?
AR: Yes, I used to work for a small newspaper. That was about twelve years ago.
CB: Why did you leave that job?
AR: I left when I had my first child.
CB: Oh, I see.
AR: My children are eleven and ten now, and I'd like to have a job again.
CB: Mm. Can you use a computer?
AR: Yes. Well, I'm on a computer course now. And we've got a computer at home, so I can usually learn the new things quickly.
CB: Good. I might have some more questions later.

2a Comprehension

Write down five sentences (three true, two false) about Angela's past.

Exchange papers with another student and write T (true) or F (false) next to his/her sentences.

2b How to say it: Expressing possibility

Practise the intonation first.

> I might have some more questions later.
> I may have some more questions later.
> Perhaps I'll have some more questions later.
> I'll probably have some more questions later.

Mit *perhaps I'll*, *I might* und *I may* drücken Sie eine Möglichkeit aus. Der Grad der Möglichkeit ist bei allen drei Wendungen gleich. *I'll probably* hingegen drückt eine größere Wahrscheinlichkeit aus.

- And now you. Practise these questions and answers with a partner.

What do you think the weather will be like at the weekend?

☐ be a bit colder ☐ be sunny
☐ rain ☐ ...

Where do you want to go for your next holiday?

☐ go to Greece ☐ do a course in England
☐ stay at home ☐ ...

Where will you be at ten o'clock on Saturday evening?

☐ be in bed ☐ be at a friend's house
☐ be at the cinema ☐ ...

What do you think you'll do next weekend?

Now ask your teacher.

Before you go on ...

Here are eight jobs. Match the words to the pictures.

☐ doctor ☐ policeman
☐ waitress ☐ engineer
☐ shop assistant ☐ bank clerk
☐ farm worker ☐ taxi driver

Listen and check your answers. Then repeat the words.
Speaking practice. Listen and do the exercises on the cassette.

STEP 2 *Grammar in action*

Starter: Jobs, jobs, jobs

Choose six of the jobs from the list at the end of the last step. What might those people say in their jobs? Work in pairs and write down one sentence for each person.

Now make a group of four with two other students and compare your sentences.

1 Grammar: Used to ...

I He/She We They	**used to**	learn French (but I'm in an English course now). work for IHH (but he/she works for a bank now). live in Munich (but we live in Zurich now). play tennis (but they play golf now).
Where **did** you **use to** work? Where **did** he/she **use to** live?		I **didn't use to** work near here. He/She **didn't use to** live in the city centre.

Used to verwenden Sie, wenn Sie ausdrücken möchten, daß Sie in der Vergangenheit etwas taten, das heute nicht mehr zutrifft. ☞ G 8

1a Write some sentences.

Write six sentences with *I used to ...* about yourself. You can write sentences like this:

When I was younger I used to ...
When I was at school I used to ...
When I was a child I used to ...

Three sentences should be true, and three false.

Now read your sentences to a partner. He/She should sort them into true and false and say:

Yes, I think you used to ... when you were younger. That's true.

or

No, I don't think you used to ... when you were at school. That's false.

or

No, I'm sure you never used to ... when you were a child. That's false.

2 Grammar: Adverbs

She's a bad singer.	She sings **badly**.	She's a good driver.	She drives **well**.
She's a quick learner.	She learns **quickly**.	She's a fast walker.	She walks **fast**.
She's a careful driver.	She drives **carefully**.	She's a hard worker.	She works **hard**.

Im Unterschied zum Deutschen haben Eigenschafts- und Umstandswörter im Englischen verschiedene Formen. Grundsätzlich wird das Umstandswort gebildet, indem man an das Eigenschaftswort *-ly* anhängt. *Good, fast* und *hard* sind Ausnahmen: das Umstandswort zu *good* ist *well; fast* und *hard* ändern sich auch als Umstandswörter nicht in ihrer Form. ☞ G 2

2a Make sentences with this information.

She used to type very slowly ***five years ago****.* ***Then*** *she did a course and so* ***now*** *she types quickly.*

five years ago	**then**	**now**
type very slowly	stop her lessons	slowly
play the piano very well	do a course	beautifully
drive very fast	get a new boss	badly
sing very badly	police stop her	hard
work very slowly	marry an Italian	quickly

3 Grammar: Imperatives

Don't phone in the morning.	**Try** after lunch.
Don't look at your book.	**Look** at these words.
Don't write.	**Listen**. ☞ G 4

3a Listen and write down the imperatives.

Write the verbs only. You'll hear three new verbs: *put*, *sit* and *smoke*.

		negative imperatives	positive imperatives
1		don't drive	....
		....	....
2		....	learn ....
		....	....
3		....	....
		....	....
4		....	....
		....	....

Listen again. Can you say the complete sentences now? Say only the sentences with the imperatives!

3b The boss!

Here are ten rules that a boss has got for his workers. Write the verbs in. Seven of his rules begin with *Don't ...*, and three of them begin with *Always ...* . You need these verbs: *arrive, come, drink, go, make, stay, smoke, take (x2), use.*

MY TEN RULES!

1 .... in the office.

2 .... the phone for personal calls.

3 .... before 8.30.

4 .... to work in jeans.

5 .... personal photocopies in the office.

6 .... more than half an hour for lunch.

7 .... to see your doctor after work.

8 .... beer or wine with your lunch.

9 .... your holidays in the school holidays.

10 .... in the office until you finish your day's work.

Would you like to work for this boss? Why? Why not? Why does he say some of these things?

Before you go on ...

You often find these things in offices. Match the words to the pictures.

☐ pen ☐ calculator
☐ pencil ☐ typewriter
☐ dictionary ☐ desk
☐ photocopier ☐ office chair

Listen and check your answers. Then repeat the words.
Speaking practice. Listen and do the exercises on the cassette.

STEP 3 *Language and life*

Starter: In the office

Look at these objects (there are thirteen) for one minute. Your teacher will tell you when the minute is over. Then close your book.

Teacher! When the minute is over, tell your students to close their books and to write down all the objects that they can remember.

1 Angela's new job

Angela Read was very happy to get the job at Mega Mags. She wrote to a friend about a month after she started there. This is part of her letter.

> I'm an office assistant at Mega Mags now. The work is really interesting, and I've got a very good boss. She's very nice and helps me a lot. She really understands the problems of a working mother (she's got two children, too). I work full-time. The working hours are normal, 38 hours a week, but they have flexi-time. I must be there from 10 to 12 and from 2 to 4 every day. I can work the other 18 hours when I want. That's very good. My salary isn't very good at the moment, but I'll earn more after my computer course, and then more again after one year with Mega Mags. I get 5 weeks' holiday a year. Oh – and they give me all their magazines (the ones that I want)!!! I think Mega Mags is a good employer, and I'm happy there. The only problem is I have to work on a computer for hours and hours (no more pens and pencils for me!) I'm sure this is bad for my eyes! How's your job?

☞ *Andere Länder, andere Sitten (S. 59)*

Which words in Angela's letter are important for describing a job? Underline them.

1a Personal dictionary

You want to describe a job (your present job, a job that you used to have or a job that you'd like to have). What words do you need?

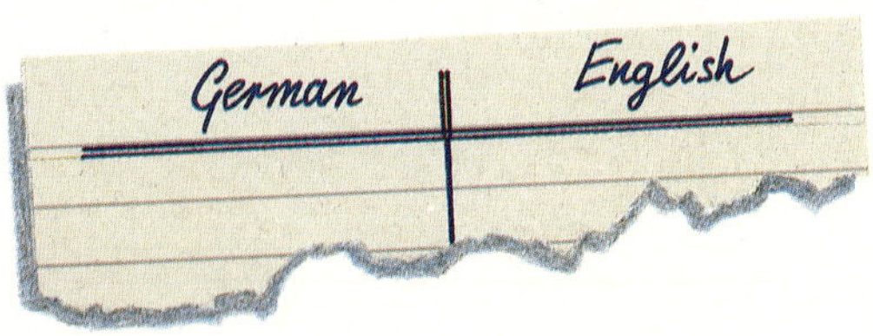

Now write a short paragraph about the job.

1b A five-minute conversation!

Work in groups of three or four. Tell the others in your group about your present job or a job that you used to have. Tell them:

- what the job is/was
- what you do/did every day
- who your employer is/was
- the good things about the job
- the bad things about the job

Answer this question: What job would you really like to have?

I'd really like to be a/an ... because ...
I'd really like to work ... because ...

2 What are their jobs?

Listen and choose the correct answers. Then match these jobs to the people:

- ☐ hotel receptionist
- ☐ taxi driver
- ☐ farm worker
- ☐ tennis teacher

a	inside	1	2	3	4	c	same place	1	2	3	4
	outside	(1)	2	3	4		different places	1	2	3	4
b	regular hours	1	2	3	4	d	other people	1	2	3	4
	irregular hours	1	2	3	4		alone	1	2	3	4

What are the good and the bad things about their jobs?

Panorama

VSO: Working in another country

Some people decide to go to other countries to work, and some go for VSO, Voluntary Service Overseas. Each year VSO sends about 600 volunteers to countries such as Bhutan, Nepal, Nigeria, Thailand and many more. They go there, usually for two years, to work in various kinds of jobs – in teaching, agriculture, technology or health, for example.

☞ *Andere Länder, andere Sitten (S. 59)*

Ann Newton's story

I went to Nigeria for VSO, 15 years ago. I was 21, and it was my first job after university. I worked as an English teacher in a secondary school in a small town called Wukari.

When I arrived in Wukari, I found the countryside very uninteresting. It was very flat, the earth was a nice red, and the people lived in tin huts – I lived in a tin hut, too. I lived with another girl volunteer – and we were the only young Europeans in the town. We had a lot of contact with Nigerians, and we made some very interesting friends.

There were some things that made life a bit more difficult than life back home. We only had electricity for four hours a day, in the evening – but you soon learn to live with a problem like that. At first I didn't like some of the food – we could only get cheese in tins, and powdered milk. We lived on tomatoes, onions, eggs, potatoes and sardines. We sometimes bought chickens in the market – but they were alive, and we had to kill them ourselves (we usually asked someone else to do it!)

I was often homesick in Nigeria and missed my family, but when I came back to Britain I had a lot of problems. I was very critical of my parents and their way of life, for example. I think I changed a lot in those two years. Looking back now, after 15 years, I really can say that it was the best and most important time of my life.

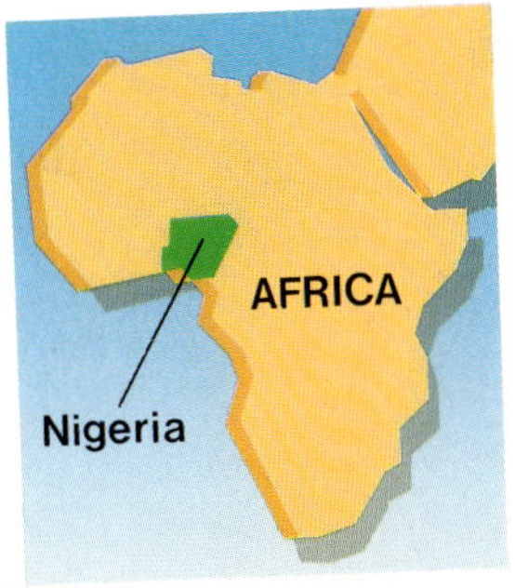

Now listen to Ann Newton's story.

Not only young people go and work abroad for VSO, people of all ages can. Would you like to do something like this?

UNIT 2 *Revision activities*

Starter: Have you ever ...?

One student asks a question with *Have you ever ...?*. The next person must answer *Yes, ...* (even if it isn't true!) and then continues with a sentence with *used to*. Then the next person asks a question, and so on.

Here are some ideas: a Rolls Royce, Japan, an Italian film, a Hilton Hotel, tennis, Californian wine, ...

1 Reactions on the phone

You might hear these things on the phone. Give two possible reactions to them.

1 Can I speak to Mr Branson, please?
2 I'm sorry, he'll be out of the office until lunchtime.
3 He can call you back at two-thirty.

2 With your partner!

Partner A, look at this page. B, please look at page 56.
Partner A. Write these verbs in the sentences:
be, cook, look, park, sit, spend.

1 Don't .... your bicycle here, ...

2 Don't .... at home all day today, ...

3 Don't .... at your books now, ...

4 Don't .... dinner today, ...

5 Don't .... all your money today, ...

6 Don't .... late, ...

You have got the first half of each sentence, and B has got the second half. Read the sentences with B and put the two halves together.

3 Please match.

Match expressions 1-9 with a-e:

1 I might ... 4 I think I'll ... 7 I don't think I'll ...
2 I'll ... 5 Perhaps I'll ... 8 I probably won't ...
3 I won't ... 6 I'll probably ... 9 I may ...

a certainly: [2]
b probably: [ ] [ ]
c possibly: [ ] [ ] [ ]
d probably not: [ ] [ ]
e certainly not: [3]

Now write five sentences (a, b, c, d and e) about next week. Choose the expression that you like best in b, c and d. Then read your five sentences to a partner.

4 Write some sentences.

Write three true and three false sentences about yourself with these words:

1 used to 3 badly 5 well
2 beautifully 4 never used to 6 slowly

Exchange papers with a partner. Which sentences are true and which are false on his/her paper? Find out more about the true things.

5 Word square

There are twelve names for jobs here, some of them with two words. Can you find them? They go across (→) or down (↓).
They start with these letters:

1 b... c... 4 f... s... 7 e... 10 w...
2 s... a... 5 d... 8 t... 11 p...
3 f... w... 6 s... 9 t... 12 w...

b	f	p	w	a	z	d	c	e	p	a	u	b
x	t	e	a	c	h	e	r	e	n	k	l	v
p	o	l	i	c	e	m	a	n	b	d	s	t
d	f	d	t	w	r	l	i	g	a	h	z	e
c	i	s	e	o	t	j	n	i	n	r	d	l
u	l	y	r	u	i	w	l	n	k	w	r	e
s	m	u	t	s	q	a	o	e	c	m	y	p
o	s	r	z	n	w	i	p	e	l	y	c	h
q	t	p	d	o	c	t	o	r	e	o	f	o
f	a	r	m	w	o	r	k	e	r	i	u	n
w	r	s	i	n	g	e	r	b	k	w	r	i
z	m	h	d	j	a	s	o	p	y	x	v	s
s	h	o	p	a	s	s	i	s	t	a	n	t

page 62

THE ENGLISH GAZETTE

Vol. 2 No. 1

Do people get enough holidays?

Has this man got a problem with his job? Or does he need a holiday?

People in some countries get a lot more holidays than people in some other countries. The Americans don't do very well at all. I saw some statistics from 1990 the other day. The average American full-time worker worked 40 hours a week, got 11 official holidays (the British call these public holidays) and 12 days paid vacation a year (the British call this holiday). This was typical for an American in the same job for five years. The British did better. They worked an average of 39 hours a week, got eight official holidays, and had 25 days paid vacation. The French did a little bit better! They worked an average of 39 hours, too. They had eight official holidays, too. But they got 25.5 days paid vacation! Half a day can make a big difference! The people who did very well were the Germans. On average, they worked 38 hours a week, got ten official holidays and 30 days of paid vacation. I think I'll leave America and I know where I'd like to live!

Facts and Figures

Free time activities

A research company asked people in Britain (all adults, no children) about their free time activities. Which activities did people like best? What do you think? Number them 1-10.

- ☐ drinking alcohol at home
- ☐ gardening
- ☐ listening to music
- ☐ playing with children
- ☐ reading books
- ☐ reading newspapers and general-interest magazines
- ☐ reading special-interest magazines
- ☐ visiting the pub
- ☐ watching television
- ☐ watching videos

Watching television was (and probably still is) a very popular free time activity. But is it really an activity?

Learners' Letters

Dear Editor,

I've often seen the words ***Mr, Mrs*** *and* ***Miss*** *that you use with a person's surname. In my English lesson we had the word* ***Ms.*** *What's this? What am I? Am I* ***Mrs, Miss or Ms?***

Yours sincerely,
LC, Innsbruck.

Dear Ms LC,

People started saying *Ms* because women often didn't like the difference between *Mrs*, for married women, and *Miss*, for single women. *Ms* doesn't tell people if you're married or single – the same as *Mr* for men.

All the best, ED.

Dear Editor,

There's something that I'd like to ask you about the present perfect: Do you always make it with the verb ***have – I've been, he's eaten, they've seen*** *... etc.? Or can you make it with be? I know you can in French.*

With my best wishes,
LK, Dusseldorf.

Dear LK,

You always make the present perfect with *have* in English – don't use *be*.

Yours sincerely, ED.

P.S. If you've got a language problem, write it down and ask your teacher when you've got time. ED.

page 62

A story

Fast Food

"Come in, come in!" the Professor said. "Oh, yes. That's right. You're here to write about my new machine."
"Yes," Tim said. "It's for our newspaper. They want a story about your work here."
"Well, as you can see," said the Professor. "It's very important. We can make food from all sorts of things. Give me that chair over there."
"Er – chair?" said Tim. "This one?"
"Yes, that's right. Now, what's your favourite food?"
"Oh, hamburger and chips," said Tim.
"One hamburger and chips," said the Professor. "That isn't a problem." He opened a door in the side of a very large machine, and a moment later the chair was inside. Tim heard something from inside the machine. The Professor opened another door in the side of the machine. "There's your hamburger," he said. "With chips."
"But – this can't be true!" said Tim.
The Professor said, "You see, we can make food from all sorts of things. Bread from toothpaste, meat from newspapers, cheese from old shoes. Just give it to me and I can make it for you."
"What about drinks?" Tim asked.

The Professor opened a door in the side of the machine.

"Beer from water, wine from water. You know, the world will have food and drink for hundreds of years!"
"My newspaper wants some photos," Tim said. "Can I take some? I'd like one or two photos of the inside of the machine. Our readers would like to know how it works."
The Professor opened the door in the side of the machine again. "You can go in," he said. "You've got enough light in there for some photos."
Tim walked in. The door clicked behind him.
"No time for a large lunch," the Professor said. "I'll just have a chicken sandwich."
And then he said, "Now, who can I invite for lunch tomorrow?".

Unit 3

Health and fitness

Do you do these things (1) every day, (2) often, (3) sometimes, (4) seldom or (5) never?

How often do you

- get some exercise (for example, jogging or swimming)? ☐
- eat too much? ☐
- feel stressed? ☐
- sit in the sun? ☐
- sit and think? ☐

Are the things in the photos good or bad for you?

STEP 1 *Language in use*

1 A letter to a doctor

Dr Day writes answers to letters in a magazine. Read both letters and underline the new words.

YOUR FAMILY DOCTOR

Dear Dr Day,
I often have terrible backache. I went to my family doctor, and he said, "There's nothing I can do. Women often have backache." I hope you can give me some help. I'm not ill, but I must have some good advice soon.
DG, Bristol

Dear DG,
If I were you, I'd change my doctor. I think you should do this immediately. Backache can be serious. I'll send you some information on chairs, shoes and beds. Perhaps you'll find an explanation there. I hope your new doctor can give you an answer to your problem – bad backache is terrible!
Dr Day

PROBLEMS WITH YOUR BACK?

Why not

☞ *Andere Länder, andere Sitten (S. 60)*

1a Vocabulary

• Find these words in the letters. Does the word *an* or the word *some* come before them?

.... advice .... explanation .... help

.... answer .... information

> *advice* (= Ratschlag), *help* (= Hilfe) und *information* (= Information) haben im Englischen keine Mehrzahlform – sie sind nicht zählbar. Deshalb wird ihnen nicht *a* oder *an* vorangestellt, sondern *some*.

• There are many different answers to the question *How are you?* Which of these words are negative and which are positive in meaning? There are four of each.

great, ill, a bit under the weather, on top of the world, fine, terrible, very well, worse and worse

I feel ☹	I feel ☺
....	....
....	....
....	....
....	....

1b Comprehension

What can you say about DG from Bristol with these words?

1 terrible
2 doctor
3 immediately
4 serious
5 explanation

1c How to say it: Giving advice

Practise the intonation first.

> If I were you, I'd change my doctor.
> I think you should do this immediately.
> Why don't you take up jogging?

• Now work in groups of four. One student should choose a problem, and the other three can give advice. Here are some ideas:

I'd like to find a new flat.

I'd like to be fit, but I'm not!

I'd like to meet some new people and make some new friends.

I'd like to speak better English.

I'd like to be very rich.

2 Dialogue: Making an appointment with the doctor

DG from Bristol took Dr Day's advice and asked a friend for her doctor's phone number. Then she phoned and made an appointment.

(R=receptionist, DG=Mrs Garrard from Bristol)

R: Good morning. Can I help you?
DG: Hello. My name's Mrs Garrard. Can I speak to Dr Smith, please?
R: I'm sorry, but he's talking to someone at the moment.
DG: Oh. Well, can I make an appointment to see him, please?
R: Yes. How about Friday, at four?
DG: Oh, Friday's not very good, I'm afraid. I'm working full-time this week, you see.
R: Well, how about next Tuesday at eleven-thirty?
DG: I'd prefer the afternoon if possible. I always work in the mornings.
R: Okay. Tuesday at three. And what's the problem?
DG: I often have terrible backache, and then I can't sleep.
R: I see. So next Tuesday, that's the 24th, at three. Is that okay?
DG: Yes, that's fine. Thank you very much. Goodbye.
R: Goodbye.

2a Comprehension

Listen. Are the sentences true (T) or false (F)? If the text doesn't tell you, write a question mark (?).

1 .... 2 .... 3 .... 4 .... 5 .... 6 .... 7 .... 8 ....

2b How to say it: Making appointments

People often use these expressions when they want to make an appointment. Find the expressions in Dialogue 2 and underline the sentences.

1 Can I speak to ...?
2 I'm sorry, ...
3 Can I make ...?
4 How about ...?
5 Friday's not very good ...
6 How about ...?
7 I'd prefer ...
8 Is that ...?
9 Yes, that's ...

Read the underlined parts of the dialogue as a mini-dialogue with a partner.

Now read it again with this information.

A	B
1 Mrs Jones	2 speaking to her husband
3 her	4 this Wednesday, 11 o'clock
5 staying with my daughter this week	6 next Wednesday, three o'clock
7 morning, tennis on Wednesday afternoons	8 good time for you
9 very good	

2c With your partner!

You are both in London. One of you is a tourist and has got a problem. The other works in London. Partner A, look at page 55. B, please look at page 57.

Before you go on ...

Here are twelve words for parts of the body. Look at the picture and number the words 1 to 12.

☐ arm ☐ finger ☐ head ☐ mouth
☐ ear ☐ foot ☐ knee ☐ nose
☐ eye ☐ hand ☐ leg ☐ shoulder

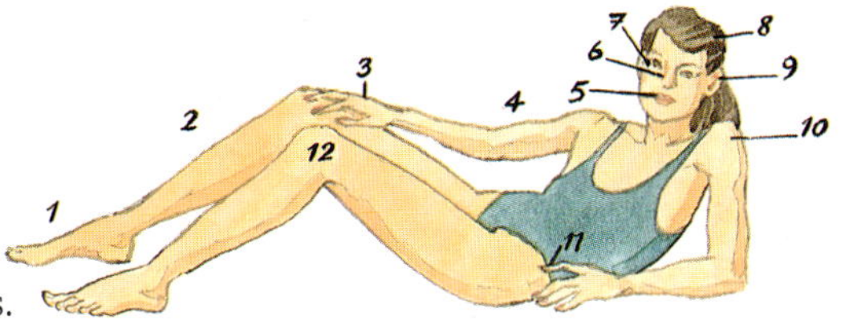

Now listen and check your answers. Then repeat the words.
Speaking practice. Listen and do the exercises on the cassette.

STEP 2 *Grammar in action*

Starter: Simon says

This is an old English game. Your teacher will start. He/She will give you instructions like this:

And all of you do what 'Simon says'.

If your teacher gives you an instruction without the words 'Simon says', then don't do it. If you do it, you're out!

After one or two minutes, one of you can take the place of your teacher and give the instructions.

1 Grammar: The present progressive

Are you **reading** a German book? What **are** you **reading**?	No, **I'm not**. **I'm reading** an English book.	**I'm not reading** a German book.
Is he/she **cooking** spaghetti? What**'s** he/she **cooking**?	No, he/she **isn't**. He**'s** / She**'s cooking** an omelette.	He/She **isn't cooking** spaghetti.
Are you **learning** Spanish? What **are** you **learning**?	No, we **aren't**. We**'re learning** English.	We **aren't learning** Spanish.
Are they **singing** a new song? What **are** they **singing**?	No, they **aren't**. They**'re singing** an old song.	They **aren't singing** a new song.

In Band 1 haben Sie die einfache Gegenwart kennengelernt. Zur Erinnerung: diese Form benutzen Sie, wenn Sie Dinge beschreiben, die regelmäßig oder gewohnheitsmäßig (*regularly, always, often sometimes*) geschehen. Sprechen Sie aber über Handlungen oder Ereignisse, die gerade im Gange oder vorübergehend sind, verwenden Sie die Verlaufsform der Gegenwart. Diese Form hat noch weitere Anwendungsmöglichkeiten, doch keine Sorge – diese lernen Sie später. ☞ G 5

1a Listen. What are the people doing?

Discuss what you hear with your partner and write your answers down.

1–4: Mrs Garrard
5–8: her husband
9–12: their children

1 She's reading a newspaper.
2 ...

What questions can you ask your teacher about the things that the people are doing?

Example: 1 Mrs Garrard's reading a newspaper.

You can ask:
Is she reading a German newspaper?
Is she reading today's newspaper?

Ask two questions for each sentence.

1b Talk about the people in these pictures.

Look at the example carefully first.

1 She usually drives a taxi in the mornings. It's half past ten now, but she isn't driving her taxi this morning. The sun's shining so she's working in the garden instead.

2 Grammar: Must, mustn't, don't have to

Doctor's orders!	Doctor's orders!	It isn't necessary.
I **must** eat more vegetables.	I **mustn't** smoke.	I **don't have to** go to hospital.
You **must** buy better shoes.	You **mustn't** sit all day.	You **don't have to** see the doctor again.

Dem deutschen Wort *müssen* entspricht im Englischen *must*. Doch Vorsicht: *mustn't* heißt nicht *muß nicht*, sondern *darf nicht*. Versuchen Sie sich zu merken: *mustn't* = darf nicht, *don't have to* = muß nicht. ☞ G 6

2a A change in your life?

People sometimes want to make a change in their lives – but not a very big change, perhaps!

What would you like to change? Write one sentence with *I must* ... and one with *I mustn't* ... .
If possible, write a second sentence with *But I don't have to* ... , too.
Read your sentences to two other people in your class.

2b You mustn't ...

Look at these signs. What mustn't people do? Where can you see these signs?

Before you go on ...

Here are eight health problems. Match the sentences to the pictures.

- ☐ I've got a headache. (Is it migraine?)
- ☐ I've got toothache. (You must go and see your dentist.)
- ☐ I've got a temperature. (Is it more than 38° C?)
- ☐ I've got a sore throat. (You mustn't speak too much today.)
- ☐ I've got backache. (Have you got a bad office chair?)
- ☐ I feel sick. (Do you think the fish in the restaurant was bad?)
- ☐ I feel tired. (Perhaps you work too much.)
- ☐ I've got a cold. (Please don't give it to me!)

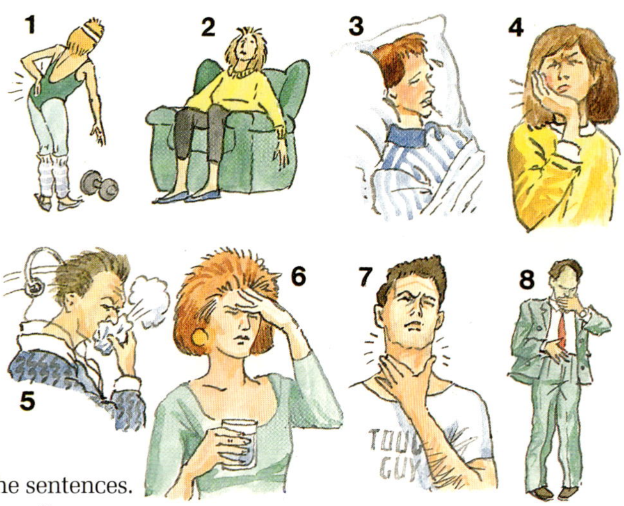

Now listen and check your answers. Then repeat the sentences.
Speaking practice. Listen and do the exercises on the cassette.

STEP 3 *Language and life*

Starter: Parts of the body and health problems

Work in groups of three or four. Fill in the word square below with ten words for parts of the body or for health problems. You can start like this if you want:

e	x	d	h	e	a	l	t	h	b

Here's your word square:

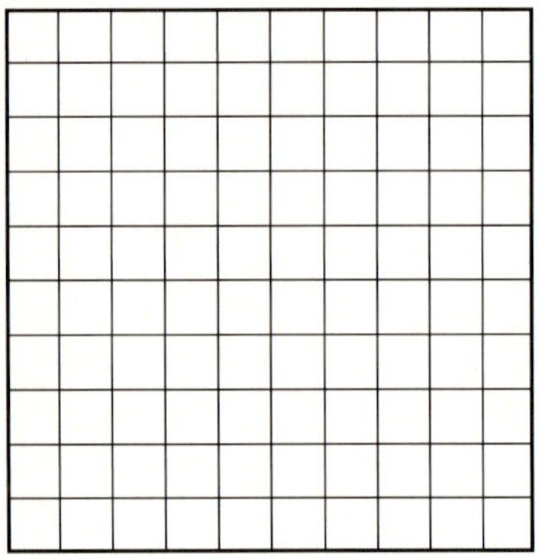

Now exchange your word square with another group and try to find all their words. (Time: five minutes.)

1 A long and healthy life

Samuel Simpson is a hundred and one years old today. He's in good health and is fit. How does he do it? This is what he told us:

A hundred and one today!

I don't believe that there's a secret to good health. It's different for each person. I drink a glass of red wine every evening, but no whisky or other drinks like that! I smoke one cigarette after lunch and two or three in the evening. That's all. I get some exercise every day – when I was younger I used to swim a lot, now I walk for an hour every morning. That's very important. My diet is important, too. I don't eat meat, and I don't eat a lot of sugar. I eat fish, vegetables and fruit. Every morning I drink a glass of hot water with lemon juice in it. Tea or coffee in the morning isn't good for you. I've never been in hospital, and I've never had an accident. And perhaps the most important thing – I don't worry. I worked as a gardener for 45 years, and I didn't worry once about my job. Not once! Every evening before I go to bed, I sit and think about the day, so I can always sleep – I sleep very well.

Ask your teacher questions. Use ideas from the text.

Do you drink wine every evening? How often ...? How much ... ?
Do you smoke? How many ...?

1a What are the differences?

What do you know about Mr Simpson from the newspaper article?

Write about:

- drink
- exercise
- illness
- sleep
- smoke
- hospital
- food

Now listen to Mrs Garrard. (Remember? The lady with backache.) She's telling the doctor about her health. What does she say about these things? Write down what you hear about her.
What are the differences between Mr Simpson and Mrs Garrard?

1b Personal dictionary

You want to tell the other students in your class about your way of life and your health (for example: food, exercise, general health, ...). What words do you need?

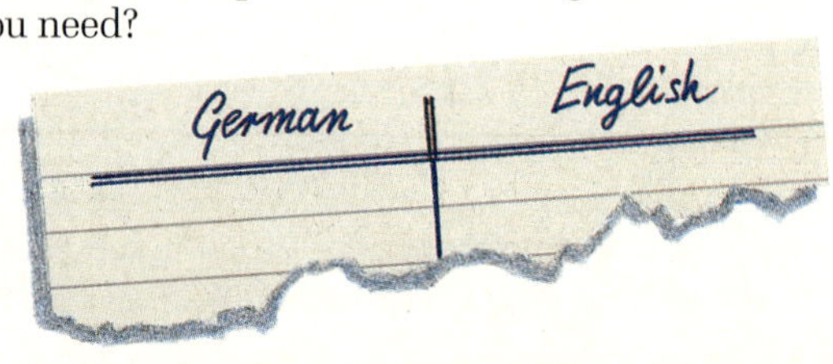

1c A five-minute conversation!

Work in groups of three or four. Tell the others in your group about your health and your way of life. Tell them about:

- things that you do which are not good for you
- things that you do which are good for you
- your diet
- the exercise that you get
- your health in general

Panorama

Alternative medicine

Alternative medicine is the name for methods that general doctors and hospitals don't usually use. But times are changing! People are becoming more and more interested in alternative medicine.

Homeopathy

A German doctor, Samuel Hahnemann (1755–1843), invented homeopathy. *Homeo* comes from the Greek language and means *like* (or *the same*). A large dose of homeopathic medicine will produce the symptoms of the illness. But doctors give a small dose of that medicine, and that cures the illness. A lot of people try homeopathy because they don't like the bad side-effects of traditional medicines. Sometimes people take medicines and in the end have another problem. One homeopath said, "I knew a child who took medicine for anaemia (a problem with the blood) and after that she became diabetic!"

ACUPUNCTURE

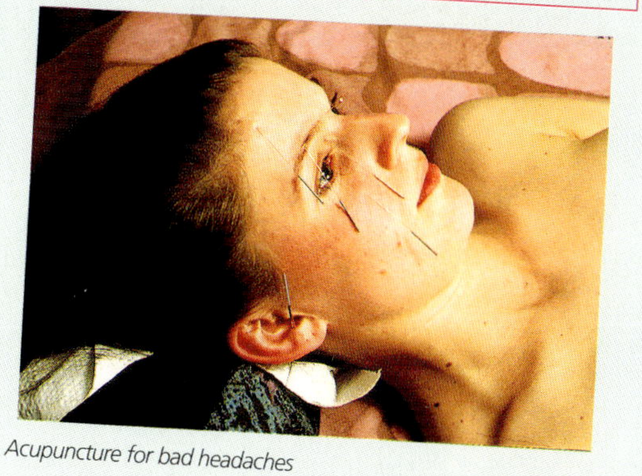

Acupuncture for bad headaches

Acupuncture comes from China. The Chinese used it already 5,000 years ago. The acupuncturist puts fine needles into the body at special points. Doctors have sometimes used acupuncture to stop pain. In China some doctors have done very big operations when the patient wasn't asleep – they stopped the pain with acupuncture! Some people have tried acupuncture to stop smoking, drinking alcohol or eating too much. This is what one man said:

"I went to an acupuncturist once. I wanted to give up smoking. He talked to me for about 20 minutes and explained his methods. He said that acupuncture is 90% successful with heavy smokers, but less successful with lighter smokers. I was a light smoker! He put two needles into my nose, two into my ears and two into my hands – between the thumbs and the first fingers. I felt some electricity in the needles in my nose, but it wasn't painful. After that I didn't smoke for three months. But then I started again. I didn't go back to him when I started again – perhaps that was a mistake."

Now listen to what the man said about acupuncture.

Have you ever tried acupuncture or homeopathy?

UNIT 3 *Revision activities*

Starter: If I were you, I'd ...

Each student must have a small piece of paper (not bigger than a postcard).
Write a problem or a wish on your piece of paper. The sentences can start like this:

I don't like (my) ...
I'd like to ...
I want to ...
I hate (my) ...
I don't know how to ...

Teacher! Please collect all the papers, and give them out again – to different students.

Read what is on your paper. The other students will give you advice. Listen to what they say:

If I were you, I'd ...
I think you should ...
Why don't you ... ?

When you hear some good advice, say: "Now that's really good advice". Give the paper to the person who gave you the best advice.
In the end you can see – the person with the most papers is the best 'advice-giver' in your class!

1 Write some sentences.

Read these three situations. Then work with a partner and write the lists. Can you find two or three sentences for each situation?

1 Your holiday starts tomorrow morning. You'll be away for three weeks. What *must* you do before you leave?

I must ...

2 You work from Mondays to Fridays, but not on Saturdays or Sundays. What things *don't* you *have to* do at the weekends?

I don't have to ...

3 You've got an important interview tomorrow morning. What *mustn't* you do this evening or tomorrow morning?

I mustn't ...

2 With your partner!

You and your partner have both got pictures, but there are some things in the pictures that are different. Partner A, look at page 55. Partner B, your picture is on page 57.

3 Think about these sentences.

Look at this picture. Are the sentences true (T) or false (F)? If the picture doesn't tell you the answer, write a question mark (?).

1 She works in a shop.
2 She's working in a shop.
3 She's working in the garden.
4 She often works in the garden.
5 She doesn't work in a shop.
6 She never works in the garden.
7 She isn't working in a shop.
8 She often drinks beer.
9 She drinks beer.
10 She's drinking a beer.

4 A crossword

1 You've got eight and they aren't in your shoes.
2 When you speak you open your ....
3 You've got one in each of your shoes.
4 She cried on his .... !
5 Migraine is a very bad ....ache.
6 You've got two and you can see with them.
7 You've got two and you can hear with them.
8 Cats have four, people have two.
9 The dentist can look at that .... for you.
10 It's at the end of your arm.

Write the words for parts of the body in here:

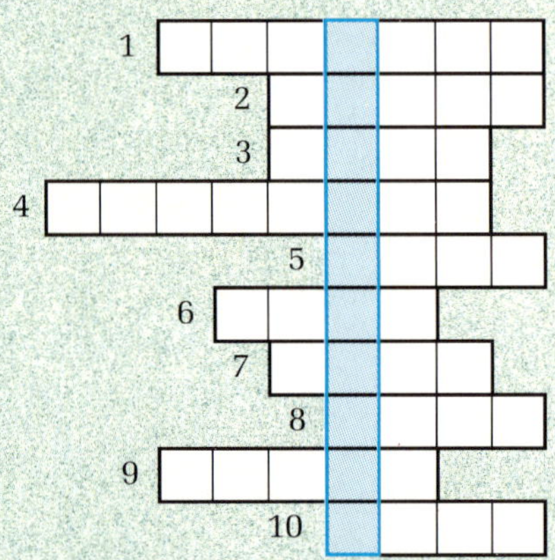

Write the words in the coloured boxes in this sentence:

.... is very important for all of us!

page 62

Unit 4

Homes and houses

Where do you think this house is?

☐ in a small town
☐ in the centre of a big town
☐ in a suburb of a big town
☐ in the country

Would you like to live in or near this house?

STEP 1 *Language in use*

1 A letter from Doris

Doris lives in Munich. She wants to go to Cambridge for six months to learn English. She wrote to a friend called Thomas. He lives in Cambridge. Here's part of her letter:

Do you think you can help me? I'd like a flat that's got two rooms, a bathroom and a kitchen. The flat should have central heating, it must be furnished, and I'd like a balcony, too – but no garden. I won't be able to work in a garden while I'm there – I'll have to work hard to learn as much English as possible! The rent??? Not too high, please. I'm not a millionaire!

Thomas saw this advert:

> My **2-rmd flt**, Cambridge, will be free 6 mths from Jan. Interested? Tel. Erica Smith, 96021 (day)

☞ *Andere Länder, andere Sitten (S. 60)*

1a Comprehension

What things about a flat are important to Doris?

1b ▬ Vocabulary

Listen to Thomas. He's talking about his flat. Number these words 1-11.

- ☐ balcony
- ☐ bathroom
- ☐ bedroom
- ☐ dining room
- ☐ door
- ☐ entrance hall
- ☐ kitchen
- ☐ living room
- ☐ stairs
- ☐ toilet
- ☐ window

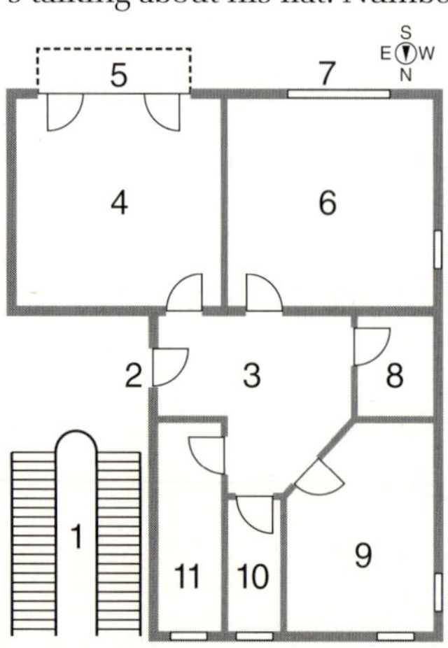

1c ▬ How to say it: Needs and wishes

Practise the intonation first.

I'd like a balcony.	(just a wish)
I need two rooms.	(important)
The flat should have central heating.	(important)
It must be furnished.	(very important)

Now work with a partner and write down four sentences like this for:

- a flat that you'd like to live in full-time (you've got four children).
- a flat that you'd like to rent for a holiday (for the two of you).

2 Dialogue: Looking at the flat

Thomas phoned Erica Smith. He made an appointment to go and see the flat. He's there now.

(ES=Erica Smith, T=Thomas)

ES: This is the living room, with the balcony there.
T: Oh, what a lovely balcony!
ES: Yes, it gets a lot of sun. It faces south, you see.
T: That's very nice. May I see the bedroom?
ES: Yes, of course – it's here, next to the living room.
T: What super big windows!
ES: Yes, both rooms have got big windows. That's very nice. And here's the bathroom and the kitchen next to it.
T: Nice – and modern, too.
ES: Well, the flat is furnished as you can see and ...
T: I think it's perfect for Doris. If you agree, I'll phone her and tell her about it.
ES: Oh yes, that's fine.
T: I'll phone her this evening. If she wants the flat, I'll call you immediately. Is that okay?
ES: Yes, I won't be in bed before about 11.30 this evening, so you can call me late if you want.

2a Comprehension

What do you know about Erica's flat?

2b How to say it: Making compliments

Find the two compliments that Thomas made when he was in Erica's flat. Write them in here:

....	Yes, it gets a lot of sun.
....	Yes, both rooms have got big windows. That's very nice.

☞ *Andere Länder, andere Sitten (S. 60)*

What can you say as a reaction to these compliments?

1 What a super flat!
2 What great photos!
3 What a lovely garden!
4 What lovely shoes!

2c With your partner!

Draw a plan of your flat or house, like the plan in the Vocabulary section of this unit. Don't write any words on the plan. Give the plan to your partner. He/She will ask you questions and label your plan.

What is the first room on the right/left when I go into the flat? Which room is next to ...? Where is ...?

2d How to say it: Asking permission

Look at the dialogue. What does Thomas say when he wants to see the bedroom? How does Erica say *yes*?

Work with a partner. Ask him/her if you can:

- look at his/her book.
- have his/her dictionary until next week.
- borrow his/her car at the weekend.
- have his/her pen for the next exercise.

He/She can answer:

Yes, of course. or I'm sorry, but I need it.

Before you go on ...

Write these words in the sentences: *attic, basement, downstairs, garage, lift, upstairs.*

1 In most houses the kitchen is ....
2 The car is always in the .... at night.
3 We live on the top floor, and there's no .... !
4 In most houses the bedrooms are ....
5 The .... is at the top of the house.
6 The .... is under the ground floor.

Now listen and check your answers.
Speaking practice. Listen and do the exercises on the cassette.

STEP 2 *Grammar in action*

Starter: Find someone who ...

Find people in your class who can answer *yes* to these questions. The first question is: *Do you live in a flat?* If someone answers *Yes, I do*, then write his/her name on the line. Careful! You can only write each person's name once!

Find someone who ...

- lives in a flat. ....
- lives on the second floor. ....
- has got a garage. ....
- hasn't got a lift. ....
- lives in a house with the bedrooms upstairs. ....
- hasn't got an attic. ....

1 Grammar: Sentences with *who*, *that* and *which*

The person	**who** / **that**	lives upstairs plays the piano every evening.
We're good friends with the people	**who** / **that**	live at number 10.
I'd like a flat	**that** / **which**	has got three large rooms.
I'd prefer one	**that** / **which**	isn't too expensive.

Als Faustregel gilt: *who* wird nur bei Personen verwendet, *which* nur bei Sachen. *That* kann sowohl für Personen als auch für Sachen benutzt werden. ☞ G 11

1a Who are/were these people?

Make a sentence about them like this:

He / She	is/was the	man / woman	who/that ...	in ... .

marry write walk climb win	Eine kleine Nachtmusik Wimbledon on the moon Mount Everest Prince Charles	1787 1969 1953 1981 1988

1 Edmund Hillary
2 Princess Diana
3 Mozart
4 Steffi Graf
5 Neil Armstrong

1

2

3

4

5

1b What do you want, need or would like?

Put these words in the correct order and make sentences:

1 car has doors that got four a
I need ....

2 fast car that a very goes
I'd like ....

3 near flat the is station a that
I'd like ....

4 isn't a big that garden too
I want ....

Make sentences like these for:

- a holiday flat (for next summer)
- an English book
- a flat
- a new bed
- a hotel in Paris (for next weekend)
- a robot

2 Grammar: The first conditional; the future of *can* and *must*

If he **comes** on Saturday, I'**ll be** very happy.
If he **doesn't arrive** before lunch, I'**ll eat** his lunch, too.
If the weather **is** good, he'**ll come** by car.
If the weather **is** bad, he'**ll come** by train.

If the sun **shines**, we'**ll be able to** play tennis.	(future of *can*)
If it **rains**, we **won't be able to** play.	(future of *can*)
If it **rains**, we'**ll have to** stay at home.	(future of *must*)
If the sun **shines**, we **won't have** to stay at home.	(future of *must*)

Beschreiben Sie ein Ereignis, das in der Zukunft eintreffen kann, steht im *if*-Satz das Verb in der einfachen Gegenwart. Die Konsequenzen davon werden hingegen im anderen Satzteil mit der Zukunft ausgedrückt. Die Zukunft von *can* (*will/won't be able to*) und von *must* (*will/won't have to*) ist bei allen Personen gleich. ☞ G 6, G 12, G 13

2a What will you do if ...?

Ask and answer these questions with a partner. Answer like this: *If ..., I'll ...*

What will you do
- if it rains next weekend?
- if you can't come to the next lesson?
- if your teacher gives you too much homework this week?
- if you can't sleep tonight?
- if you don't understand something in your homework?

2b What will be different?

These people are very rich. Add some more things that might be true about them to this list. Can your class add five more things?

They drink good wine every day.
They drive a very expensive car.
They live in a castle.
They always travel first class.
They stay in five-star hotels.

Their company is losing a lot of money at the moment. What will be different for them if they go bankrupt?

If they go bankrupt, they won't be able to drink good wine every day. They'll have to drink tea or water instead.

2c What about you?

What will be different for you? Complete this sentence with *I won't be able to* and *I'll have to*:

If I lose all my money next week, I ...

But you might win a lot of money next week. What will be different then? Complete this sentence with *I'll be able to* and *I won't have to:*

If I win a lot of money next week, I ...

Now tell a partner about the things that will be different.

Before you go on ...

You can find these things in most flats. Match the words to the pictures.

☐ sofa ☐ fridge
☐ lamp ☐ cooker
☐ table ☐ cupboard
☐ stereo ☐ washing machine

1

2

3

4

5
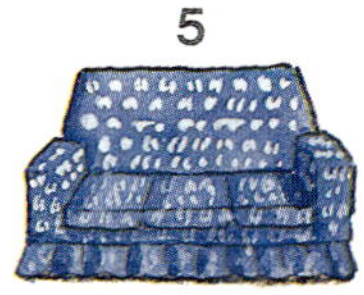
6

7

8

Now listen and check your answers. Then repeat the words.
Speaking practice. Listen and do the exercises on the cassette.

STEP 3 *Language and life*

Starter: What words do you know?

Which words do you associate with these four words here? Write them in the blue boxes.

upstairs

kitchen

home

living-room

Ask other students about their words. If there are some different words that you like, write them in the yellow boxes.

Compare your lists with a partner.

1 Advertisements for flats and houses

Which of these places can you buy? Which of them can you rent?

THE FLATS AND HOUSES COMPANY ☎ 37956

Room to let
Furn rm in 3-bed flt, share K+B, 4th fl *F236*

↑ **Flat to let**
2 bed, 1 liv, K+B, CH, no children, furn *F556*

↑ **Flat to let**
Sm 1-bed flt in att, sm K, WC+shwr, no B *F201*

House to let
3 bed, 2 liv, K+B+WC, CH, furn, lge gdn, gge *H329*

Flat for sale
1 bed, 1 liv + balc, K/din, B, 1st fl *F26*

↓ **House for sale**
4 bed, 2 liv, lge K, 2 B +WC, CH, lge gdn + dbl gge, party rm in bsmt *H15*

What do these abbreviations from the advertisements mean? Write the words on a piece of paper.

furn	K	CH	shwr	balc
rm	B	sm	lge	K/din
bed	fl	att	gdn	dbl
flt	liv	WC	gge	bsmt

1a ▭ Information about a flat

Thomas was in town, so he also went to The Flats and Houses Company. He wanted to find a flat for Doris. While he was there a woman in the office gave some information to someone on the phone. Listen and write down as much information as you can. Then compare with another student.

Which of the above advertisements did the person on the phone ask about?

1b Personal dictionary

You want to write to someone about your home and what you like and don't like about it. What words do you need?

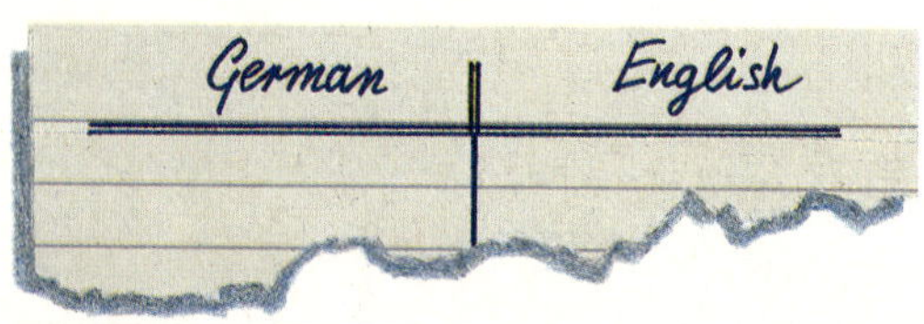

Now write a description of your home and give it to another student to read. When you read his/her description think of two more things that you'd like to know. Ask your partner about these two things.

1c A five-minute conversation!

Work in groups of three or four. Tell the others in your group the best thing and the worst thing about:

- your neighbours
- the area near your home

Panorama

The way people live

Eve, from Scotland, lived in Canada for a year. This is what she said about the cold winters there.

"The way that a lot of people live shocked me at first, but when winter came I began to understand them. It's very cold in Toronto in winter. It can be windy, too, and that makes it even colder. You can often go directly down from your flat to an underground garage to get your car, or to an underground station to catch a train. When you arrive at your workplace you can go directly up to your office. Big business centres and shopping centres are often in the same building so you can do your shopping before you go home. In fact, if you want to, you need never go outside – for weeks and weeks! I must say, I always chose just a few minutes of freezing fresh air a day!"

Man lives on train

In Italy one man always spends nearly 15 hours a day on trains. He buys a monthly ticket from Turin to Savona, and he does the 7-hour return journey twice a day. Between journeys he has a short stop in Savona (twice a day). He spends over six hours in Turin where he gets lunch at a hostel for the poor. He can sometimes work for a few hours and earn a bit of money – for his train ticket. He says it isn't bad on the train. He can sleep, go to the toilet and have a wash. It's warm, and he can always find someone to talk to!

Compact, 1-roomed flat, 1 metre wide, 2.4 metres long and 2.3 metres high.

This advertisement was in a newspaper in Tokyo, where nearly 12 million people live.
As you can see, there's a bed, a television, a desk and a wash basin. A perfect flat, perhaps, for one of the thousands of weekend commuters. They live in Tokyo from Monday to Friday, and go home to their families at the weekends.

Question: Where's the toilet?
Answer: The photographer's standing on it.

Now listen to what Eve said about the cold winters in Canada.

Which of these reports do you think is the most interesting?

UNIT 4 *Revision activities*

Starter: A new home

You want to find a new home. Write down four things that are important to you (be realistic!). Start with:

I'd like ... *I need ...*
It should have/be ... *It must have/be ...*

Now ask other people in your class about their homes. For example, if your first sentence is *I'd like to have a garden*, then you should ask: *Have you got a garden?*

Is there a person in your class who has got the ideal home for you?

1 Write some sentences.

Write two true sentences about yourself on a piece of paper like this:

I go jogging every day. I've never been to New York.

Give your paper to your teacher. Your teacher will read out some of the sentences that the people in your class wrote. Some of these sentences will be true for you and some will be false. Write them down under *true* or *false* like this:

True	False
I go jogging every day.	*I work for a computer company.*
I ate in a restaurant yesterday.	*I used to smoke.*
I've never been to New York.	

Now tell a partner about the things in the false column:
I'm not the student who works for a computer company. I work for a bank, but I've got a computer at home. I'm not the student that used to smoke. I've never smoked.

2 Complete these sentences.

Complete each of these sentences twice. Use all these expressions:

I'll be able to ..., I won't be able to ..., I'll have to ..., I won't have to ...

1 If I win a lot of money next week, ...
2 If I don't finish all my work tomorrow, ...
3 If it rains at the weekend, ...
4 If I find a bigger home, ...

Now read the last parts of your sentences to a partner. He/She should say the beginnings.

3 What are the missing sentences?

1 What a lovely cupboard! / ...
2 ... / Thank you. I bought them in Paris.
3 ... / Thanks. My mother gave it to me.
4 What big rooms! / ...

4 With your partner!

You and your partner have both got pictures, but there are some things in the pictures that are different. Partner A, look at page 55. Partner B, your picture is on page 57.

5 A crossword

Write in nine words for things that you can find in most homes. All the words have the letter **o** in them, and the first letter is already there. Here are the other letters that you need.

For the first 3 words: d e e i n o r r t w
For the second 3 words: a b d d e i k o p r s u
For the third 3 words: a e e e f i i k l n o r s v

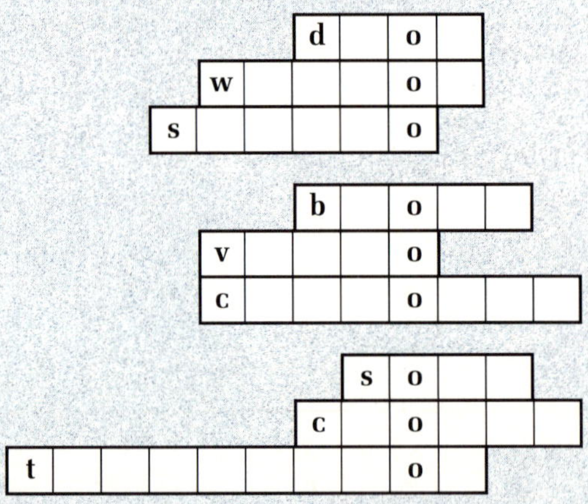

page 62

THE ENGLISH GAZETTE

Vol.2 No.2

A song: Kumbaya

Listen to the song and fill in the verbs.

Kumbaya my Lord, Kumbaya,
Kumbaya my Lord, Kumbaya,
Kumbaya my Lord, Kumbaya,
Oh Lord, Kumbaya.

Someone's ...., Lord, Kumbaya, (x3)
Oh Lord, Kumbaya.

Someone's ...., Lord, Kumbaya, (x3)
Oh Lord, Kumbaya.

Someone's ...., Lord, Kumbaya, (x3)
Oh Lord, Kumbaya.

Someone's ...., Lord, Kumbaya, (x3)
Oh Lord, Kumbaya.

Kumbaya my Lord, Kumbaya,
Kumbaya my Lord, Kumbaya,
Kumbaya my Lord, Kumbaya,
Oh Lord, Kumbaya.

Facts and Figures

Ways of keeping fit

Do you want to keep fit? These are the ten most effective activities. Which ways of keeping fit are the most popular? What do you think? Number them 1-10.

- ☐ cycling
- ☐ dancing
- ☐ football
- ☐ gymnastics
- ☐ jogging
- ☐ judo
- ☐ rowing
- ☐ squash
- ☐ swimming
- ☐ walking (quickly)

Do you do any of these things?

Body expressions

What do you think these expressions mean?

1 I'm up to my eyes in work.
- ☐ I haven't got very much work.
- ☐ I've got a lot of work (perhaps more than I can do!).

2 How expensive was it? It cost me an arm and a leg.
- ☐ It cost a lot of money (perhaps too expensive for me!).
- ☐ It wasn't very expensive.

3 He really put his foot in it at the meeting.
- ☐ He said the right thing.
- ☐ He said the wrong thing.

Learners' Letters

Dear Editor,

We talked about flats and houses in our lesson two weeks ago. Our teacher said the word ***bungalow*** *– but we say this in German! Is it a German word or an English word that we use in German?*

With thanks,

JP, Stuttgart.

Dear JP,

The word *bungalow* comes originally from India! It's from the Hindu word *banglā*, which means a house with one floor (and often with a veranda). The word *bungalow* is used in English, German and French, too.

Yours sincerely, ED.

Dear Editor,

What must I say if I'm in a person's house and want to go to the toilet? I don't like the word ***toilet****. Is there a different expression?*

Yours sincerely,

KG, Basel.

Dear KG,

Yes – in a private house you can ask for the *loo*. This word is used very often in Britain. But the word *toilet* is okay, you know. Be careful with Americans! They often ask for the *bathroom*. Don't show them the room with the bath, if there isn't a toilet in it, too! In a public place you can ask for the *Ladies* or the *Gents* (this is short for *gentlemen*).

Yours sincerely, ED.

P.S. If you've got a language problem, write it down and ask your teacher when you've got time. ED.

page 63

A story

H-o-liday Photos

"An excellent dinner!" Betty said. She looked at her husband, Steve. "Yes," Steve said. "A really great Spanish omelette. A bit like the one we had in Madrid. Thank you very much."

My wife was pleased. Betty and Steve travel a lot and know different sorts of food. It's really a problem to cook for them because they always say things like "the steak in Paris was a lot better" or "we both love Italian spaghetti – in Rome, of course." That's the problem with world travellers. They always know where things are better. And they're always right, of course. Spanish omelettes are better in Madrid. We don't travel very much. We haven't got the money. Holidays in other countries cost a lot. So we just listen to Betty and Steve's stories and travel with them (in their wonderful stories) to Rome, Madrid and Paris. It's a cheap way to travel, isn't it?

"Can I smoke?" Steve asked and took out cigarettes. "Would you like one?" he asked. "No, thanks," I said. "I used to smoke but I don't now." "These are special Turkish cigarettes," Steve said. "They were much cheaper in Istanbul."

"Oh – you *must* see our last holiday photos," Betty said. I looked at Betty on the beach, Betty in a blue swimming costume, in a red swimming costume, in a green swimming costume. "They're this year's colours," Betty said. I looked at another photo of Betty in the garden of the hotel. "Do you like these photos?" Steve asked. "I've got a new camera. It's Japanese and it was very expensive. I took photos for hours and hours every day. It was great." "Yes, it was," Betty said.

"Well, these photos are very nice," I said. Then I looked more carefully at one of the photos. "But who's the man in this photo?" I asked. "Man?" Steve asked. "Where?" "There," I said. "Just behind Betty." Steve looked. "I don't know," Steve said. "He's here, too," I said. "In this photo. And in this one, too." "I can't understand it," Betty said slowly.

"He's in **all** of them," Steve said. "Who is he, Betty?"

"He's in *all* of them," Steve said. "Who is he, Betty?"

"If you ask me, he likes you, Betty," I said. "It's in his eyes."

"Oh, that's enough," Betty said quickly. "I don't know him. Perhaps he's one of the – one of the waiters."

"Are you sure you don't know him, Betty?" Steve asked coldly.

My wife came back from the kitchen with the coffee. Steve and Betty weren't there. "Where are they?" she asked. "On the way home," I said. "Steve isn't very happy. I can't think why. He says he wants to have a holiday at home next summer – like us."

Unit 5

Shopping

Where do you go shopping for food, for clothes or for Christmas presents?

Do you like shopping when you're in other countries?

STEP 1 *Language in use*

1 Dialogue: A complaint

(M=man, R=receptionist)

M: I'm sorry, but I have a complaint to make.
R: Oh, what's the matter, sir?
M: Well, I was having a shower when I heard someone in my room, and I thought it was room service. Then I was getting dressed in the bathroom when that lady walked in.
R: Oh dear.
M: Now – she says the room is hers, and I say it's mine.
R: Oh dear, I'm sorry. What's your name and your room number, please?
M: My name's Pelman, Charles M. Pelman, and it's room 401.
R: Just a moment, I'll have a look. Oh, I see what's happened. The lady's name is also Pelman. She and her husband are in another room.
M: Oh, I see. So room 401 *is* mine.
R: Yes, sir, it is. I'm very sorry for the mistake.
M: Oh, it doesn't matter. By the way, can you tell me where I can buy clothes – for me ...?

☞ *Andere Länder, andere Sitten (S. 60)*

1a Comprehension

Tell the story of what happened at the hotel. Start with: *Mr Pelman arrived at the hotel and went to his room. He decided to take a shower. Before he had his shower he called room service and asked for a ...*

1b How to say it: Complaining

Practise the intonation first.

I'm sorry, but I have a complaint to make. I ...
I'm sorry, but I must complain about my ...
Excuse me, I'd like to complain about the ...

Work with a partner. What complaints might people make in a hotel? Start your list with:

no television
too cold
too near the kitchen

Briten sind oft sehr vorsichtig und zurückhaltend, wenn sie eine Beschwerde vorbringen. Fast immer leiten sie die Beschwerde mit *I'm sorry, but ...* ein. Die direkte Äußerung *I want to complain about ...* wird oft als zu aggressiv empfunden.

1c Two complaints

On the cassette you'll hear two dialogues. Listen to the complaints that the two people make. Answer these questions for each of the dialogues.

1 Where did the person make the complaint?
2 Who was the person that listened to the complaint?
3 What was the complaint about?
4 What did the 'listener' do about the complaint?

1d How to say it: Apologizing and reacting to apologies

Practise the intonation first.

I'm sorry.	Oh, it doesn't matter. That's all right.
I'm sorry about that. I'll ...	Thank you.

Now find a partner. One of you should make all the complaints that you wrote in exercise 1b. The other is the receptionist and must offer some help with: *I'll ask ..., I'll tell ..., I'll call ..., I'll ...*

2 Dialogue: In a clothes shop

(CP=Charles Pelman, SA=shop assistant)

SA: Good afternoon, sir. Can I help you?
CP: Yes, I'd like some pants, please.
SA: Some pants, sir?
CP: Yes, I'd like some pa... . Ah, you British, you don't call them pants, do you? Stupid of me. I'm sorry.
SA: Oh, that's all right. I think it's a pair of trousers that you want, sir.
CP: Yes, trousers. Not pants.
SA: What size do you take?
CP: 40 I think. Is that a British size?
SA: Yes, it is. And what colour would you like?
CP: Blue, please. Oh, these are good. Can I try them on?
SA: Certainly, sir, over there. Is there anything else you'd like to try on? A jacket or a shirt and tie perhaps.
CP: I'll just try the pa... – the trousers first, if that's okay.
SA: Of course.

☞ *Andere Länder, andere Sitten (S. 60)*

2a Comprehension

Which of these questions are in the dialogue? Which of them did Mr Pelman (CP) ask and which did the shop assistant (SA) ask?

1 Can I help you? ....
2 Have you got a ...? ....
3 What size do you take? ....
4 What colour would you like? ....
5 Is this the only colour that you've got? ....
6 Can I try them on? ....
7 Have you got a longer pair? ....
8 How much are they? ....
9 Is there anything else you'd like to try on? ....
10 Do you take credit cards? ....

2b With your partner!

You are both in a shop in England. One of you works there, and the other wants to buy something. Partner A, look at page 55. B, please look at page 57.

3 Vocabulary

Match the British English words with the American words. Sometimes the word is different, sometimes it's only the spelling that is different!

GB:

1 autumn	6 colour	11 kilometre
2 bank note	7 film	12 lift
3 bill	8 flat	13 shop
4 chips	9 ground floor	14 taxi
5 cinema	10 hello	15 theatre

USA:

☐ theater	☐ bill	☐ apartment
☐ movie	☐ store	☐ kilometer
☐ hi	☐ movie theater	☐ first floor
☐ fall	☐ French fries	☐ color
☐ check	☐ elevator	☐ cab

Now listen and check your answers.

Before you go on ...

Match these British English words to the clothes in the pictures.

☐ shirt	☐ jacket	☐ shoes
☐ coat	☐ pullover	☐ tights
☐ skirt	☐ trousers	☐ socks
☐ tie	☐ blouse	☐ dress

Now listen and check your answers. Then repeat the words.
Speaking practice. Listen and do the exercises on the cassette.

STEP 2 *Grammar in action*

Starter: Clothes

Work in groups of three. Write down as many words for clothes as you can. After five minutes exchange your paper with another group. Sort their words into: clothes for men, clothes for women and clothes for men and women.

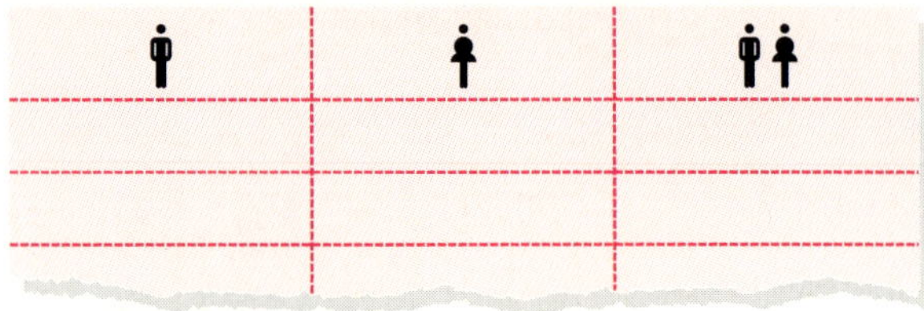

1 Grammar: The past progressive

I **was drinking** a coffee when he arrived at my house. You **were singing** when I walked past your window. He **was getting dressed** when she came in. She **was working** when her boss came in.	We **were drinking** wine when the police came. You **were reading** when the phone rang. They **were standing** on the corner when she drove past.
What **were** you **doing** this morning at eight? **Were** you **driving** to work alone?	I **was driving** to work. Yes, I **was**.
What **was** she **doing** yesterday at three? **Was** she **writing** a letter?	She **was working**. No, she **wasn't**.

Die Verlaufsform der Vergangenheit beschreibt ein Ereignis oder eine Handlung, die zu einem bestimmten Zeitpunkt in der Vergangenheit gerade im Gange war. Sie drückt auch eine Handlung aus, die bereits ablief, als eine neue eintrat. Die neu eingetretene Handlung steht hingegen in der einfachen Vergangenheit. ☞ G 9

1a What were you doing?

Ask a partner questions 1-5 below. Example:

What were you doing yesterday evening at seven?

I was walking home.

Write down the answers on a piece of paper.
Karin was walking home yesterday evening at seven.

What were you doing ...
1 yesterday evening at seven-thirty?
2 this morning at eight?
3 last Sunday at three in the afternoon?
4 on 31st December at midnight?
5 yesterday afternoon at two-thirty?

Now ask other people questions and find someone who was doing something different.

Example:
Were you walking home yesterday evening at seven?

When you find someone who was doing something different, write a sentence like this:
Karin was walking home yesterday evening at seven, but Franz was watching a film.

1b A man with a gun!

Look at this short dialogue. Do you understand why the verb forms in the red and blue boxes are different?

(W = woman, M = man)

W: I was in a boutique yesterday afternoon when a man came in with a gun in one hand and a big bag in the other hand. He looked at the shop assistant and said, "Give me all the money you've got!"
M: What was the shop assistant doing when the man came in?
W: She was talking to me.
M: And what did she do when she heard what the man said?
W: She gave him the money, of course.

The shop assistant was talking to me | when the robber came in.

2 Grammar: Possessive pronouns *mine, yours*, ...

Whose ticket is this?	It's **mine**. It's **yours**. It's **his**. It's **hers**.	Look, my name is on it. Look, your name is on it. Look, his name is on it. Look, her name is on it.	It's **ours**. It's **yours**. It's **theirs**.	Look, our names are on it. Look, your names are on it. Look, their names are on it.

☞ G 3

2a Mine or yours?

Use each of these words in the sentences:
mine, yours, his, hers, ours, yours, theirs.

2b Is this yours?

One student should go out of the room. The others, some as individuals and some in pairs, put personal objects on a table. The person who was outside then comes in and asks *Is this / Are these yours?*

The others can answer, for example: *Yes, it is mine, thank you.* or *No, they aren't ours, but they might be hers.* The questions continue until all the objects are back with the right students.

Before you go on ...

Where can you buy these things?
Match the pictures to the shops, one picture to each shop.

- ☐ baker's
- ☐ butcher's
- ☐ chemist's
- ☐ department store
- ☐ florist's
- ☐ newsagent's
- ☐ market

🖭 Now listen to the sentences and check your answers.
Speaking practice. Listen and do the exercises on the cassette.

STEP 3 *Language and life*

Starter: A shopping list

Sit in a circle if possible. It's Saturday morning, you're in the street and walking to the shops. A friend stops and asks you, "Where are you going?" Start with one student's answer. The next student repeats that, and adds a bit more. And the next one adds a bit more, like this:

Where are you going?

I'm going to the baker's.

I'm going to the baker's to buy some bread.

I'm going to the baker's to buy some bread and a sandwich for lunch.

I'm going to the baker's to buy some bread and a sandwich for lunch, and to the butcher's.

I'm going to the baker's to buy some bread and a sandwich for lunch, and to the butcher's to buy ...

When you've got two things on the list for a shop, you can change to a different shop. But add more than two things if you can.

Teacher! Please write the shopping list on the board, it might get too long to remember.

☞ *Andere Länder, andere Sitten (S. 61)*

1 A letter home

Charles Pelman wrote a letter home to his family in America. Part of his letter was about his day shopping in London. Read the letter. What does it tell you about Harrods and Covent Garden?

I took a cab to the well-known Harrods. They say Harrods is expensive, traditional and exclusive – and it is! No cheap boutiques there! There are a lot of excellent specialist departments – one that sells houses, for example! They say you can even buy an elephant there! Harrods opened in Knightsbridge (that's the name of a part of London) in 1849 and so the building is really old – but I liked it better than the other more modern department stores and chain stores.

In the afternoon I went to Covent Garden. Years ago this used to be a big fruit and vegetable market, and now there are lots of unusual, small shops there and a market, too. It's a great place. A lot of it is traffic-free, and you can watch musicians on the street all day! You'll have to come with me next time – and bring an empty suitcase with you! Tomorrow I think I'll do some sightseeing (no more shopping!) – I think I'll go to

Read the letter again. Find twelve adjectives that Mr Pelman wrote when he described places in London. Underline these adjectives. The first one is *well-known*. The others begin with *e, t, e, c, e, s, o, m, b, u, s, g* – in that order.

Which of these words can you use to talk about a MacDonald's restaurant?

1a Personal dictionary

You want to send a speaking letter (on a cassette) to someone in England. You want to tell them something about a day when you went shopping (at home or in another place). What words do you need?

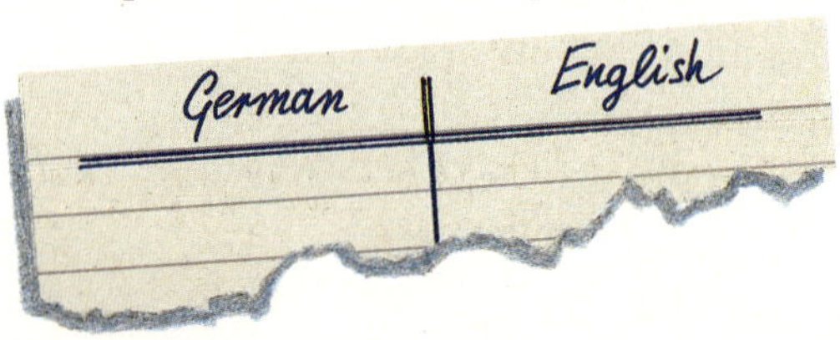

Write a few sentences for your speaking letter.

Now work in groups of four. Read your sentences to the others, and listen to their speaking letters. Make a list of all the shops (*department store, specialist shop, baker's* etc.) that were in your group's speaking letters.

1b A five-minute conversation!

Work in groups of three or four. Tell the others in your group about:

- things that you like buying
- things that you hate buying
- a shop that you go to very often
- your favourite shop

Panorama

Harrods: The Store and the Legend

Enter a different world -
There are larger stores in the world;
not many but just one or two.
There are more modern stores.
There are some with a longer history.
This one is unique, the most famous
of all, in a class by itself. It is
Harrods

One night in 1975, there was a midnight phone call to Harrods. It was an order for a baby elephant – for Ronald Reagan. That was before he was President of the USA. Of course, there aren't any elephants in the shop, you have to order one. One person who didn't believe the elephant story, phoned Harrods and said that he wanted to buy an elephant. He was shocked to get the immediate answer: "Yes, sir, an Indian elephant or an African one?"

Some facts about Harrods:

Henry Charles Harrod was born in 1800 and opened his first shop in 1835. Harrods in Knightsbridge opened in 1849. He sold the shop to his son Charles in 1861. He didn't give the shop to him – one of his mottos in life was "nothing of value comes for free"!

In 1898, Harrods introduced the first moving stairs to London – the first escalator. Now shoppers could go upstairs without walking. At the top there was a man to help nervous shoppers. He gave them a glass of cognac on arrival!

Harrods has always been big in the export business. They send the things that people buy anywhere in the world. They've had some strange export orders:

- a Persian carpet to Persia,
- French wine to France,
- a handkerchief to Los Angeles (the cost of the handkerchief was 35 pence, the cost of sending it was £17.50),
- a fossil found in Texas, bought by Harrods, sold to a Texan who re-exported it to Texas.

Now listen to these texts. There is one more short text on the cassette. What is it about?

UNIT 5 *Revision activities*

Starter: What can you buy?

Work in groups of four. There's a big and modern department store near your home. Make a list of clothes that you can buy there, or of things that you can buy a friend for his/her birthday. Follow the alphabet: a, b, c ... . Can you think of one thing for each letter?
Your teacher will stop you after five minutes.

1 I'm sorry ...

Work with a partner. Think of situations when you might hear these reactions to a sentence with *I'm sorry ...* . Practise your three situations together. Then act them to the others in your class.

Well, perhaps you should buy me a new one!

Well, I'll forget it this time, but please don't do it again.

Sorry! What good does that do?

2 With your partner!

Partner A, look at this page. B, please look at page 58.
Partner A. You are in a restaurant and you want to leave now. You have a complaint to make about the bill. Number these sentences 1-8 in the order you *think* that they should come.

- ☐ But I didn't have a salad. And there's this, too. What's this?
- ☐ The computer doesn't know what I ate or what I drank.
- [1] Excuse me, can I have the bill please?
- ☐ Yes, but the bill isn't right. What's this here – the starter?
- [8] That's what you think. I want to speak to your boss. Now!
- ☐ Listen. I didn't eat salad and I didn't drink wine. Okay?
- ☐ I'm sorry, but I must complain about this bill. It isn't mine!
- [5] But I didn't drink wine with my lunch.

Now read the dialogue with your partner. You should start with your first sentence. Perhaps you'll have to change some numbers when you hear B's part.

Now continue the dialogue with your partner. Don't write, just speak! You are the person in the restaurant, but your partner has changed roles. He/She is the boss now.

3 What were the people doing?

Look at these pictures. In all these situations you walked into the room. What was/were the person/ people in the room doing when you walked in?

Example:

1 *He was getting dressed when I walked into the room.*

4 British or American English?

Look at these words. Seven of them are English and seven are American. Write them in the correct column. Write their 'partners' in the other column, too. If you need help, look at the end of this exercise. There's a list of the first letters of all the 'partners'.

apartment, autumn, banknote, cab, check, cinema, color, elevator, ground floor, hi, movie, shop, theatre, trousers

GB	USA

The 'partners': b, c, c, f, f, f, f f, h, l, m t, t, p, s, t.

page 63

Unit 6

The future

What has replaced these things?

STEP 1 *Language in use*

1 Kath's future

Kath Williams is in her late forties and has got two children aged 19 and 17. Read this letter from Kath to an old friend of hers called Nancy.

There are going to be some changes very soon in our lives. As you know, both of the children are going to leave home next year. Tim's going to start at Manchester University. I think he'll probably live with my sister-in-law there - that'll be cheaper than a flat, *and* he gets on very well with her. Emma's going to start her training as a nurse. She might go to Bristol or to Liverpool - she doesn't know yet. She hopes she'll be able to live in a nurses' home. And what about us? What are *we* going to do? We've got some ideas, but no plans. Our heads are full of "We hope we'll...", "We might...", "We'd like to..." but there's no "We're going to..."! HELP! Is this a crisis, Nancy? I'd love to talk to you about this. Why don't you come and spend a day here soon?

☞ *Andere Länder, andere Sitten (S. 61)*

1a Comprehension

What do you know about Tim and Emma? Why has Kath written this letter to Nancy?

1b Vocabulary

Kath has got a sister-in-law in Manchester. Write in the words for the other in-laws.

Peter ♥ Caroline — Edgar ♥ Dorothy

Sharon ♥ John — Kath ♥ Mark — Anne ♥ Fred

Tim — Emma

Anne is Kath's *sister-in-law*.

Dorothy is Kath's ....

Edgar is Kath's ....

John is Mark's ....

Kath is Edgar and Dorothy's ....

Mark is Peter and Caroline's ....

Now listen and check your answers.

1c How to say it: Ideas for the future

Practise the intonation first.

I'd like to change my job next year.
I hope I'll be able to find a more interesting job.
I might look for a job in a different town.
I'll probably have a holiday between jobs.

Now write sentences to talk about the future. Write about ideas, not certain plans. Use these expressions: *next week, next year, when I'm old.*

Then read your sentences in groups of three or four.

1d With your partner!

Partner A, look at this page. B, please look at page 58.
Partner A. What would you like to do in the future? Write down your ideas. Then ask B.
1 Which country would you like to visit?

1 A country that you'd like to visit.
2 A person that you'd like to meet.
3 Something that you'd like to buy.
4 A crazy thing that you'd like to do.
5 Something that you'd like to change in your life.

2 Dialogue: Plans for the future

Nancy is at Kath's house. They're talking about their ideas and plans for future holidays.

(K=Kath, N=Nancy)

K: And one other thing we'd like to do is travel round the world – when we retire, of course. That's the best time for a long holiday.
N: Oh, I'm afraid I don't quite agree with you there, Kath. Why don't you go next year? It's impossible to know now what you'll want to do in twenty years!
K: Yes, you're probably right.
N: Simon and I are going to take an eight-week holiday next year. We're going to Australia.
K: To Australia! For eight weeks! That'll be expensive, won't it?
N: Well – not too expensive. We're going to swop homes with an Australian family.
K: You mean, you're going to stay in their home, and they're coming here to England. Oh, that's a good idea.
N: Yes, it is, isn't it? For me Australia's the most wonderful country in the world. It's great.
K: Oh, do you think so? I think I'd prefer to go to Canada.

2a Comprehension

Look back at Kath's letter and her conversation with Nancy, and find ideas and plans for the future. Find four that are certain (with *going to*) and four that aren't certain yet and add them to these lists.

They have decided	They're not sure yet
Tim's going to start at university next year.	*Tim will probably live with Kath's sister-in-law.*

2b How to say it: Agreeing and disagreeing

Practise the intonation first.

All university students should work part-time to pay for the university education.

Oh, I'm afraid I don't quite agree with you there.
Yes, I think you're probably right.
That's a good idea!
Oh, do you think so?
Oh yes, I agree with you there.

Die Briten verwenden meist milde Formen des Widerspruchs, wie z.B. *Oh, do you think so?* oder *Oh, I'm afraid I don't quite agree with you there.* Ein direkter Widerspruch wird als schroff empfunden. ☞ *Andere Länder, andere Sitten (S. 61)*

What are your reactions to these statements?

1 Winter holidays are much better than summer holidays.
2 Life is harder now for young people.
3 I think that all our shops should be open on Sundays.
4 Everybody works too much here.
5 Munich is the nicest city in Germany.
6 London is more interesting than New York.

Before you go on ...

In what order might this little girl do these things? Number them 1-14.

- ☐ train as a nurse
- ☐ have children
- ☐ leave school
- ☐ become a nurse
- ☐ get married
- ☐ take some examinations
- ☐ stop work for a while
- ☐ bring up her children
- ☐ start school
- ☐ start work
- ☐ go back to work again
- ☐ leave home
- ☐ retire
- ☐ take more examinations

Now listen to the little girl's grandmother, she did all these things, too. Did she do them in the same order?
Speaking practice. Listen and do the exercises on the cassette.

STEP 2 *Grammar in action*

Starter: Past, present and future

One student chooses a person and an age. The others try and say things for that person. The things that you say must be possible comments about the past, present or future for that person.

a man aged 20

I'm going to become a farm worker next year.

I think I'll retire when I'm sixty.

I left school three years ago.

I'm training as a farm worker now.

I'll probably get married before I'm thirty.

I might have two children, but not more.

1 Grammar: The future with *going to*

What **are** you **going to do** on Friday evening?	I'**m going to stay** at home.	I'**m not going to stay** at home on Saturday.
When **is** Mark **going to arrive** at your house?	He'**s going to arrive** at six.	He **isn't going to arrive** with the others.
And how **is** Kath **going to travel** there?	She'**s going to travel** by train.	She **isn't going to drive**.
What **are** you **going to do** then?	We'**re going to cook** dinner together.	We **aren't going to eat** in a restaurant.
What **are** they **going to bring** with them?	They'**re going to bring** some wine.	They **aren't going to bring** only one bottle (I hope!)

Die Zukunft mit *going to* wird bei festen Vorsätzen oder sicheren Plänen für die Zukunft verwendet. Diese Form wird auch bei gerade bevorstehenden Handlungen benutzt; z.B. steht ein Mann mit Münzen in der Hand vor dem Fahrscheinautomat, können Sie sicher sagen: *He's going to buy a ticket.* Mit den Verben *come* und *go* wird die Zukunft mit *going to* seltener verwendet, da sie umständlich klingt (*she's going to come ..., they're going to go ...*). Stattdessen sagt man: *she's coming ..., they're going ...* ☞ G 14

1a What are these people going to do?

1b Ask your partner.

Ask and answer these questions with your partner. If the plan is certain, answer with *I'm going to ...* . If it isn't certain, answer with *I might ...* or *I'll probably ...* . Write your partner's answers down.

Example:

What are you going to do tomorrow morning?

I'm going to write some letters.

1 after the lesson?
2 tomorrow morning?
3 tomorrow afternoon?
4 on Saturday evening?
5 on Sunday?
6 in your next summer holidays?

Now work with a new partner. Tell him/her about yourself and your first partner.
We're both going to have a drink after the lesson.
Karin's going to write some letters tomorrow morning.
I might go to the fitness club.

1c A poem: My Mum

Listen to the poem and write in the missing words.

When I was very young, I often said to my Mum,
"I'm .... become a pilot.
I'm .... the world."
"That's nice dear," said my Mum.

When I was twenty-one, I often said to my Mum,
"I'm .... an important man.
You're .... proud of me."
"That's nice dear," said my Mum.

When I was thirty-one, I often said to my Mum,
"I'm .... when you're old.
You're .... gran."
"That's nice dear," said my Mum.

I didn't do all those things, of course
And she never became a gran, my Mum
But I'll always hear those words of hers
"That's nice dear," she always said ... my Mum.

• What do you know about the writer (I) of this poem?

2 Grammar: Question tags

The weather **is** bad today, **isn't** it?
I **can** ask her about it, **can't** I?
You **have** got a bad cold, **haven't** you?
He **lives** very near the station, **doesn't** he?
We **work** too much here, **don't** we?
They **went** to Spain last year, **didn't** they?

It **isn't** very sunny, **is** it?
I **can't** ask him, **can** I?
You **haven't** got a temperature, **have** you?
He **doesn't go** to work by car, **does** he?
We **don't have** enough free time, **do** we?
They **didn't have** very good weather, **did** they?

‚Frageanhängsel' werden verwendet, wenn Sie auf Ihre Frage eine Bestätigung erwarten.
Ein bejahter Satz wird im Frageanhängsel verneint, ein verneinter Satz bejaht. ☞ G 10

2a Write in the question tags.

1 They've got a lot of money, ... ?
2 She left her job last week, ... ?
3 It isn't too expensive, ... ?
4 He wants to go there again, ...?
5 You don't really like it, ...?
6 He can't finish it today, ...?

2b Listen and write down the question tags.

1 .... 5 ....
2 .... 6 ....
3 .... 7 ....
4 .... 8 ....

Listen again and say your question tag to a partner. Have you both got the same answers?

Now listen and check your answers.

Before you go on ...

Match the words on the left with those on the right.

1 last year
2 a month ago
3 the day before yesterday
4 yesterday
5 yesterday evening
6 early this morning
7 before this lesson

☐ the day after tomorrow
☐ tomorrow
[7] next year
☐ after this lesson
☐ in a month
☐ tomorrow evening
☐ late this evening

Now listen and check your answers.
Speaking practice. Listen and do the exercises on the cassette.

STEP 3 *Language and life*

Starter: Time expressions

Here are some words that you can use to talk about the present:

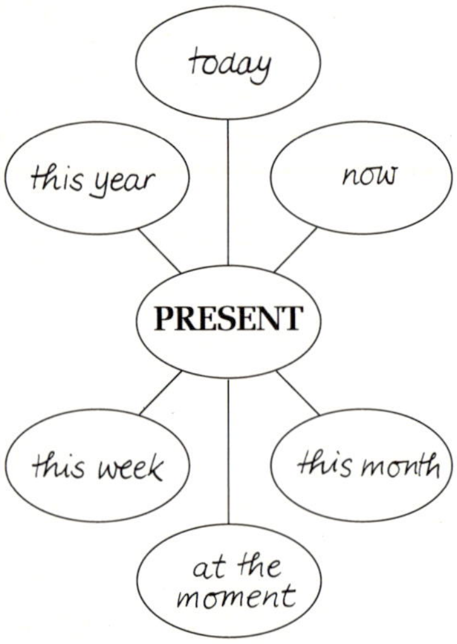

Work in two groups and do the same thing for:
PAST and **FUTURE**

You know more than six time expressions for the past and for the future. How many can you write down in five minutes? Which group has the most expressions?

1 Dreams for the future

One day, when Kath Williams was a young girl she wrote a list of plans for her future. She found that list yesterday. Here it is:

1. I'm going to get married before I'm 25.
2. I'm going to marry a very rich and handsome man.
3. I'm going to live by the sea.
4. I'm going to travel round the world.
5. I'm going to have long hair until I'm very old.
6. I'm going to have two children.
7. I'm going to have a dog, a cat and a horse.
8. I'm going to get married in Westminster Abbey in a beautiful, long, white dress.
9. I'm going to be a famous film star.
10. I'm going to have tea with the Queen one day.

Which of these plans and dreams nearly never come true for young girls?

1a Have these things come true for Kath?

When Kath's children came home they wanted to read the list, too. They asked her about the things on it. Listen. Have these things come true for Kath?

1	got married ☑	before 25	☒	6	two children			☐
2	rich husband		☒	7	dog ☐	cat ☐	horse	☐
	handsome husband		☐	8	Westminster Abbey			☐
3	by the sea		☐		long, white dress			☐
4	round the world		☐	9	film star			☐
5	long hair until old		☐	10	tea with the Queen			☐

Listen again. What details did Kath give about these plans and dreams?

1b Personal dictionary

What plans and dreams were on your list at the age of twelve? Some of them have probably come true and some of them probably haven't! Make a list of those plans and dreams. What words do you need?

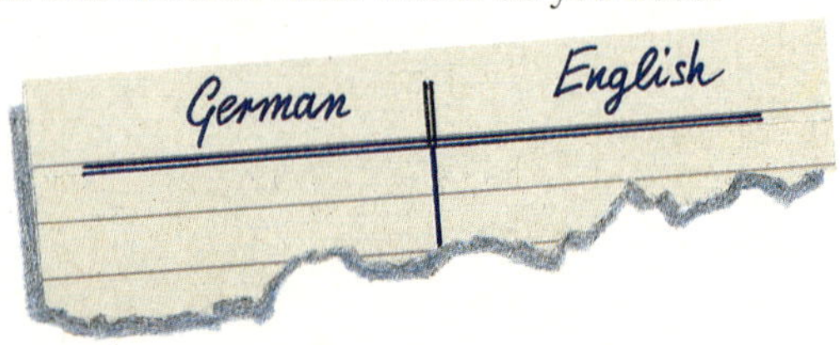

Now write six plans and dreams like this: *I'm going to ...*

Exchange papers with a partner and go through the lists like this:

A: *You wrote "I'm going to buy a big house in the country" – has this come true?*

B: *Yes, it has. I've got a big house in ...* **or**
No, it hasn't. Big houses are too expensive. I live in a ...

1c A five-minute conversation!

Work in groups of three or four. Tell the others in your group about some plans that you've got in your head for your future. Use these expressions:

I'm going to ... *I hope I'll be able to ...*
I'll probably ... *I think I'll ...*

Tell your group about:
- next week/month
- your work
- your home
- a holiday
- a big change
- the time when you retire

Do you think it's good to have plans and dreams?

Panorama

Past, Present and FUTURE

The Past

Alexander Graham Bell (1847-1922), a Scottish inventor who lived in America, made the first successful telephone in 1876. He demonstrated this first telephone over a distance of 170 metres! It was not possible to phone over long distances with it, but telephones soon got better. The first dial telephones arrived in 1896. Then people didn't have to ask the operator for every number.

The Present

The telephone is now an everyday thing in many parts of the world. The countries with the most phones per 1,000 people are:

MONACO	733
SWEDEN	657
SWITZERLAND	535
DENMARK	529
CANADA	524

The USA comes 6th in this list with 520. Great Britain isn't in the top ten – the British have got 'only' 409 telephones per 1,000 people.

At the other end of the list: in China there are 7, in Pakistan 6, in India 5, in Indonesia 4 and in most of Africa 1.4 phones per 1,000 people.

There are a lot of people today who have telephone answering machines – not only at work, but also at home. Sarah, a phone enthusiast, said this:

"I bought my first answering machine about 14 years ago – and I love it! I know some people don't like leaving messages, but I think it's so practical. It's difficult to contact me in the daytime – and I'm often out in the evenings, so the machine is perfect for me. When I'm away from home I can call my number and listen to my messages. It's never necessary for people to dial my number more than once! I listen to the messages and then phone the people who've asked me to call them back. This means that I pay for more phone calls, of course! But that's okay with me."

THE FUTURE

Sarah saw something new in a shop a few days ago – here's what she said about it: "I saw a picture phone in a shop a few days ago. You stand it next to your phone and if the other person has got one, too, you can see him or her on your little screen. You can show the other person documents, children and other things, too. I don't really know if I'd like one of these phones. I wouldn't like all my friends to see me at 11 o'clock on

a Sunday morning – in my pyjamas! But I think you can switch it off – the picture, I mean! I wonder if the picture phone will be an everyday thing in twenty years from now."

Now listen to what Sarah says about telephone answering machines and picture phones.

Have you got an answering machine? Would you like to have one? What about a picture phone?

UNIT 6 *Revision activities*

Starter: Find someone who ...

Have any people in your class done these things? Ask other students questions: *Have you ever been to America?* If someone answers *Yes, I have*, write his/her name on the line. Then ask another student the next question. Important! You can only write a person's name once. Think about all the questions before you start.

Find someone who ...

- has been to America. ....
- used to play the piano. ....
- is feeling a bit tired at the moment. ....
- was sleeping yesterday evening at 10.15. ....
- is going to walk home after the lesson. ....
- hasn't got a bicycle. ....
- doesn't smoke. ....
- wasn't at home on Sunday evening. ....

1 Do you agree or disagree with these statements?

Write your reactions in the empty speech bubbles.

1 Every family with children really needs to have a car.

2 People should not eat meat.

3 The best summer holidays are by the sea.

4 It's a nice day today.

Now work with a partner and write down two more statements. Say these things to two other students. Do they agree or disagree with you?

2 With your partner!

Partner A, look at this page. B, please look at page 58. Partner A. Interview your partner. He/She is going to start something new next year.

Find out:

- what he/she is going to start
- when he/she is going to start it
- how long he/she is going to do that
- where he/she is going to stay

3 What are they saying?

All these people are at a party. They're talking about:

- the people who are giving the party
- the weather
- a new department store in the town
- a film that was on television last night
- last week's football match in the nearest big town

1 ..., isn't he?

2 ..., didn't they?

3 ..., wasn't it?

4 ..., didn't they?

5 ..., is she?

6 ..., was he?

7 ..., do they?

8 ..., haven't they?

9 ..., is it?

10 ..., did they?

11 ..., doesn't she?

12 ..., weren't they?

What do you think they are saying? For example:
1 He's a very nice man, isn't he?

4 Family members

How many words for members of the family can you remember? Write them down in these three groups:

Can you remember twenty words?

page 63

THE ENGLISH GAZETTE

Vol. 2 No.3

Facts and Figures

Household budgets

When people are on holiday they often spend more money than when they're at home. This 'holiday money' is usually part of a budget. Do you know how much you spend on food and drink, clothes, holidays etc?

The money that you get	Food/drink	Clothes	House/ energy	Household items	Health	Transport/ communic.	Free time/ holiday
100%	%	%	%	%	%	%	%

This is how people in Britain and America spend their money:

	Food/drink	Clothes	House/ energy	Household items	Health	Transport/ communic.	Free time/ holiday
Britain	18.5%	7.1%	19.8%	6.6%	1.3%	15.9%	30.8%
America	13.3%	6.5%	19.5%	5.7%	14.7%	14.8%	25.5%

Do you make a budget?

British and American weights and measures

The situation is very complicated! There are some new weights and measures, but a lot of people still sometimes use the old ones. You'll often see two forms (for example, in Britain and America you can buy a pound of apples or half a kilo of apples!). Here is some help for you:

Linear measure

1 inch = 2.54 cm
1 foot (12 inches) = 30.48 cm
1 yard (3 feet) = 91.44 cm
1 mile (1,760 yards) = 1.609 km

Weights

1 ounce = 28.35 g
1 pound (16 ounces) = 453.59 g
1 stone (14 pounds) = 6.35 kg

If you ask a British person how heavy they are, they might say, for example, 10 stone 6 pounds. An American with the same weight will probably say 146 pounds. They are both about 66.2 kilos!

Liquid measure

Here, the British and the American measures are different!

1 pint = 0.57 litres (US 0.475)
1 quart (2 pints) = 1.14 litres (US 0.95)
1 gallon (4 quarts) = 4.56 litres (US 3.8)

Oh dear! How complicated. In supermarkets in Britain you now find milk or orange juice in litres and not in pints anymore. You can also buy petrol for your car in litres. But the British say that there's one thing that will never change. They say that you'll always be able to buy a *pint* of beer!

Learners' Letters

Dear Editor,

When do you write a big letter at the beginning of a word in English?

Best wishes,

TM, Salzburg.

Dear TM,

It isn't exactly the same as in German. In English you write a capital letter (that means a big letter)

– at the beginning of a sentence,
– with names: Peter, Mrs Smith, the River Thames, Hyde Park, London, Germany, British Airways, The Times (a newspaper), Monday, April, Oxford Street.

And don't forget that the word '*I*' is always a capital letter! Okay? By the way, the word *capital* has got a second meaning: Paris is the capital of France, London is the capital of Great Britain.

Yours sincerely, ED.

P.S. If you've got a language problem, write it down and ask your teacher when you've got time. ED.

A story

The Man in the Tunnel

There were three of us in the pub, George, Albert and me. We used to meet every Thursday evening and we always told stories. The best story of the evening won a prize. The prize was a beer. George used to tell very good stories and he often won the beer. Of course, Albert and I thought our stories were good, too. But George's were usually better. Of all his stories, we thought "The Man in the Tunnel" was the best.

Here it is:

I was on my way home from work. That was when I lived south of the river and worked on the other side. I used to go on my motor-bike through the tunnel under the river. It was an evening in winter and very late. And it was foggy, too. It's usually very foggy near the river. I went along River Road to the tunnel – and then I saw something unusual. There was a man in the middle of the road. I stopped.

There was a man in the middle of the road.

"Can't you be more careful?" I said.

"Oh, I'm very sorry," the stranger said. "But I've had an accident with my car and I must get home quickly. I live on the other side of the river. It isn't far. Can you take me with you?" He told me his address. It was true. It wasn't far. The street where he lived was near my house.

"Okay," I said. "Sit behind me and be careful!" The stranger got on and we started. There wasn't much traffic in the tunnel. I tried to talk to the man behind me. I told him something about my work and where I lived but he didn't answer.

On the other side of the river I stopped at the crossroads. "Okay?" I asked. The stranger didn't speak. I turned to look at him. He wasn't there. Where was he? The street was deserted. I started to worry. Where can the man be? In the tunnel? I turned the motor-bike and went back through the tunnel, but I didn't see the stranger there. Five minutes later I was back on the other side of the river. It was still very foggy and the road was still deserted. So where was the man?

I was really worried, I can tell you. I went home. I don't remember how. The next day was Saturday. I got up late and had breakfast. And then I remembered. That address! I know his address! He told me last night. I'll go to his house and find him.

The weather was a lot better that morning. I arrived at the house where the man lived. It was a large house on a busy road. I walked up to the door of the house and rang the bell. An old woman opened the door slowly. "Well, what do you want?" she asked. I started to tell her my story about the stranger. "He said he lived here." "I'm the only person who lives here," she said after she heard the story, so I thought I didn't have the right address. But then she asked, "What was this man like? Can you tell me?" I tried to give her a description. "But that's my husband," she said. "Oh, I see," I said. "Did he get home all right? I was worried about him." "Worried about him?" she said. "Why? He's dead. He was in a terrible car accident ten years ago. On the other side of the tunnel."

George finished his beer. "I think I'll have the same again," he said.

With your partner! – Partner A

Unit 3 / Step 1
Exercise 2c (page 21)

Partner A. You're in London for a week. You have a problem, and you must see a dentist as quickly as possible. Talk to the dentist's receptionist. Here is your side of the dialogue. B is the receptionist.

B:	...	→ A:	speak to Dr Peter?
B:	...	→ A:	back before lunch?
B:	..:	→ A:	when be back?
B:	...	→ A:	appointment for three o'clock?
B:	...	→ A:	appointment for this afternoon, another time
B:	...	→ A:	yes – ouch!, help, ouch!
B:	...	→ A:	fine
B:	...	→ A:	give an answer
B:	...	→ A:	thank the receptionist and say goodbye

Unit 3 / Revision activities
Exercise 2 (page 26)

Ask questions and find out five things that are different.

Ask questions like this:
Is there a ...? Are there any ...? Where is/are ...? What is/are ... doing? Is/Are the ...?

Unit 4 / Revision activities
Exercise 4 (page 34)

Ask questions and find out ten things that are different.

Ask questions like this:
Is there a table in your picture? Where is the table? Is it next to the window? Is it on the right of the window or on the left? Are there any chairs near the table? How many ...?

Unit 5 / Step 1
Exercise 2b (page 39)

Partner A. You want to buy a pair of shoes that are good for walking. You're in the shoe shop in England where B works. B will start the conversation.

B:	...	→ A:	tell the shop assistant what you want
B:	...	→ A:	answer his/her question
B:	...	→ A:	too big, ask the shop assistant if he/she can bring you a smaller pair
B:	...	→ A:	too small, ask if the assistant has got half sizes
B:	...	→ A:	ask if you can try on one of the other colours
B:	...	→ A:	these shoes are good, ask how much they are
B:	...	→ A:	say that you'll take them, pay and leave the shop

women					
Europe	36	37	38	39	40
GB	3	4	5	6	7
men					
Europe	41	42	43	44	45
GB	7-7.5	8-8.5	9-9.5	10-10.5	11-11.5

With your partner! – Partner B

Unit 1 / Step 1
Exercise 2b (page 3)

Partner B. You want to find out the missing information about these other hotels on the island of Corfu. Ask A questions like this:
How many ...? *How much is ...?*
How far is ...?

Name of hotel	Lido	Palace	Beach
Number of rooms		398	
Km from the airport	14km	25km	
Km from the town centre			15 km
Double room for 2 weeks + flight		£754 per person	£738 per person
Extra cost of a single room	£84		

Unit 1 / Revision activities
Exercise 2 (page 8)

Partner B. Listen to A's list of words. Match A's words with your list here. Then read your list of words to A.

New York ... Munich ....
The Thames ....
Russian ....
Rolls Royce ....
Switzerland ....

Now work *with* your partner. Write two sentences and compare the things. The two sentences must begin with different words:

New York is more international than Munich.
Munich is smaller than New York.

If you're not very sure, then start with: *We think ...* .

Unit 2 / Step 1
Exercise 1d (page 10)

Partner B. Write a short telephone conversation with your partner. A is a telephonist in a big company.

A:	...	→ ↙	B:	ask to speak to a person in that company (think of a name)
A:	...	→ ↙	B:	ask when he/she will be free
A:	...	→ ↙	B:	you don't want to give A a message, it's personal
A:	...	→ ↙	B:	this time isn't good (say why) give another time
A:	...	→	B:	say goodbye

Unit 2 / Revision activities
Exercise 2 (page 16)

Partner B. Write these verbs in the sentences:
go, leave, listen, park, phone, save.

1 ..., ... for the station before five.
2 ..., ... to your partner.
3 ..., ... it over there.
4 ..., ... a bit for next week.
5 ..., ... and reserve a table.
6 ..., ... for a walk in the park.

You have got the second half of each sentence and A has got the first half. Read the sentences with A and put the two halves together. (The sentences are not in the same order!)

With your partner! – Partner B

Unit 3 / Step 1
Exercise 2c (page 21)

Partner B. You're a dentist's receptionist in London. Your phone is ringing. Here is your side of the dialogue:

B:	answer the phone, say the number and "This is Dr Peter's receptionist.", offer to help	→ A:	...
B:	not here at the moment	→ A:	...
B:	no, at the hospital all morning	→ A:	...
B:	not before three o'clock	→ A:	...
B:	has got an appointment for three	→ A:	...
B:	ask if the problem is really serious	→ A:	...
B:	offer an appointment at 5.30	→ A:	...
B:	name?	→ A:	...
B:	say the time of the appointment again, say goodbye	→ A:	...

Unit 3 / Revision activities
Exercise 2 (page 26)

Ask questions and find out five things that are different.

Ask questions like this:
Is there a ...? Are there any ...? Where is/are ...? What is/are ... doing? Is/Are the ...?

Unit 4 / Revision activities
Exercise 4 (page 34)

Ask questions and find out ten things that are different.

Ask questions like this:
Is there a table in your picture? Where is the table? Is it next to the window? Is it on the right of the window or on the left? Are there any chairs near the table? How many ...?

Unit 5 / Step 1
Exercise 2b (page 39)

Partner B. You work in a shoe shop in England. A comes into your shop.

B:	start the dialogue and offer to help	→ A:	...
B:	colour?	→ A:	...
B:	size?	→ A:	...
B:	give the customer some shoes to try on	→ A:	...
B:	bring the next size smaller	→ A:	...
B:	no half sizes in this shoe, half sizes in another shoe but not in the colour that the customer wants, offer two other colours	→ A:	...
B:	bring the shoes, tell him/her that these are the best walking shoes that you've got	→ A:	...
B:	choose a price: £29.95, £34.95 or £49.95	→ A:	...
B:	take the money and say goodbye to your customer	→ A:	...

With your partner! – Partner B

Unit 5 / Revision activities
Exercise 2 (page 44)

Partner B. You work in a restaurant. Your partner finished lunch five minutes ago and wants to leave now. A has a complaint to make about the bill. Number these sentences 1-8 in the order that you *think* they should come.

- ☐ But the computer says that you ate salad and drank wine.
- [7] The bill? Yes, certainly – here you are.
- [4] That's the wine.
- ☐ This *is* your bill – table 24.
- [8] Certainly. If you want to speak to my boss – that's fine with me!
- ☐ That's the salad.
- ☐ What the computer says is right.
- ☐ Yes, you did – salad and wine. Look, it's here in black and white.

Now read the dialogue with your partner. The dialogue starts with A's first sentence. Perhaps you'll have to change some numbers when you hear A's part.

Now continue the dialogue with your partner. Don't write, just speak! A is the person in the restaurant, but you are the boss now. You aren't the waiter anymore!

Unit 6 / Step 1
Exercise 1d (page 46)

Partner B. What would you like to do in the future? Write down your ideas first.

Then answer A's question 1 and ask him/her your question 1.

1 Something that you'd like to buy.
2 A crazy thing that you'd like to do.
3 A country that you'd like to visit.
4 A person that you'd like to meet.
5 Something that you'd like to change in your life.

Unit 6 / Revision activities
Exercise 2 (page 52)

Partner B. You have decided that you are going to start something new next year. Choose one of these possible futures and answer A's questions. Answer in full sentences.

six months	at the university	April
at home	October	training as a nurse/baker/ policeman
a course in Italian/ photography/ cooking/...	four years	with some friends of your family
January	a university course	three years

Andere Länder, andere Sitten

Unit 1 / Step 1
1 A letter from Greece

Würden Sie mit 55 Jahren Ihr Haus verkaufen und in einem fremden Land, dessen Sprache Sie nicht sprechen, etwas ganz Neues anfangen, so wie Sue und John in unserem Text? Man kann wohl sagen, daß Deutschsprachige in dieser Hinsicht eher bodenständig sind, jedenfalls, nachdem sie einmal Wurzeln geschlagen haben. Dies wird auch daran deutlich, daß Briten und Amerikaner sehr viel häufiger in ihrem Leben umziehen, wobei sie in der Regel jedesmal ihr Haus verkaufen, in den Vereinigten Staaten sogar oft mit der gesamten Einrichtung, außer den ganz persönlichen Dingen natürlich. Deutsche bemühen sich dagegen oft, ihr Haus zu behalten, indem sie es z.B. für die Zeit einer Versetzung vermieten. Diese britische und amerikanische Mobilität fördert sicher auch die Bereitschaft, schnell Kontakte zu knüpfen, z.B. dadurch, daß die „Alteingesessenen" auf die „Zugereisten" zugehen, *to make them feel at home*, damit sie sich wie zuhause fühlen.

Unit 1 / Step 3
Starter

Ob und wie man über das Wetter redet, ist von Land zu Land unterschiedlich. In manchen Gegenden der Welt wäre es ziemlich sinnlos, überhaupt darüber zu sprechen. Wenn man z.B. seinen Sommerurlaub am Mittelmeer verbringt und jeder Tag gleichermaßen schön ist, wäre die Bemerkung *Nice day today, isn't it?* nicht besonders originell. In Großbritannien jedoch, wo das Wetter oft sehr wechselhaft ist, gibt der „Wetterkommentar" einen guten Einstieg in ein Gespräch ab, im Gegensatz übrigens zum deutschen Sprachgebiet, wo es bei vielen als Anzeichen von mangelnder Phantasie gilt, über das Wetter zu reden. Man möchte im Englischen eigentlich nur Interesse am Gesprächspartner zeigen und einen unverfänglichen Gesprächsstoff haben. Lernen Sie also möglichst viele Ausdrücke über das Wetter, und man wird Sie für einen angenehmen Gesprächspartner halten.

Unit 2 / Step 1
1 A new job

In den deutschsprachigen Ländern ist man oft besonders genau mit den Berufsbezeichnungen; man sagt z.B.: Ich bin Betonfachwerker, EDV-Fachwirt, Datentypistin, MTA, Bürokauffrau oder Starkstromelektriker. Man ist oft besonders stolz auf seinen Beruf und verwendet deshalb die genaue Bezeichnung. Für diese vielen Berufe gibt es nicht immer genaue englischsprachige Entsprechungen, weil das Ausbildungswesen anders ist. Aber selbst wenn es „offizielle" Entsprechungen in irgendwelchen Listen gibt, würde man sie in einer Unterhaltung kaum verwenden, vielleicht, weil es nicht so wichtig genommen wird, „was" man ist. In Großbritannien oder Amerika benutzt man eher Ausdrücke wie diese: *He's on the marketing side, I'm in plastics* oder *I work for a bank*. Die zum Teil sehr energisch vorgetragene Forderung, stets sowohl die männliche als auch die weibliche Form der Berufsbezeichnung (Verkäufer/in, Lehrer/in, Arzt/Ärztin, Frisör/in, Ingenieur/in, Regierungsobersekretär/in usw.) zu verwenden, ist in englischsprachigen Ländern sehr viel leichter zu erfüllen, weil Berufsbezeichnungen, von wenigen Ausnahmen abgesehen, geschlechtsneutral sind: *shop assistant, doctor, gardener, teacher, telephonist* etc. Zu den Ausnahmen gehören z.B. *waiter/waitress* (Kellner/in) und *actor/actress* (Schauspieler/in).

Unit 2 / Step 3
1 Angela's new job

In unserem Text freut sich Angela über die flexible Arbeitszeit (*flexi-time*). Der Arbeitsbeginn liegt in Großbritannien oft später als in den deutschsprachigen Ländern, wie die klassische Formel *nine-to-five job* (eine Bürotätigkeit, von neun Uhr bis fünf Uhr) es ausdrückt.
In den USA fängt der Arbeitstag jedoch eher früher an. In beiden Ländern nimmt man als Pendler (*commuter*) oft lange Fahrten zur Arbeit in Kauf, nicht selten bis zu zwei Stunden pro Strecke! Der Jahresurlaub in Großbritannien hat sich deutschen Verhältnissen angenähert; in den USA jedoch kann man sich über den langen deutschen Urlaub nur wundern; Amerikaner haben selten mehr als zwei bis drei Wochen Urlaub im Jahr. (Vgl. zu diesem Thema auch *The English Gazette*, S. 17.)

Unit 2 / Step 3
Panorama

Der britische *VSO* entspricht ungefähr dem amerikanischen *Peace Corps* (Friedenskorps, s. *Homestudy*-Teil dieser Unit); beides sind Organisationen der Entwicklungshilfe, die auf dem freiwilligen Engagement junger Menschen beruhen. In der gesamten angelsächsischen Welt gibt es eine ausgeprägte Tradition, daß Hilfe für Menschen in Not von Organisationen wie Kirchen, Vereinen, den sogenannten *Service*-Clubs (wie Rotary oder Lions) und zahlreichen karitativen Organisationen, *Charities* genannt, geleistet wird. In diese Tradition gehören auch die *Open-Air*-Konzerte bekannter Stars der Unterhaltungsmusik, deren Erlöse karitativen Zwecken zufließen.

Andere Länder, andere Sitten

Unit 3 / Step 1
1 A letter to a doctor

Dr Day ist, wie Sie auf dem Photo erkennen, eine Frau. Man kann auf englisch nicht sagen: *Frau Dr Day*, weil Titel wie *Dr* oder *officer* nicht mit *Mr* oder *Mrs/Ms/Miss* kombiniert werden können; die Anrede *Frau Ministerin* oder *Frau Minister* gibt es in dieser Form im Englischen nicht, die Regierungschefin wird als *Prime Minister* (*Yes, Prime Minister*) angeredet. Der Doktortitel wird eigentlich nur bei Ärzten verwendet, und auf gar keinen Fall in der (falschen!) Form *Mr Dr Smith als Entsprechung zu *Herr Dr. Schmidt*!
In den USA hat sich die neue Form *Ms* (vgl. *The English Gazette*, S. 17) statt entweder *Miss* (früher für unverheiratete Frauen verwendet) oder *Mrs* (früher für verheiratete Frauen verwendet) inzwischen vollkommen durchgesetzt; in Großbritannien ist dies nicht ganz so deutlich; junge Frauen schreiben unter oder hinter ihren Namen gelegentlich (*Miss*), um zu zeigen, daß sie so angeredet werden möchten.
Die Anrede *Yes, madam* oder *What can I do for you, sir?* wird vor allem im Kundenkontakt, z.B. von Verkäufern oder Kellnern, gegenüber unbekannten Personen gebraucht. Sie ist nicht die Entsprechung zum altertümlichen deutschen *Jawohl, meine Dame* oder *mein Herr*, und sie hat auch nichts Unterwürfiges, sondern ist im Bereich der Dienstleistungen völlig normal. Jeder, der Kunde ist, wird dann *Sir* oder *Madam*, auch wenn er oder sie sonst nur eine bescheidene Position im Leben einnimmt.

Unit 4 / Step 1
1 A letter from Doris

Die Anzahl der Hauseigentümer in Großbritannien und den USA liegt im Vergleich zu den deutschsprachigen Ländern höher, was im Fall von Großbritannien etwas verwundert, wenn man bedenkt, daß der Lebensstandard sonst eher niedriger ist. Außer in den großen Städten werden dort Wohnungen in der Regel als für Familien weniger erstrebenswert oder als Übergangslösung angesehen. Das Mehrfamilienhaus mit mehreren Wohnparteien ist weniger üblich, was auch der Grund dafür ist, daß Balkone und Aufzüge (außer in Wohnblocks) selten anzutreffen sind.
Auch sonst entspricht die Ausstattung in Großbritannien nicht unbedingt mitteleuropäischen Vorstellungen. Wohnungen und Häuser haben häufig keine Isolierverglasung – *double glazing* wird in Anzeigen meist extra erwähnt – und bisweilen keine Zentralheizung. Dafür trifft man den offenen Kamin (auch als elektrische Attrappe!) häufig an. Kaum ein Haus ist unterkellert. Im Badezimmer ist die Badewanne die Standardausrüstung, extra Duschwannen gibt es verstärkt erst in letzter Zeit. Wohnungen werden häufiger als bei uns möbliert (*furnished*) vermietet, auch für relativ kurze Zeit, wie in unserem Text, und in den USA mit Möbeln verkauft! Übrigens: wenn es im Englischen (*entrance) hall* heißt, dann ist damit nicht, wie oft angenommen wird, eine Halle gemeint, sondern schlicht der Flur, nicht zu verwechseln mit *floor*, dem Fußboden.

Unit 4 / Step 1
2b How to say it: Making compliments

Im Englischen benutzt man routinemäßig bestimmte Formeln für Komplimente. Im allgemeinen wird häufiger komplimentiert als im Deutschen, in den USA noch mehr als in Großbritannien. In Amerika wäre es z.B. nicht ungewöhnlich, etwas Nettes über die Kleidung zu sagen, die jemand trägt: *What a nice dress!* oder *I like your jacket!*. Im Deutschen gibt es eine Neigung, Komplimente abzuwehren, etwa, indem man den Wert des Gegenstandes herunterspielt: *Ach, das war ein Sonderangebot.* oder *Ach, das hab' ich schon ganz lange.* Man möchte bescheiden wirken und findet daher das Kompliment oft unangenehm. Im Englischen bedankt man sich demgegenüber zunächst einmal oder man freut sich jedenfalls, wie in unserem Text. Eine weitere Möglichkeit ist es, das Kompliment zurückzugeben: *I like yours, too.*, übrigens auch dann, wenn man nicht unbedingt restlos begeistert ist: Es schadet ja nicht, etwas Nettes zu sagen.

Unit 5 / Step 1
1 Dialogue: A complaint

Mr Pelman ist US-Amerikaner; er nennt seinen vollständigen Namen, mit dem Vornamen und dem meist abgekürzten *middle name*, wie man das z.B. von John F. Kennedy kennt. Sehr häufig würde man den Namen auch buchstabieren, weil in den USA so viele Namen im Gebrauch sind, die man nicht so leicht versteht wie Jones oder Miller. Auch deutsche Namen sind für Englischsprachige schwer zu verstehen; daher sollte man seinen eigenen Namen (mit Vornamen) flüssig buchstabieren können.

Unit 5 / Step 1
2 Dialogue: In a clothes shop

Als Amerikaner verwechselt Mr Pelman *pants* = Hose mit dem britischen *pants* = Unterhose. Solche falschen Freunde gibt es zwischen amerikanischem und britischem Englisch selten. Überhaupt sind die Unterschiede zwischen den beiden großen Varianten des Englischen in den Bereichen Wortschatz und Grammatik sehr gering, was erstaunen mag, wenn

Andere Länder, andere Sitten

man die geographischen Entfernungen und die Tatsache betrachtet, daß amerikanisches Englisch die Sprache eines ganzen Kontinents ist. Dafür sind die Unterschiede in der Aussprache innerhalb der USA wie auch des verhältnismäßig kleinen Großbritanniens z.T. recht groß. Übrigens: auch folgender „Fehler“ hätte Mr Pelman beim Kleidungskauf unterlaufen können: *vest* im amerikanischen hat dieselbe Bedeutung wie deutsch *Weste,* im britischen Englisch meint man damit aber ein Unterhemd!

Unit 5 / Step 3
Starter

Einrichtung und Warenangebot britischer und amerikanischer Geschäfte unterscheiden sich z.T. von denen ihrer mitteleuropäischen Entsprechungen. Die britische Apotheke *(chemist,* heute auch *pharmacy)* ist eine kombinierte Apotheke und Drogerie und bietet sogar z.T. auch Fotoapparate oder Entwicklungsservice an. Der oder die *chemist* genießt einen geringeren Sozialstatus (und auch ein deutlich geringeres Einkommen) als sein/ihr mitteleuropäischer Partner. Der amerikanische *Drugstore* bietet neben Medikamenten auch Kosmetika, Filme und Snacks an. In britischen Metzgereien liegt das Fleisch z.T. im Schaufenster oder hängt an der Wand, was nicht immer mitteleuroäischen Hygienevorstellungen entspricht und bisweilen an den Orient erinnert!

Unit 6 / Step 1
1 Kath's future

Kath Williams' Sohn verläßt die Schule und geht zur Universität. Schüler und Schülerinnen in Großbritannien verlassen die Schule mit einem zum Studium befähigenden Abschluß in der Regel schon mit 18 Jahren. Die Studienzeiten sind selten länger als drei Jahre, so daß Universitätsabgänger bereits in den frühen Zwanzigern in das Berufsleben eintreten. Ob Kath Williams berufstätig ist, erfahren wir nicht, es ist jedoch anzunehmen. Der Prozentsatz berufstätiger Frauen liegt in Großbritannien und den USA deutlich höher als in den deutschsprachigen Ländern.

Unit 6 / Step 1
2b How to say it: Agreeing and disagreeing

"Why are the English always afraid?" So hat es einmal ein Franzose ausgedrückt, als ihm aufgefallen war, wie häufig Engländer Ausdrücke wie *I'm afraid I don't quite agree with you there* verwenden. Natürlich haben sie keine „Angst“; solche Formeln darf man nicht wörtlich verstehen. In dem Bemühen, in der Öffentlichkeit einigermaßen reibungslos und friedlich miteinander umzugehen, verwendet man gerne solche Formeln, die dafür sorgen, daß der andere „nicht das Gesicht verliert“. Im Deutschen ist man im allgemeinen etwas deutlicher, wenn man nicht der gleichen Meinung ist. Haben Sie Probleme damit, diesen zurückhaltenden Umgangston zu übernehmen, wenn Sie Englisch sprechen? Das wäre völlig normal. Ein wenig übernimmt man wohl immer von einer anderen Kultur, wenn man eine fremde Sprache spricht. Sie müssen ja deswegen nicht aufhören, deutsch zu empfinden. Sie machen es sich jedoch etwas leichter, wenn Sie solche Formeln nicht überbewerten, sondern als höfliche Umgangsformen betrachten. Vielleicht wäre ein „Import“ derartiger Ausdrucksweisen ins Deutsche gar nicht so schlecht?

Schlüssel

English Gazettes und Revision activities (Schlüssel für die letzte Übung)

Unit 1 / Revision activities
Exercise 4 (page 8)

Places where you can have a holiday: in the country, in the mountains, by the sea, on an island

Things that you can take to the beach: towel, beach shoes, suntan cream, sunglasses

Things that you can do in your free time: learning English, watching films, cooking, reading

Sports: riding a bicycle, swimming, walking, playing tennis

Weather: sunny, rain, foggy, snow

Unit 2 / Revision activities
Exercise 5 (page 16)

b	f	p	w	a	z	d	c	e	p	a	u	b
x	t	e	a	c	h	e	r	e	n	k	l	v
p	o	l	i	c	e	m	a	n	b	d	s	t
d	f	d	t	w	r	l	i	g	a	h	z	e
c	i	s	e	o	t	j	n	i	n	r	d	l
u	l	y	r	u	i	w	l	n	k	w	r	e
s	m	u	t	s	q	a	o	e	c	m	y	p
o	s	r	z	n	w	i	p	e	l	y	c	h
q	t	p	d	o	c	t	o	r	e	o	f	o
f	a	r	m	w	o	r	k	e	r	i	u	n
w	r	s	i	n	g	e	r	b	k	w	r	i
z	t	h	d	j	a	s	o	p	y	x	v	s
s	h	o	p	a	s	s	i	s	t	a	n	t

The English Gazette 1 (page 17)

Facts and figures. Free time activities

[7] drinking alcohol at home
[9] gardening
[3] listening to music
[10] playing with children
[4] reading books
[2] reading newspapers and general-interest magazines
[5] reading special-interest magazines
[8] visiting the pub
[1] watching television
[6] watching videos

Unit 3 / Revision activities
Exercise 4 (page 26)

		1	f	i	n	g	e	r	s
				2	m	o	u	t	h
				3	f	o	o	t	
4	s	h	o	u	l	d	e	r	
					5	h	e	a	d
			6	e	y	e	s		
				7	e	a	r	s	
					8	l	e	g	s
		9	t	o	o	t	h		
					10	h	a	n	d

Good health is very important for all of us!

Unit 4 / Revision activities
Exercise 5 (page 34)

			d	o	o	r
	w	i	n	d	o	w
s	t	e	r	e	o	

		b	o	o	k	s	
v	i	d	e	o			
c	u	p	b	o	a	r	d

							s	o	f	a	
						c	o	o	k	e	r
t	e	l	e	v	i	s	i	o	n		

Schlüssel

The English Gazette 2 (page 35)

A song: Kumbaya

crying, laughing, singing, sleeping

Body expressions

1 I've got a lot of work.
2 It cost a lot of money.
3 He said the wrong thing.

Facts and figures. Ways of keeping fit

[2] cycling	[5] judo
[6] dancing	[3] rowing
[7] football	[10] squash
[4] gymnastics	[1] swimming
[8] jogging	[9] walking (quickly)

Unit 5 / Revision activities Exercise 4 (page 44)

GB	USA
flat	apartment
autumn	fall
banknote	bill
taxi	cab
cheque	check
cinema	movie theater
colour	color
lift	elevator
ground floor	first floor
hello	hi
film	movie
shop	store
theatre	theater
trousers	pants

Unit 6 / Revision activities Exercise 4 (page 52)

women	men	men and women
mother	father	parents
daughter	son	children
sister	brother	grandparents
aunt	uncle	cousins
grandmother	grandfather	
sister-in-law	brother-in-law	
mother-in-law	father-in-law	
daughter-in-law	son-in-law	

Wegweiser Homestudy

Übrigens: Wenn Sie in den Sommerferien Ihre Kenntnisse festigen möchten, können Sie mit *English Network 2 Break* auf unterhaltsame Weise Grammatik, Wortschatz und Redewendungen aus dem Kursbuch wiederholen. Damit sind Sie für das neue Semester bestens vorbereitet!

Was gibt es im *Homestudy*-Teil?

Der *Homestudy*-Teil umfaßt ausschließlich Materialien, die Sie zu Hause alleine für sich außerhalb des Unterrichts bearbeiten können. Enthalten sind zusätzliche Übungen zu jedem Step der Units vorne im Buch. Es sind in der Regel schriftliche Übungen, doch sind einige zur gezielten Schulung des Hörverstehens gedacht und durch Cassette bzw. CD gesteuert. Die Aufnahmen dazu finden Sie auf den Lernercassetten bzw. Lerner-CDs, die es zu diesem Lehrwerk gibt (Cassetten: Bestell-Nr. 57 567 und 57 568; CDs [Dreierpaket]: Bestell-Nr. 57 525).

Zu allen Übungen des *Homestudy*-Teils gibt es ab Seite 101 einen Lösungsschlüssel. In Ihrem eigenen Interesse sollten Sie natürlich erst dann die Lösungen einsehen, wenn Sie die Aufgaben bearbeitet haben und mit Ihren eigenen Lösungsvorschlägen zufrieden sind. Auch die Tonbandtexte der Hörverstehensübungen finden Sie im Anhang, ab Seite 105. Sie sind übrigens nur für den Fall abgedruckt, daß Sie wirklich große Verständnisschwierigkeiten haben. Sie müssen nicht jedes Wort verstehen, um die Aufgaben lösen zu können.

Ferner finden Sie im *Homestudy*-Teil zu jeder Unit eine Seite mit Lerntips, die Ihnen Hilfen und Techniken an die Hand geben, mit denen Sie Ihr Lernen verbessern können. Außerdem gibt es nach jeweils zwei Units die Sektion *Test Yourself*, die es Ihnen ermöglicht, in regelmäßigen Abständen Ihre Fortschritte und Ihren Lernerfolg selbst zu überprüfen.

Wie arbeite ich mit dem *Homestudy*-Teil?

Besonders wichtig ist der Grundsatz: Lieber wenig aber oft, als viel aber selten; d.h. mehrere kurze Lern- und Übungsphasen pro Woche, z.B. täglich 10 Minuten, sind effektiver als nur einmal die Woche eine lange. Weitere Informationen, wie Sie den Lernerfolg der Gruppenstunden zu Hause untermauern können und was Sie unterlassen sollten, finden Sie in Lerntip 3 auf Seite 81.

Wenn Sie zu Hause üben, ist es sinnvoll, zunächst die Teile der Unit, die Sie in der Gruppenstunde bearbeitet haben, noch einmal durchzusehen. Dann können Sie die Übungen zu dem jeweiligen Step hier im *Homestudy*-Teil machen. Nehmen Sie dazu einen Bleistift und tragen Sie Ihre Lösungsvorschläge ein. Wenn Sie mit ihnen zufrieden sind, vergleichen Sie sie mit dem Schlüssel, unterstreichen Sie die Fehler (falls es welche gibt!) und korrigieren Sie sie. Falls Ihnen nicht klar ist, warum Ihre Lösung nicht stimmt, fragen Sie Ihre Kursleiterin / Ihren Kursleiter in der nächsten Stunde. Alle Lösungen könnten Sie dann noch einmal ausradieren und die Übungen einige Tage später wiederholen, auch wenn sie vorher richtig waren. So sichern Sie Ihren Lernerfolg ab.

Wie arbeite ich mit den Lernercassetten?

Ehe Sie die Übungen im *Homestudy*-Teil machen, sollten Sie zunächst die Teile der Unit, die Sie im Unterricht bearbeitet haben, noch einmal durchsehen. Aus diesem Grund sind die Texte, Dialoge und Übungen aus dem *Unit*-Teil, die mit einem weißen Cassettensymbol versehen sind, auch auf den Lernercassetten und Lerner-CDs zu finden. Die Nachbereitung nach jeder Gruppenstunde sieht somit folgendermaßen aus: Sie wiederholen als erstes mit Hilfe der Lernercassetten oder -CDs die Teile, die Sie im Unterricht durchgenommen haben. Danach gehen Sie zu den Übungen im *Homestudy*-Teil über, wobei sich die entsprechende Hörübung (falls vorhanden) aus dieser Sektion unmittelbar an die Übungen des *Unit*-Teils anschließt. Das folgende Beispiel – anhand von Unit 2, Step 1 – kann Ihnen helfen, die Übungen auf den Lernercassetten oder -CDs denen des Buches zuzuordnen.

Lernercassette	Seite im Buch
Unit 2, Step 1	
1 Dialogue: A new job	S. 10
2 Dialogue: An interview	S. 11
Before you go on: Speaking practice	S. 11
Homestudy: Exercise 1: What was the question? Exercise 2: A message for Mr Brown	S. 70

UNIT 1 *Step 1*

1 We like ...ing

Füllen Sie bitte die Lücken des nachstehenden Textes mit den vorgegebenen Wörtern des Kastens aus.

a staying being taking swimming walking playing reading

b doesn't like enjoys likes (3x) like

a Look here, please. This is a photograph of my last birthday party. Lots of my friends came, and we all had a wonderful afternoon in my garden. What is interesting, you know, is that we all have got one hobby now, we like .... (1) tennis. We enjoy .... (2) active and .... (3) young. When we were children, we liked different things, we liked .... (4) books, ... (5) in the sea and .... (6) in the mountains, because that was great fun, and our parents didn't have the money for tennis clubs. On my left is Vanessa, our friend from Canada, she likes .... (7) photos of people, dogs, and cats.

b Her hobby is her camera. She .... (8) taking photographs and walking in the country. She .... (9) walking in big cities because she hates big houses and streets full of people. But she .... (10) going to museums, parks and zoos. Vanessa really is a nature lover, she .... (11) working in her garden, her beautiful garden. I'm sure you will .... (12) it, too. It is a fantastic garden. Vanessa is an interesting person and very kind, and she .... (13) making new friends.

2 Invitations

Was würden Sie in den folgenden Situationen sagen? Einladungen können verschieden ausgesprochen werden, deshalb gibt es für jede Situation mehrere Lösungen. Vergleichen Sie anschließend Ihren Vorschlag mit den Cassettenaufnahmen.

1 You want to invite your boss to dinner next Thursday evening.

a I'd like .... next Thursday evening.

b Would you .... next Thursday evening?

c Can I .... next Thursday evening?

2 You want to invite a friend to the cinema tomorrow to see "Casablanca" again.

a Would you .... to see "Casablanca" again?

b Why don't we .... to see "Casablanca" again?

c Let's go .... to see "Casablanca" again.

3 You want to invite some of the people that you work with to go for a drink after work.

a Would ....

.... ?

b I'd ....

....

c Let's ....

....

d Why ....

.... ?

"I'm sorry, but I've still got the migraine. Why don't you try again?"

UNIT 1 *Step 1 / Step 2*

3 The Belgian coast is wonderful ...

Der folgende Text ist einem Ferienprospekt entnommen. Füllen Sie die Lücken mit dem Eigenschaftswort aus dem Kasten, das am besten für einen Werbetext paßt.

1	attractive expensive big wonderful
2	bad interesting mild fine
3	beautiful friendly excellent typical
4	good nice mild warm
5	expensive large beautiful excellent
6	old cheap fantastic modern
7	great small unfriendly tired
8	excellent expensive interesting cheap
9	attractive modern large fantastic
10	unfriendly expensive interesting true
11	modern friendly excellent big

Belgium is a .... (1) country for a holiday. Ideal for tourists in summer and winter. Visitors like our .... (2) climate, the .... (3) people, the .... (4) summer sun, ... (5) hotels and .... (6) beaches. You will find .... (7) cities, ... (8) small towns, and .... (9) villages. There are .... (10) parks for families with children, and .... (11) places for all forms of sport. Why not come and see?

Step 2

1 Comparisons

Fügen Sie bitte die nachstehenden Satzteile zu sinnvollen Aussagen zusammen, in denen Vergleiche gemacht werden.

1 ☐ New York is more interesting ...
2 ☐ People often say that Japanese cars ...
3 ☐ Hotels in America are very expensive, but ...
4 ☐ People hated "J. R." in "Dallas" on TV, but ...
5 ☐ This camera is more modern than that one and ...
6 ☐ "Psycho" is a Hitchcock thriller and ...
7 ☐ I like playing tennis in Great Britain because it's ...
8 ☐ People enjoy watching sport on TV, but ...

a it's one of the best films that I know.
b certainly more expensive.
c are more modern and cheaper than German cars.
d than the place where I live.
e not as expensive as tennis here in Germany.
f he was the most interesting person in the series.
g often more comfortable than hotels in Europe.
h jogging is better for your health.

2 A quiz show

Hören Sie den Text der Cassette mehrere Male. Das erste Mal schreiben Sie bitte noch nichts, erst beim zweiten und dritten Mal sollten Sie die Lücken des Textes mit den Wörtern von der Cassette ausfüllen.

And here are the winners of today's quiz, the Hamiltons. Mrs Hamilton will get one of the .... (1) Japanese cameras. She likes taking photos. And for her husband a very good book about one of the .... (2) countries in the world – Italy. One of the .... (3) monuments there is the Collosseum in Rome, it's about 2,000 years old. The Hamiltons will visit that beautiful country and meet the .... (4) people in the world. And for the children, what have we got? Video cassettes of one of the .... (5) pop singers of our time. And that's not all. Beautiful sunglasses, some say, the .... (6) sunglasses by our star designer Roberto Merlotti. People say he has got the .... (7) and .... (8) car in Europe. And that's their extra prize. The Hamiltons will drive that wonderful car, they will have it for three weeks, the .... (9) weeks of their lives. I am sure the Hamiltons will be happy, not only happy, they will be the .... (10) people in the world.

UNIT 1 *Step 2 / Step 3*

3 Have you ever ...?

Wie lauten die Fragen auf die ausgedruckten Antworten?

1 ....

.... No, I haven't been to London.

2 ....

.... Yes, I have. I learned Spanish two years ago, when I was in Madrid.

3 ....
No, I haven't. I have never met a film star.

4 ....

.... Yes, they have. They read the English book "Gone With the Wind" last year.

5 ....

.... No, I haven't. I went to the cinema last Wednesday but I didn't see "Rain Man".

6 ....

....
No, he hasn't. He has always driven German cars.

7 .... Yes, I have.
I love French wine and drink it very often.

4 Which words belong together?

Ordnen Sie die Wörter des Kastens zu Sinngruppen von je drei Wörtern.

> airport, big, cinema, city, flat, France, Greece, holiday, house, jazz, large, learning, listening, month, museum, music, plane, pop song, reading, room, small, Spain, summer, suntan, theatre, ticket, town, village, week, year

1 airport	....	....
2 France	....	....
3 music	....	....
4 summer	....	....
5 room	....	....
6 museum	....	....
7 week	....	....
8 reading	....	....
9 city	....	....
10 small	....	....

Step 3

1 A boat tour to Hampton Court

Ein Tourist fragt nach Bootsfahrten auf der Themse nach Hampton Court, wo es einen berühmten Palast gibt. Hören Sie das Gespräch zweimal an und füllen Sie die Lücken der Informationstafel aus.

> **Boat Tours on the Thames**
>
> **to Hampton Court**
>
> **£ .... (children: £ ....)**
>
> **Every day**
>
> **at ....**
>
> **and ....**
>
> **from .... to September.**
>
> **Extra weekend tour at ....**

2 Oh, these prepositions

Können Sie sich noch an all die kleinen Wörter erinnern, die in den nachstehenden Sätzen fehlen?

1 He's our boss .... the hotel now.

2 Our room is not big enough .... us all.

3 Would you like to have a drink .... me after work?

4 This is the best hotel .... this beautiful island.

5 They decided to go .... France .... three weeks.

6 Here is the missing information .... our trip.

7 Why don't we go there .... train?

8 We had a fine holiday .... the sea last autumn.

9 I like watching tennis .... television.

UNIT 1 *Step 3*

3 What is wrong here?

In diesen Broschürentext haben sich sieben sinnentstellende Fehler eingeschlichen. Finden Sie sie heraus und berichtigen Sie den Text.

This brochure gives you a lot of information about London. London, the capital of England, is one of the world's smallest towns and certainly one of the greatest. A famous man said once:
"When a man is tired of London, he is tired of life; ... there is in London all that life can afford[1]." And this is true.
London is a friendly city, visitors feel unwelcome because Londoners will take time and trouble to help them.
Shopping in London means the elegant and cheap specialist shops of Bond Street, St James, and Saville Row, but also street markets like Petticoat Lane and Chapel Market in Islington. One of the most beautiful and most elegant places to shop is Burlington Arcade.
You can walk about the streets and have a terrible day. And, it is still possible to leave the streets, walk in parkland and think of the traffic. London has a very special character. Perhaps this is why Americans are happy in London. London is the country they like most: it has lots to offer, it is traditional and modern, old and new, a fantastic place.
What did the Scotsman, William Dunbar, say 500 years ago? "London, you are the flower[2] of cities all." He was right and still is wrong.

[1] *Etwa: Wenn jemand Londons überdrüssig ist, ist er des Lebens überdrüssig; es gibt in London alles, was das Leben bieten kann.*
[2] *Blume*

	False	True
1	*smallest towns*	*largest / biggest cities*
2	....	....
3	....	....
4	....	....
5	....	....
6	....	....
7	....	....

4 Please complete.

- Tell me about your holiday in Waizoona.
- Waizoona? I've never .... (1) there. That was just a competition.
- Where .... (2) you go then?
- To New England.
- Oh, that's nice.
- .... (3) you ever .... there?
- No, I haven't. .... (4) go?
- In October. The autumn is the ....(5) beautiful time.
- Was the weather OK?
- Well, it was c..............................y (6) on one day in the morning, but it .... (7) rain. And on one other day by the coast it was f.......................... (8). We couldn't see anything! But most of the time it was warm and s.............................. (9), but not too h.............................. (10).
- So you .... (11) a good time.
- Yes, we .... (12).
- .... (13) stay?
- Two weeks.
- .... (14) you travel?
- By plane, then by car. Look, ... (15) you like to come to dinner tomorrow and see some photos?
- I'd .... (16) to, but I'm .... (17) I can't.

Lerntip 1

Speziell für Quereinsteiger

1 Sie haben nun schon einige Kursstunden hinter sich und Erfahrungen mit Ihrem neuen Lernmaterial machen können. Hoffentlich konnten Sie sich gut in Ihre Lerngruppe einfinden. Auch wie Sie in Ihrem Kurs arbeiten und wo Sie was im Kursbuch finden, werden Sie inzwischen festgestellt haben. Hier erhalten Sie nun einige Informationen, die Ihnen helfen, weiterhin mit dem Buch erfolgreich zu arbeiten und auch Spaß dabei zu haben.

2 In *English Network 1* befinden sich nach den einzelnen Units im *Homestudy*-Teil auf den Seiten 68, 73, 80, 85, 92 und 97 sechs Lerntip-Seiten zu den verschiedenen Themen. Lassen Sie sich bitte einmal *English Network 1* zeigen, und lesen Sie sorgfältig die Einleitung zu dem Band und die Lerntips durch. Sie sollten Ihnen nicht nur Mut machen, Ihr Vorhaben, die Fremdsprache Englisch gezielt zu lernen oder zu vertiefen, in die Tat umzusetzen, sondern Ihnen auch den Anschluß an die Lerngruppe, zu der Sie neu hinzukommen, erleichtern. Beherzigen Sie bitte diese Hinweise; Ihre Mitlernenden haben danach gelernt und sind damit nicht schlecht gefahren. Fragen Sie sie ruhig einmal. Sie werden Ihnen bestimmt sagen, welche Hinweise besonders hilfreich waren.

3 Wir alle wissen, daß man Erfahrungen nicht widersprechen kann. Nicht alle sind aber gleichermaßen auf jede Person und jede Situation übertragbar. Finden Sie deshalb Ihren eigenen Lernrhythmus, Ihr persönliches Lernverfahren, sich den Stoff anzueignen. Bei Schwierigkeiten wird Ihnen Ihr Kursleiter/Ihre Kursleiterin gern behilflich sein, und unter Umständen sind dann die Erfahrungen Ihrer Mitlernenden eine auch für Sie nützliche Hilfe.

4 Ganz gleich wie interessant ein Lehrwerk gestaltet ist und der Unterricht durchgeführt wird, in jedem Lernprozeß gibt es Durststrecken, die durchgestanden sein wollen. Grammatik, selbst wenn sie kurzweilig in Situationen verpackt ist oder sich hinter spielerischen Übungen versteckt, ist nicht jedermanns Sache, und auch das Auswendiglernen von Wörtern läßt nicht jedes Mal das Herz vor Freude schneller schlagen. Zeigen Sie etwas Durchhaltevermögen, lassen Sie sich nicht sofort entmutigen, wenn etwas nicht so klappt, wie Sie es gerne möchten. Diese Selbstüberwindung, diese Mühe, der regelmäßige Kursbesuch und das ständige Zurhandnehmen des Lehrwerks werden zweifellos zum Erfolg führen.

5 Langzeituntersuchungen, die sich mit diesem Thema beschäftigen, bestätigen immer wieder das, was bereits 1928 festgestellt wurde:

- Fast alles ist zu jeder Zeit erlernbar. Die häufig gehörte Klischeevorstellung „Was Hänschen nicht lernt, lernt Hans nimmermehr" ist nachgewiesenermaßen falsch.

- Die wirklichen Schwierigkeiten beim Lernen Erwachsener sind in den meisten Fällen geringer als erwartet und in jedem Fall zu meistern.

- Erwachsene lernen in der Regel viel weniger, als sie könnten.

6 Sie selbst werden die Richtigkeit dieser Aussagen am eigenen Leibe verspüren; Sie werden Ihren Lernfortschritt bewußt erleben und für Ihre Belange nutzen können. Dies ist ein Versprechen, das die Autoren des Lehrwerks und mit ihnen die Kursleiter und Kursleiterinnen guten Gewissens geben können, wenn Sie Ihrerseits aktiv und regelmäßig mitarbeiten und Lernschwierigkeiten oder Motivationsprobleme in der Lerngruppe offen ansprechen.

UNIT 2 *Step 1*

1 What was the question?

Während Sie auf einen Termin warten, hören Sie aus einem Nebenraum einen Teil eines Vorstellungsgesprächs. Die Antworten können Sie gut verstehen, die Fragen sind jedoch nicht so deutlich zu hören. Wie lauten sie? Hören Sie dann zur Kontrolle das Gespräch auf der Cassette, bzw. vergleichen Sie Ihre Lösungen mit dem Schlüssel auf Seite 101.

(M = man, S = Miss Smith)

M: .... (1) do when you left school, Miss Smith?

S: Well, the first thing I did was to take a long holiday, and then I worked as a telephonist.

M: .... (2) work as a telephonist?

S: About three years.

M: .... (3) that job?

S: I left because I wanted to take a computer course.

M: Where .... (4) work now?

S: I work for a big company in London.

M: .... (5) ?

S: Yes, I like my job, but I don't earn enough money. That's why I'm here.

2 A message for Mr Brown

Im Büro hören Sie den Anrufbeantworter ab und notieren eine Mitteilung für Ihren englischen Chef, Herrn Brown.

MEMO

Date: *October 10* Time: *11.15 am*

Message for ....

Message from ....

Telephone number ....

She won't be in ....

Please .... *her tomorrow between*

.... *and* .... *o'clock.*

3 Expressing possibilities

Sie sind etwas unsicher darüber geworden, ob sich der Zeitplan wirklich einhalten läßt. Möglich ist es, aber nicht sicher. Schreiben Sie deshalb die Sätze mit *might* oder *perhaps* um.

1 The meeting will start at 3.00 pm.
The meeting might start at 3.00 pm.
Perhaps the meeting will start at 3.00 pm.

2 Mr Brown will be about half an hour late.

....

....

3 The others will arrive by two o'clock.

....

....

4 Mrs Smith will leave by train at 11.42.

....

....

5 I'll take an earlier train.

....

....

6 I'll see you tomorrow afternoon.

....

....

4 Find the right sentence.

Finden Sie den Satz, der am besten zu der Zeichnung paßt.

- Can I help you?
- Thank you for calling.
- I'll put you through.
- Can I give her a message?
- Shall I ask her to call you back?
- Hold on, please.
- Would you like to come and visit us next summer?
- Have you ever been to London?
- Have you ever driven an American car?
- How many people were there in your class?
- It's the middle of the night and this is not the Apollo Hotel.
- Let's go and have a coffee in the restaurant.

UNIT 2 *Step 2*

1 Adjectives and adverbs

Setzen Sie die fehlenden Wörter ein, hören Sie dann das Gespräch von der Cassette an, oder schauen Sie im Schlüssel auf Seite 101 nach.

I think your friend Jim is a really good writer.

Yes, he writes very ....

But I've heard he's a slow worker.

That's not true! He doesn't work ....

But he is very careful about his work, I know.

Yes, he works .... , but he's not slow!

Okay, okay. I'm sorry. I'll only say nice things about him next time.

Yes, please talk .... about him. He's a very nice person.

2 Crossword puzzle

Across (→):

1 In English, a .... is not only someone who is studying at a university.

6 The .... brought us our food very quickly.

10 The .... said: "Don't drive so fast."

Down (↓):

2 The .... said: "Don't smoke so much."

3 The .... said: "Always arrive before 8.30."

4 A .... worker lives in the country and works very hard.

5 The .... said: "Don't forget your homework."

7 When I was a child, I used to get .... early every morning.

8 Her daughter is ten years ....

9 How .... is the airport from here?

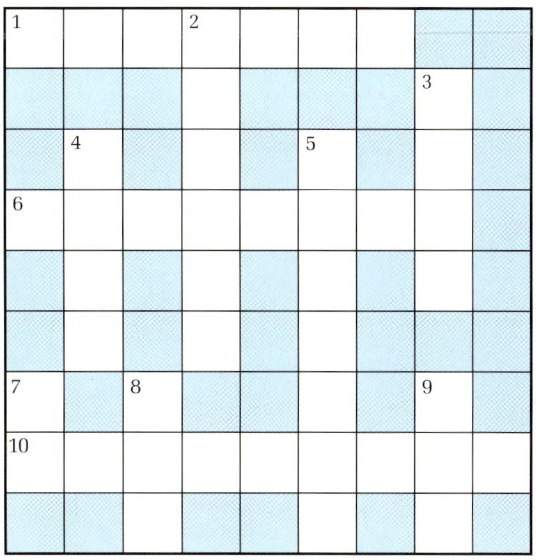

UNIT 2 *Step 2*

3 Tips for telephoning

Mit der Fernmelderechnung verschicken die privaten amerikanischen Telefongesellschaften manchmal Merkblätter mit Hinweisen zum richtigen Umgang mit dem Telefon. Ergänzen Sie in jedem Satz die erste Lücke mit *don't* (3x) oder *always* (6x) und die zweite Lücke mit einem der Wörter aus dem Kasten.

be, call, forget, go, look, put, say, talk, write

Tips for telephoning

The friendly people at your Valley Area Bell Telephone Company want you to be happy with your telephone. Follow these simple rules for trouble-free telephoning:

1 .... in the telephone book to find the right number before you call.

2 .... down important telephone numbers so you won't forget them.

3 .... careful to call the right number.

4 .... you're sorry if you don't get the right number.

5 .... to the telephone quickly when it rings.

6 .... too long; other people might need the telephone.

7 .... people through quickly if they want to talk to someone else.

8 .... to make a list of telephone numbers that you might need again.

9 .... people in the middle of the night.

4 Find the differences.

Auf der Cassette ist dieser Text etwas anders als im Buch. Hören Sie den Text mehrmals an. Beim ersten Mal hören Sie nur zu, beim zweiten Mal unterstreichen Sie die sieben Wörter, die auf der Cassette anders sind. Dann hören Sie noch ein paarmal (ohne die Cassette dauernd anzuhalten) und vervollständigen die untenstehende Tabelle.

speed limit = Geschwindigkeitsbegrenzung

My husband and I went to America last summer for a holiday. What I didn't know about America was that they all drive so fast over there. The speed limit is 55 miles an hour, that's only about 88 kilometres. Most Americans drive faster than that. They're all very unfriendly when you see them out on the roads, and they all drive very badly, if you ask me. We got a car in New York and drove all the way to Arizona. It was a very long journey, and I hope we can do it differently next year.

	She didn't say ...	She said ...
1	*fast*	*slowly*
2		
3		
4		
5		
6		
7		

UNIT 2 *Step 3*

1 The Peace Corps

Lesen Sie den Text. Welches ist das passende Bild?

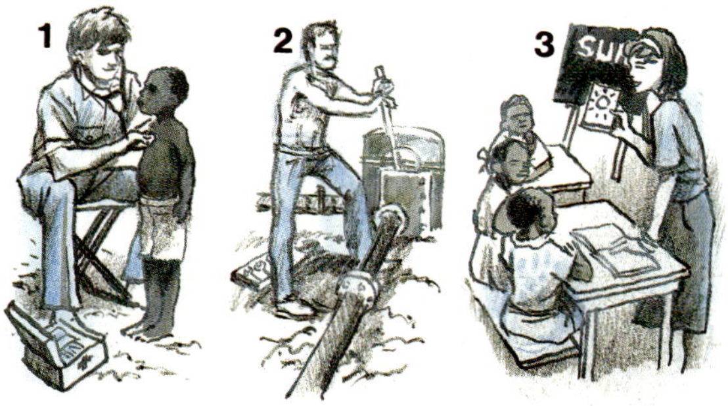

The speaker, a 24-year-old person from Chicago, Illinois, USA, is working as a Peace Corps volunteer in Africa. The Peace Corps is an American organization much like the British VSO.

"I've always wanted to help people, and now I can. The people here are very nice. Some of them speak French or English – British English, not American. I don't speak their language very well, but I've started to learn, and I'm sure I can learn quickly. I live in a small village, far from the nearest city. The work is interesting but very hard, and the weather is hot. It never gets cold here, not even in the middle of the night. I get up at five o'clock every morning and start working before it gets too hot. Sometimes I work ten or twelve hours a day, but usually I sleep a little bit after lunch. My big problem is that it takes a very long time to get the things that I need for my work. Sometimes I have to wait for weeks and weeks. Look at this pump, for example. We need it to bring good water to the village, but it's been out of order for a long time. I need some special parts for it, and I can't do anything until the parts arrive from the city."

2 Where is the stress?

Teil 1: Unterstreichen Sie bitte bei den folgenden Wörtern die Silbe, die besonders betont wird (Stress = Betonung). Hören Sie die Cassette zur Kontrolle.

1 prefer	4 assistant	7 moment
2 hotel	5 interesting	8 excellent
3 expensive	6 information	9 student

Teil 2: Hören Sie, wie die Sätze gesprochen werden. Ahmen Sie das Modell nach und betonen Sie richtig.

- I'd prefer a cheaper hotel.
- This one's too expensive.
- My assistant can give you some interesting information.
- Just a moment, I'll put you through to Mr Smith.
- Your daughter is an excellent student.

3 Scrambled sentences

1 a – be – Bob – Chicago – in – student – to – used

....

....

2 always – has – he – help – people – to – wanted

....

....

3 a – America – big – city – he – in – in – live – to – used – very

....

....

4 early – every – gets – he – morning – up – very

....

....

5 doesn't – he – language – speak – their – very – well

....

....

4 Fill in the words.

1 A table in an office.
2 You can write with this.
3 This machine copies papers and letters.
4 This rings a lot.
5 He or she helps the boss.
6 This is where they all work.
7 You can write with this, too.
8 The money that they all get.
9 What they do all day.
10 You can write with this machine.

Key word: A special book that students often use.

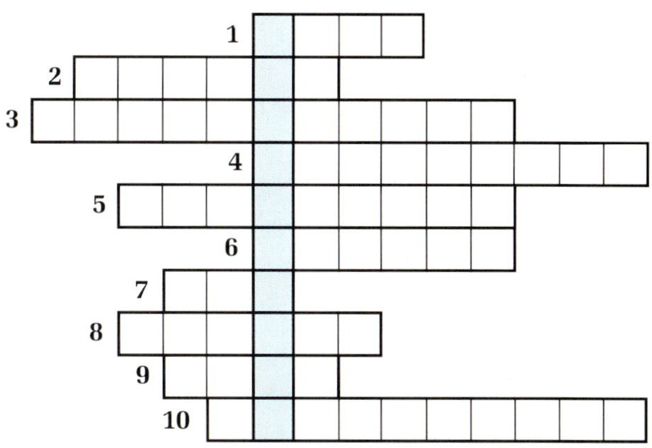

Lerntip 2

Kurse versäumt = Anschluß verpaßt?

1 Sie kennen dies alle: Wir nehmen uns vor, bestimmte Dinge prompt zu erledigen – nicht mehr soviel zu arbeiten, etwas mehr für unsere Gesundheit zu tun, um nur einige wenige gute Vorsätze zu nennen –, doch in Wirklichkeit kommt natürlich oft etwas dazwischen. Diese Erfahrung werden Sie auch mit Ihrem Englischkurs machen. Durch private oder berufliche Verpflichtungen können (und werden) Sie manchmal daran gehindert werden, Ihren Kurs regelmäßig zu besuchen. Es sollte Ihnen ein Trost sein zu wissen, daß es den anderen Kursmitgliedern nicht besser ergeht als Ihnen. Nehmen Sie auf keinen Fall ein einmaliges oder mehrmaliges Fehlen zum Anlaß, die Flinte ins Korn zu werfen und gar nicht mehr auf der Bildfläche zu erscheinen. Es gibt genügend Möglichkeiten, sich über die Kursstunden auf dem laufenden zu halten und Versäumtes eigenständig nachzuholen.

2 Zunächst einmal einige Hinweise, die banal klingen mögen, es aber wert sind, daß wir uns an sie erinnern: Vom Aufbau des Lehrbuchs und von den bisherigen Kursstunden her wissen wir, wieviel Stoff in einer Unterrichtsstunde bearbeitet wird, so daß wir uns leicht ausrechnen können, was wir versäumt haben und wo die Lerngruppe steht. Das erleichtert unsere Planung, uns den versäumten Stoff selbst anzueignen. Hinzu kommt, daß die Steps einer Unit miteinander verzahnt sind. Sie haben unterschiedliche Schwerpunkte; in allen dreien aber sind die Lernziele aufeinander bezogen. Aus diesem Grunde ist die Furcht, den Anschluß zu verlieren, wirklich unbegründet, wenn Sie relativ regelmäßig das Kursangebot nutzen können.

3

Bei längerer Abwesenheit, z. B. nach einem dreiwöchigen Urlaub, bitten Sie Ihren Kursleiter/Ihre Kursleiterin um Unterstützung und eine kleine Zusammenfassung des versäumten Stoffs, und scheuen Sie sich auch nicht, Ihre Mitlernenden um Mithilfe zu bitten. Diese werden gern die Gelegenheit nutzen, Ihnen bei einer Tasse Kaffee oder einem Glas Wein (auf Ihre Kosten natürlich, und das ist aber auch schon die ganze „Strafe“ für Ihr Fehlen) den Lernstoff zu erklären und damit auch für sich selbst zu wiederholen. Und Lernen zu zweit oder in der Gruppe macht viel mehr Spaß als allein im Kämmerlein.

4 Die beiden Lernercassetten dienen dem Hör- und Sprechtraining, so daß Sie keine Angst haben müssen, ohne das Sprachmodell Ihres Kursleiters/Ihrer Kursleiterin kämen Sie nicht zurecht. Gerade für das eigenständige Nacharbeiten sollten Sie die Lernercassetten gezielt zum mehrfachen Hören und Nachsprechen einsetzen. Überprüfen Sie durch das Arbeiten mit dem dreispaltigen Wortschatzanhang, ob Sie die neu gelernten Wörter behalten haben und beherrschen. Das sind Arbeitsvorlagen, die Sie ja sonst auch einsetzen und die sich als nutzbringend erwiesen haben. Mit dem Übungsangebot des *Homestudy*-Teils können Sie das Gelernte weiter festigen und dann anschließend die Lösungen mit dem Schlüssel überprüfen.

5 In den Steps des Lehrbuchteils selbst können Sie die Dialoge zunächst bei geschlossenem Buch zweimal hören und danach auf der Grundlage dieses Sprachmodells die Texte laut lesen. Die step- oder unitbegleitende Wortschatzliste bietet Ihnen die erforderliche Verständnishilfe. Die Grammatikkästen erklären Strukturen und zeigen Verwendungszusammenhänge auf. Mit ein wenig Phantasie wird es Ihnen auch gelingen, sich still oder sogar laut mit einem vorgestellten und nicht wirklich existierenden Gesprächspartner zu unterhalten, wenn Sie in Ihrer Familie oder Ihrem Freundeskreis kein geeignetes Opfer finden. Auf diese Weise können Sie vielleicht nicht alle, aber doch eine Menge Übungsangebote des Lehrwerks im Notfall auch allein nutzen. So werden Sie ganz schnell wieder den Anschluß an Ihre Lerngruppe finden.

Test yourself 1

1 Listening

Lesen Sie Pamelas Postkarte an ihre Mutter. Dann hören Sie mehrmals, was Pamela auf der Cassette zu erzählen hat. Kreuzen Sie an, welche Aussagen auf der Postkarte richtig und welche falsch sind.

Dear Mum,

Thanks for your nice letter. Yes, of course I'm OK, Mum. I am 18 now, you know. The weather isn't very good here this summer, but I like my job at the hotel. It's a very expensive hotel. I work in the restaurant and I'm a fast worker.
My boss is very nice and helps us a lot. He has a big dog. I go swimming every day and I am not eating too much!

Love, Pamela

	True	False
1 The weather isn't very good here this summer,		
2 but I like my job at the hotel.		
3 It's a very expensive hotel.		
4 I work in the restaurant		
5 and I'm a fast worker.		
6 My boss is very nice and helps us a lot.		
7 He has a big dog.		
8 I go swimming every day		
9 and I am not eating too much!		

2 Please complete.

Setzen Sie die fehlenden Wörter ein.

1 .... you ever been to Canada?

2 No, I've .... been there. What's it like?

3 It's wonderful. Canada's the .... interesting country that I've ever visited.

4 When .... you go there?

5 I .... to Canada last summer.

6 My uncle .... to live in Canada, but now he lives in the United States.

3 A crossword

Schreiben Sie zu jedem Bild das richtige Wort. Das Lösungswort (senkrecht) ist ein Glückwunsch.

4 Adverbs

Vervollständigen Sie die Antworten.

1 Is he a good singer?

Yes, he sings very ....

2 Is he a bad cook?

Yes, he cooks very ...., I'm afraid.

3 Is he a hard worker?

Yes, he works very ....

4 Is he a slow driver?

Yes, he drives very ....

5 Is his wife a fast driver?

Yes, she drives very ....

6 Is she a quick learner?

Yes, she learns very ....

Test yourself 1

5 Comparatives and superlatives

Schreiben Sie die richtige Form des Adjektivs in die Lücke.
His office is *smaller* than yours. (small)

1 I have the .... office of all. (small)

2 His computer is .... than my computer. (good)

3 Our boss has got the .... computer in the company. (expensive)

4 This job is .... than my last job. (interesting)

5 That man is the .... person here. (nice)

6 The weather is .... today than it was yesterday. (bad)

6 Pronunciation

Unterstreichen Sie die stummen Buchstaben, d.h. solche, die nicht ausgesprochen werden. In den vier Wörtern gibt es vier stumme Buchstaben.

autumn	comb	island	walk

7 Say it in English.

Schreiben Sie die Unterhaltung zwischen John und Sue. Die Redewendungen, die Sie dazu benötigen, haben Sie größtenteils in den Dialogen und Abschnitten *How to say it* kennengelernt. (Die in Klammern aufgeführten deutschen Hinweise sollen Sie nicht wörtlich übersetzen, sondern nur als Anhaltspunkt benutzen, um die jeweils passende Redewendung zu finden.)
(J=John, S=Sue)

J: Would .... ?
(John lädt Sue ein, mit ihm morgen abend ins Kino zu gehen.)

S: I'd ....
(Sue würde liebend gerne, bedauert aber, daß sie nicht kann.)

Why .... ?
(Sie schlägt vor, am nächsten Dienstag zu gehen.)

J: That's ....
(John findet die Idee gut.)

Have .... ?
(Er fragt, ob sie jemals den Film „Casablanca" gesehen hat.)

S: Yes, ... three times.
(Sie hat ihn dreimal gesehen.)

I ....

....
(Sie mag alte Filme, würde es aber vorziehen, am Dienstag einen moderneren Film zu sehen.)

J: Okay, ...
(Er schlägt vor, ins Apollo-Kino zu gehen.)

They ....
(Er sagt, daß sie dort immer die neuesten Filme haben.)

S: The ....
(Sie sagt, daß das Kino möglicherweise voll sein wird.)

Let's ....
(Sie schlägt vor, zu versuchen, früh dort zu sein.)

UNIT 3 *Step 1*

1 Make pairs.

a Ordnen Sie die Wörter paarweise einander zu.

1 ☐ only	a magazine
2 ☐ single	b explanation
3 ☐ possible	c room
4 ☐ weekly	d backache
5 ☐ helpful	e child
6 ☐ terrible	f specialist
7 ☐ famous	g receptionist

b Setzen Sie nun die gefundenen Wortpaare in die Satzlücken.

1 The .... in the big hotel showed me my ....

2 She had .... and went to a ....

3 Which .... do you read?

4 All my friends have got brothers and sisters, but I'm an ....

5 Let's look for a ....

2 If I were Mrs Lloyd I would ...

Die allein lebende gebrechliche Mrs Lloyd hat sich ihr linkes Bein gebrochen und ist deshalb auf die Hilfe ihrer Nachbarn und all ihrer lieben Angehörigen angewiesen. Vervollständigen Sie die Ratschläge von Tochter Sandra.

Mum, if .... (1), I'd ask Mr Hogan to go shopping for you. He is very friendly. I'm sure he will do it. .... (2) ask Ann to cook the lunch for you? I think you .... (3) ask brother Paul to do the work in the flat. And why .... (4) ask Mrs Gress to help you get up in the morning? If .... (5) I'd ask Mary to visit you in the afternoons. And Joe and I will come after work and do the garden for you.

3 Making an appointment

Mr Partington ist Vertreter und ruft montags in einer Firma an, um einen Gesprächstermin mit seinem Geschäftspartner Dr Keach zu verabreden. Ordnen Sie seine Gesprächsanteile, die in dem Kasten aufgelistet sind, richtig ein.

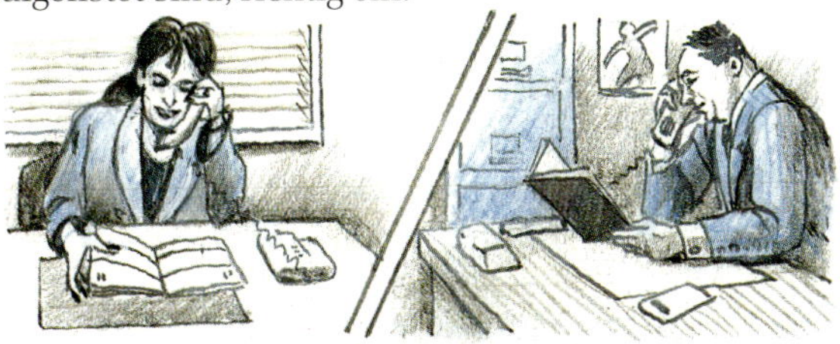

1 Wednesday is fine, but I'd prefer the afternoon if possible.
2 Good morning. My name's Fred Partington. Can I speak to Dr Keach, please?
3 Yes, that's fine. Thank you very much. Goodbye.
4 Well, I'd like to make an appointment to see him, please.
5 Tomorrow is not very good. I won't be here, I'm afraid. I'll be out of town.

(S = Mrs Sommer, P = Mr Partington)

S: Dr Keach's office.

P: ....

....

....

S: Oh, I'm sorry. Dr Keach is away today. Can I help you?

P: ....

....

....

S: Yes, Mr Partington. How about tomorrow at three?

P: ....

....

....

S: Well, would you like to come on Wednesday then, at eleven?

P: ....

....

S: Okay. Wednesday at half past three?

P: ....

....

S: Goodbye, Mr Partington.

UNIT 3 *Step 2*

1 What are they doing right now?

Mrs Stafford ist der gute Geist im ganzen Mietshaus und nimmt am Leben ihrer Mitbewohner regen Anteil. Jetzt aber muß sie etwas für ihre eigene Gesundheit tun und ist deshalb zur Kur, ruft aber täglich ihren Mann an und läßt sich über alles „Wissenswerte“ informieren.

Sagen Sie, was die abgebildeten Personen gerade tun.

1 Andrew and Lena .... in the garden.

2 Susan .... in her room.

3 Paul ....

4 Mrs Bryant .... Italian meal.

5 The Wilsons ....

6 Diana ...., she's not at home.

2 An interview

Hören Sie die Cassette und kreuzen Sie an, welche Aussagen wahr und welche falsch sind.

	True	False
1 Sue is a reporter for a newspaper.		
2 Mrs Lamb is making lunch at the moment.		
3 Mr Lamb is helping her in the kitchen.		
4 Mr Lamb normally goes to work by bus.		
5 Mrs Lamb usually works at a hotel.		
6 Sue always helps her mother at home.		
7 Mrs Lamb enjoys being a housewife.		
8 Mrs Lamb is enjoying her work today.		

3 Questions and answers

Ordnen Sie die Antworten den entsprechenden Fragen zu.

1 ☐ Is John coming home?
2 ☐ What's Barbara doing in the office?
3 ☐ Are the children doing their homework in their room?
4 ☐ Is Peter smoking a cigar?
5 ☐ Is Mary getting up?
6 ☐ Are Andrew and Mark playing golf?
7 ☐ Where is Al drinking a beer?
8 ☐ Are Susan and Paula travelling by plane?

a Yes, they are. They don't like travelling by car or by train.
b Yes, they are. Golf is their favourite sport.
c He's drinking a beer in the pub round the corner.
d No, she isn't. She's still sleeping.
e No, he isn't. He's still working with a colleague.
f Yes, they are. They're sitting in their room; they are doing their exercises.
g No, he isn't. He's smoking a cigarette now.
h She's making an appointment for her boss.

UNIT 3 *Step 2 / Step 3*

4 You must (+), mustn't (!), don't have to (–) ...

Mr und Mrs Marshall machen an einem verlängertem Wochenende Urlaub. Ihre halbwüchsigen Kinder wollten schon immer einmal allein zu Hause sein. Aber natürlich müssen sie ... (must = +), müssen sie nicht ... (don't have to = –) und dürfen sie nicht ... (mustn't = !). Welche Anweisungen haben ihnen ihre Eltern gegeben? Schreiben Sie ganze Sätze.

1 + do homework
2 ! watch TV all evening
3 – work in the garden
4 ! forget to go for a walk with the dog
5 + phone Uncle Thomas
6 ! stay out too long
7 + remember tennis lessons
8 + go shopping
9 ! smoke cigarettes and drink alcohol
10 – make the beds

They must do their homework.

....

....

....

....

....

....

....

....

....

....

Step 3

1 What must you do? / mustn't you do? / don't you have to do?

Wir alle wissen, was Körper und Geist guttun soll. Auf vieles müssen wir verzichten und auch manchmal unsere Trägheit überwinden, um gesteckte Ziele zu erreichen.

Vervollständigen Sie bitte die begonnenen Aussagesätze.

You know, we all feel tired from time to time. We .... (1) have enough sleep. We .... (2) work too hard, and to stay fit we .... (3) get regular exercise. We .... (4) see our doctor so often, if* we live carefully. We .... (5) drink too much alcohol, but one glass of wine per day is fine. And doctors tell us we .... (6) smoke cigarettes.

To learn a foreign language is an excellent idea. We .... (7) learn the new words in our units. But we should not learn single words, we should learn the words in sentences and situations. We should practise our pronunciation, but we .... (8) speak English perfectly.

We .... (9) repeat all the new words every day, but we should use them often.

If* we really do all this, we will be okay. Perhaps.

* *if = wenn, falls*

UNIT 3 *Step 3*

2 That's interesting, it's the same in German.

Sie kennen mittlerweile schon recht viele Wörter, die Teile unseres Körpers beschreiben. Diese Wörter tauchen auch in bildhaften Ausdrücken auf, für die es im Deutschen Entsprechungen gibt. Wie lauten sie?

1 What beautiful chips. They really *make my mouth water.*

....

....

2 He always *lives from hand to mouth.*

....

....

3 She took the *words out of my mouth.*

....

....

4 It's nice to *put your feet up* after a long day.

....

....

5 My son *tries to stand on his own two feet.*

....

....

6 He *only has eyes for* his girlfriend.

....

....

7 They did it *under the nose of* the police.

....

....

8 Always try to *keep a cool/clear head* in difficult situations.

....

....

9 I can't *get* all these new words *into my head.*

....

....

10 He didn't want to know that. He *hid* his head in the sand.*

....

....

11 *Heads will roll.*

....

....

**hide (hid, hidden) = verstecken*

12 He *didn't lift a finger* to help them.

....

....

Und damit ist das gute Dutzend voll. Wenn Sie mit Ihren Übersetzungen beherzt zugepackt haben, haben Sie sich bestimmt nicht die Finger verbrannt, *you didn't burn your fingers.*

Sehr oft entsprechen sich die englischen und deutschen idiomatischen Redewendungen aber nicht. Vorsicht ist also geboten, wenn Sie „Bilder" direkt übersetzen wollen. Das kann für den anderen sehr lustig klingen. Schauen Sie also lieber einmal im Wörterbuch nach.

3 Giving advice

Sie hören vier Gespräche zwischen Personen mit gesundheitlichen Beschwerden und Freunden oder Ärzten. Ordnen Sie die Gespräche den Bildern zu.

Dialogue ☐

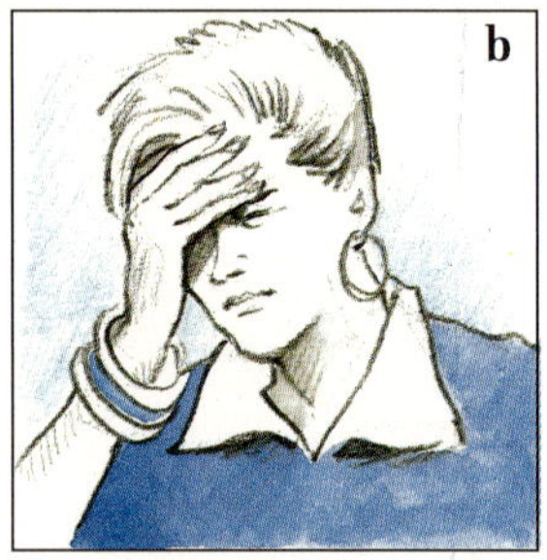

Dialogue ☐

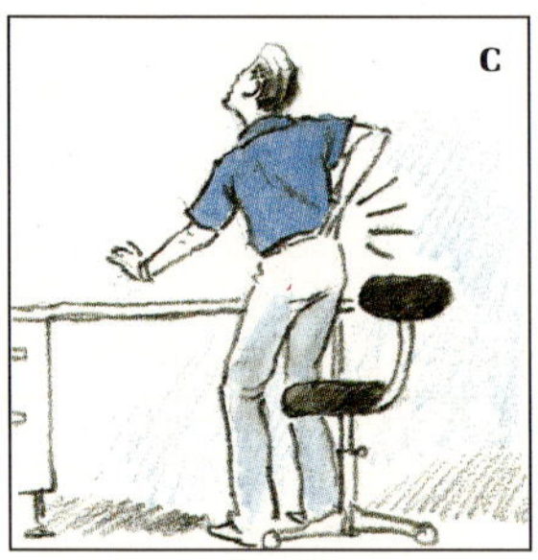

Dialogue ☐

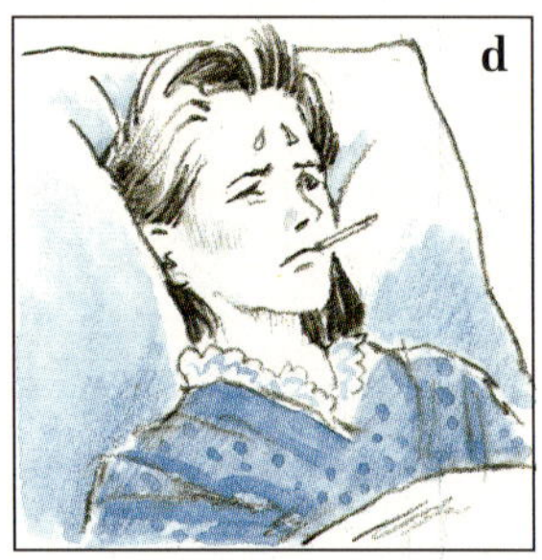

Dialogue ☐

Hören Sie nun die Cassette noch einmal und ergänzen Sie die folgenden Sätze.

1 Why don't you ....

2 I think we should ....

3 You really must ....

4 If I were you ....

Lerntip 3

Die Arbeit zu Hause – *DOs* and *DON'Ts*

1 „Was sollen wir denn zu Hause machen?“ ist eine der Standardfragen, die ständig gestellt werden. Und auch Sie möchten wahrscheinlich auf einige Hinweise nicht verzichten. Doch eins vorweg: Zu Hause bestimmen Sie selbst Ihre Lernumgebung, Ihr Lernverfahren und -tempo und lösen sich von der leitenden Hand Ihres Kursleiters/Ihrer Kursleiterin. Im Ernstfall müssen Sie ja auch mit Ihrem eigenen Sprachvermögen und Können zurechtkommen. Einige Empfehlungen jedoch möchten wir Ihnen vermitteln, was Sie zu Hause tun können und was Sie besser oder sogar unbedingt vermeiden sollten, dies nennt man im Englischen die *DOs* and *DON'Ts*.

2 Sie möchten Erfolge sehen. Gerade für das selbstverantwortliche Lernen ist es wichtig, sorgfältig zu planen, Lücken zu erkennen und diese auszufüllen. Dabei hilft Ihnen der *Homestudy*-Teil von *English Network*. Die Übungen bieten Ihnen eine zuverlässige Erfolgskontrolle. Arbeiten Sie deshalb den Stoff der Unterrichtsstunden bitte nach und beziehen den *Homestudy*-Teil in Ihre Wiederholung mit ein. Es sollte gewährleistet sein, daß Sie sich möglichst jeden Tag eine Viertelstunde mit dem Englischen beschäftigen, so daß Sie gleichsam ständig im Training sind.

3 Während das Schreiben innerhalb Ihres Kurses eine eher untergeordnete Rolle spielt, kommt ihm in der häuslichen Nachbereitung eine größere Bedeutung zu. Sollten Sie die Angebote Ihres Lehrwerks ergänzen wollen, bieten sich z. B. die folgenden Verfahren an, die von den Texten in Step 1 oder Step 3 ausgehen:

- Text lesen und einprägen.
- Satzanfänge schreiben und die Sätze selbständig ergänzen.
- Kopieren Sie den Text und löschen Sie auf der Kopie die Ihnen schwierig erscheinenden Wörter mit Korrekturflüssigkeit. Nach ein oder zwei Tagen füllen Sie die Lücken aus.
- Bilden Sie eigenständig Sätze mit dem neuen Wortschatz. Es macht zunächst gar nichts, wenn Sie sich eng an die Originalvorgabe anlehnen.
- Schreiben Sie Stichwörter zu dem Text auf.
- Fassen Sie auf der Grundlage dieser Stichwörter den Text zusammen und finden Sie eine neue Überschrift.

Es wäre schön, wenn Sie diese Anregungen aufgreifen und auch für sich selbst weitere Verfahren entwickeln könnten.

4 Dieser Hinweis ist umso wichtiger, wenn Ihnen keine Hausarbeiten aufgegeben werden. Dann liegt es an Ihnen, mit Ihren Mitlernenden Ideen auszutauschen, was Sie allein oder zu mehreren zu Hause tun können. Die zu lösenden Aufgaben sollten sich sinnvoll aus dem Unterrichtsgeschehen ergeben. Es ist folglich in diesem Bereich Ihre Eigeninitiative gefragt. Versuchen Sie, das Neue mit bereits Bekanntem zu verknüpfen, dann erscheint es nicht mehr so schwierig, sondern kommt einem schon vertraut vor. Und man versteht und behält es viel besser.

5 Vermeiden Sie bitte:

- das Auswendiglernen von Einzelwörtern;
- das Vorlernen. Sie laufen Gefahr, sich etwas Falsches anzueignen, wenn Sie auf die Einführung durch Ihren Kursleiter/Ihre Kursleiterin verzichten;
- das Lernen von grammatischen Regeln ohne Anwendungsbezug, d. h. mindestens ein einleuchtender Beispielsatz sollte zur Verdeutlichung einer Regel mitgelernt werden:

Regel Past tense	+	“I went to Paris last year.”
Regel Present perfect	+	“Have you ever been to London?”

Halten Sie sich bitte an diese Empfehlungen, denn nichts ist trügerischer und störender als eine falsche Sicherheit.

DOs	DON'Ts
Text lesen und einprägen	~~Einzelwörter auswendig lernen~~
Satzanfänge schreiben und selbständig ergänzen	~~Vorlernen~~
schwierige Wörter löschen und Lücken ergänzen	~~grammatische Regeln ohne Beispielsatz lernen~~
Sätze mit neuem Wortschatz bilden	
Stichwörter zum Text aufschreiben	
Text mit neuer Überschrift zusammenfassen	

UNIT 4 *Step 1*

1 In the tourist bus

Setzen Sie die Wörter aus dem Kasten in die Lücken des Textes ein.

along at at at for for for in of of on on on on to to to

"Good morning and welcome .... (1) the beautiful city .... (2) Vienna. We are happy that you have come .... (3) Vienna .... (4) your holiday, and we'll show you all the most important parks and buildings. We are driving .... (5) the famous Ring Street. .... (6) your right you can see the New Castle, and next .... (7) the castle are the castle gardens. .... (8) your left there are two museums. They are both open .... (9) the weekend but are closed .... (10) Mondays. If you can't find them again, you can ask .... (11) help .... (12) the tourist office. Later we'll see one .... (13) the houses where Wolfgang Amadeus Mozart used to live. He lived .... (14) the top floor, but he only lived there .... (15) six months. Mozart and his family had eighteen different flats .... (16) Vienna .... (17) different times."

2 Crossword

Das erste Wort haben wir für Sie schon eingesetzt.

1 P	2 A	I	N	3 T		4	5		6
				7					
8									
					9		10	11	
12			13						
							14		15
	16					17			
18					19				
20	21			22					
23						24			

Across (➔):

1 To put colour on something. (streichen)
4 He doesn't live in a house, he lives in a ... .
7 His flat is ... the second floor.
8 I have a great ... . Why don't we paint the flat?
10 We can ... in the dining room.
12 You can sleep in the ... .
14 ... is her favourite colour.
16 There's no lift, so we must walk up the ... .
19 I can't ... that colour. It looks terrible.
20 She isn't home. I think she's ... holiday.
23 Her flat has got four ..., but they aren't very big.
24 Thank you for inviting me to ... house.

Down (➔↓):

2 Her ... is 14 Sterling Road.
3 Do you want ... paint the flat?
5 I don't ... this colour very much.
6 This picture isn't so nice, but ... one is beautiful.
9 His flat has got new ... and windows.
11 Some friends ... coming to visit us.
13 You can sit and ... a book.
15 How ... you find this lovely flat?
17 Why don't you ... at our house tonight?
18 Does she want to rent a flat ... ten months?
21 ..., she doesn't.
22 This ... the entrance hall, and that's the dining room.

UNIT 4 *Step 1*

3 Listening

Hören Sie dem gesprochenen Text mehrmals zu, ohne die Cassette anzuhalten. Fangen Sie beim zweiten Mal an, die Lücken im gedruckten Text zu ergänzen.

(M = Man, W = Woman)

M: Hey, I've got a great idea. Why don't we paint the flat this .... (1)?

W: Yes, okay. But what .... (2) should we paint it?

M: Well, the .... (3) should be blue.

W: Blue? Perhaps the .... (4) could be blue, but not the .... (5)!

M: Here's a nice yellow for the .... (6).

W: That's not bad, but I'd prefer green for the .... (7) and the .... (8).

M: Green? You know I can't stand green. But you can paint the .... (9) green if you want to.

W: I don't want to paint the .... (10) green. That would be terrible.

M: Well, the .... (11) has to be white, in any case.

W: White isn't a very .... (12) colour. How about brown?

M: Never!

W: I've got a better idea. We don't .... (13) have to paint the flat. We can go on .... (14) instead.

4 Asking permission

Bitten Sie um Erlaubnis mit dem Wort *may*. Benutzen Sie außerdem jeweils zwei der folgenden Wörter oder Ausdrücke in jedem Satz. Die Wörter oder Ausdrücke können nur einmal benutzt werden.

a drink, dictionary, go and have, kitchen, look at, lunch, bring, open, see, telephone, use, window

1 I'd like to ring my brother.

....

....?

2 I don't know what this word means.

....

....?

3 It's very hot in here.

....

....?

4 The dining room is very nice.

....

....?

5 You look hot and tired.

....

....?

6 Mr Jones, I'm very hungry.

....

....?

UNIT 4 *Step 2*

1 Selling a car

Hören Sie dem gesprochenen Dialog mehrmals zu und kreuzen Sie die richtigen Antworten an.

1 Who is the person who wants to sell a car?

☐ the man ☐ her daughter
☐ the woman ☐ her son

2 Who is the person who gave the address?

☐ the husband ☐ the daughter
☐ the son ☐ the mother

3 If the man wants to see the car, he'll have to come over

☐ today. ☐ tomorrow morning.
☐ this evening. ☐ tomorrow afternoon.

4 The man wants a car which has got

☐ two doors and is not more than two years old.
☐ two doors and is not more than four years old.
☐ four doors and is not more than two years old.
☐ four doors and is not more than four years old.

2 Find the right place.

Wo müssen wir *'ll* (oder *will*) einsetzen? Kreuzen Sie die richtige Stelle an – aber nur einmal in jedem Satz!

1 If ☐ the ☐ weather ☐ is ☐ good, he ☐ walk ☐ to ☐ work.

2 He ☐ walk ☐ to ☐ work ☐ if ☐ the ☐ weather ☐ is ☐ good.

3 If ☐ the ☐ train ☐ isn't ☐ late, we ☐ be ☐ able ☐ to ☐ go ☐ shopping.

4 If ☐ she ☐ isn't ☐ here ☐ now, we ☐ have ☐ to ☐ come ☐ back ☐ tomorrow ☐ morning.

5 I ☐ play ☐ the ☐ piano ☐ if ☐ you ☐ want ☐ to ☐ sing ☐ your ☐ new ☐ song.

6 You ☐ feel ☐ better ☐ if ☐ you ☐ don't ☐ smoke ☐ so ☐ much.

7 If ☐ you ☐ come ☐ to ☐ Hanover, I ☐ take ☐ you ☐ to ☐ a ☐ nice ☐ restaurant.

8 If ☐ you ☐ walk ☐ past ☐ the ☐ cinema ☐ and ☐ turn ☐ left, you ☐ soon ☐ come ☐ to ☐ the ☐ supermarket.

3 Words

Setzen Sie diese Wörter in die Lücken ein. Benutzen Sie jedes Wort nur einmal.

> dictionary, exercise, food, irregular, large, lovely, meat, nice, north, start, stop, terrible, town unfriendly, village, wine

1 A .... is a kind of[1] book.

2 .... is about the same as big.

3 The opposite[2] of wonderful is ....

4 A .... is usually smaller than a city but larger than a ....

5 .... is a kind of drink.

6 Jogging is a kind of ....

7 South is the opposite of ....

8 The opposite of friendly is ....

9 The opposite of regular is ....

10 .... is a kind of ....

11 .... is about the same as ....

12 .... is the opposite of ....

(*[1]a kind of = eine Art, [2]the opposite = das Gegenteil*)

4 *Who* or *which*?

Ergänzen Sie die Lücken mit *who* oder *which*.

1 He would like to have a girlfriend .... doesn't smoke.

2 He has a car .... is ten years old.

3 Are you the person .... doesn't eat meat?

4 He's the man .... didn't marry Pamela Brown.

5 I'm reading a book .... is very interesting.

6 My father was a man .... always worked hard.

UNIT 4 *Step 3*

1 When I was a child

Setzen Sie die Wörter aus dem Kasten in die Lücken des Textes ein.

at at at at in in in on on to to to with

"When I was a child I lived .... (1) a farm but I went .... (2) school .... (3) a big town. Every morning I used to get up .... (4) a quarter past five, but that wasn't so bad because my parents and my brothers and sisters all got up .... (5) that time. We ate breakfast .... (6) the kitchen and .... (7) six o'clock I used to leave the house and walk .... (8) the bus stop. .... (9) the winter the school bus was often late and it was terribly cold and windy while I waited there .... (10) the bus stop. But it was usually nice and warm in the bus, and I used to have long talks .... (11) my friends .... (12) the way .... (13) school."

2 Listening

Füllen Sie die Tabelle mit den Informationen von der Cassette.

Number of rooms	
Number of bathrooms	
Rent at the beginning	
Rent now	
Good things about this flat	1 .... 2 ....

3 *If* and *will*

Schreiben Sie diese Sätze um. Benutzen Sie dabei die Zukunftsformen von *can* und *must*. Den ersten Satz haben wir als Beispiel schon umgeschrieben. (Achtung: Das Wort *will* kommt nur einmal in jedem Satz vor!)

1 If it doesn't rain today, we can go swimming.
If it doesn't rain today, we will be able to go swimming.

2 If you miss the bus, you must walk.

....

....

3 If you have a backache, you must see the doctor.

....

....

4 If you have a camera, you can take some pictures.

....

....

....

5 If she gets a new job, she can go on holiday this summer.

....

....

....

6 If the lift isn't working, we must walk up the stairs.

....

....

....

7 If you go to England, you can practise your English.

....

....

....

8 You can practise your English if you go to England.

....

....

....

Lerntip 4

Die Versuchung, den Kurs abzubrechen ...

1 Auch Sie werden erleben, daß einzelne Mitlernende den Kurs schon recht bald unregelmäßig besuchen oder ihm ganz fernbleiben. Das ist für Ihren Kursleiter/Ihre Kursleiterin unangenehm, der/die dies oft als Anzeichen dafür nimmt, daß bestimmte Erwartungen bei den Kursteilnehmern nicht erfüllt wurden. Deshalb nutzen Sie bitte das ernst gemeinte Gesprächsangebot und reden Sie offen darüber, wenn Sie am Kurs etwas stört. Schnelle Schuldzuweisungen sind allerdings unangebracht, denn oft wurde die zeitliche Belastung von den Aussteigern unterschätzt, und sie brechen ihren Kurs ab, um Kollisionen mit privaten oder beruflichen Verpflichtungen auszuweichen. Und Sie selbst sollten sich auch fairerweise fragen, ob Ihre Erwartungen an den Kurs realistisch sind. Beim Fremdsprachenerwerb ist „das Unmögliche nicht sofort erreichbar“ und „auch Wunder dauern etwas länger“.

2 Manchmal ist es unvermeidlich, daß Lernende den Kurs verlassen, weil ... Und hier setzt auch schon die Ursachenforschung an. Befragungsbögen wurden erstellt und eingesetzt, um die Gründe für die sogenannte Schwundquote in den Kursen zu ermitteln. Personen, die einen Sprachkurs abgebrochen haben, konnten z.B. auf einem Erhebungsbogen die für sie zutreffenden Aussagen ankreuzen. Die Anonymität und Vertraulichkeit dieser Daten war natürlich gesichert.

Warum haben Sie den Kurs aufgegeben?

- ☐ Er war zu Ende bzw. wurde nicht fortgesetzt.
- ☐ Ich habe das Ziel, das ich mir gesetzt hatte, erreicht.
- ☐ Ich mußte wegen der beruflichen Belastung aufhören.
- ☐ Meine anderweitigen Verpflichtungen ließen mir keine Zeit.
- ☐ Ich bin umgezogen.
- ☐ Ich wurde krank.
- ☐ Ich hatte einfach keine Lust mehr.
- ☐ Ich war mit dem Unterricht unzufrieden.
- ☐ Er war zu teuer, es wurde zu wenig geboten.
- ☐ Ich fand die anderen Mitlernenden unsympathisch.
- ☐ Am Abend konnte ich mich nicht mehr konzentrieren.
- ☐ Ich mußte zu weit zum Unterricht fahren.
- ☐ Die Lernbelastung war größer, als ich gedacht hatte.

3 Natürlich spielen viele persönliche Gründe eine Rolle, und die Befragungsergebnisse aus einem Kurs sind nicht unbedingt übertragbar; und doch ist es interessant zu wissen, daß relativ viele Abbrecher die zu große Lernbelastung erwähnten und auch ihre mangelnde Konzentrationsfähigkeit am Abend beklagten. Eine Aussage wie „Ich war mit dem Unterricht unzufrieden“ müßte dann präzisiert werden, um die aufgetretenen Probleme zu benennen oder einzukreisen.

4 Häufig genannte Probleme sind anscheinend Kursleitern und Kursleiterinnen anzulasten wie z. B. ein zu hohes Tempo bei der Vermittlung, eine zu unklare Unterrichtsgestaltung oder unzureichende Berücksichtigung der Teilnehmerinteressen. Daß es schwer ist, das für alle passende Lerntempo zu finden, den richtigen Ton zu treffen, das zu erfüllen, was jeder/jede einzelne Lernende jetzt gerade erwartet, braucht hier nicht noch einmal betont zu werden. Nicht alle Bedürfnisse können unter einen Hut gebracht werden. Und deshalb sollten auch Sie etwas Toleranz üben und Verständnis gegenüber den anderen Mitgliedern Ihrer Gruppe und Ihrem Kursleiter/Ihrer Kursleiterin aufbringen.

5 Die Autoren des Lehrbuchs *English Network* haben sich ehrlich bemüht, durch ein abwechslungsreiches Stoff- und Themenangebot dafür zu sorgen, daß Unter- und Überforderungen vermieden werden, daß Sie den Unterricht und Ihr Lernen als positives Erlebnis empfinden. Wenn Sie sich in der Gruppe engagieren, auf Ihr Gegenüber zugehen, mit Lernpartnern zusammenarbeiten und vielleicht auch außerhalb des Kurses Kontakt suchen, werden Sie sich recht bald der Gruppe zugehörig fühlen. Und das ist die Grundlage für ein fruchtbares Lernen in den Kursen. Für das Lernen zu Hause hilft Ihnen eine effektive Zeitplanung, Streß, Hektik und Nervosität zu vermeiden und Erfolgserlebnisse beim Einhalten Ihres Plans zu haben, denn schließlich haben Sie sich dazu durchgerungen und ihn auch durchgehalten.

6 Es gibt viele unterschiedliche Gründe, einen Sprachkurs zu beginnen und ebenso viele, ihn auch wieder abzubrechen. Und oft sind gute Gründe darunter, die wir nicht kritisieren sollten. Die Tatsache, daß Sie beim Lesen dieser Zeilen noch dabei sind, ist natürlich Grund zur Freude, und ein Anlaß, ein bißchen stolz auf sich zu sein.

Test yourself 2

1 Listening

Dr. Smith, ein erfolgreicher Arzt, besucht seinen alten Vater und hört sich dessen Ratschläge an. Hören Sie den Dialog mehrmals. Welche Ratschläge gibt der Vater?

Dr Smith's father says he should

- ☐ 1 buy a new car
- ☐ 2 not buy a new car
- ☐ 3 buy a larger house
- ☐ 4 buy a smaller house
- ☐ 5 make some new friends
- ☐ 6 meet some important people
- ☐ 7 not eat so much
- ☐ 8 not talk so much
- ☐ 9 get more exercise
- ☐ 10 take up jogging
- ☐ 11 stop jogging
- ☐ 12 stop smoking
- ☐ 13 take up swimming
- ☐ 14 read a good newspaper every day
- ☐ 15 visit him more often
- ☐ 16 think about his advice

2 Please complete.

Benutzen Sie die richtige Form von *can* oder *must*.
If you feel sick, *you'll have to* go home. (must)

1 If you work faster,

.... to leave early. (can)

2 If you take up jogging,

.... to buy a pair of jogging shoes. (must)

3 If you have a sore throat, you won't

.... sing at the concert tonight. (can)

4 If you get a toothache while you're there,

.... go to the dentist. (must)

5 If you drink too much coffee, you won't

.... sleep tonight. (can)

6 If you type the letter now, you won't

.... do it tomorrow. (must)

3 What are they doing?

1 What's John doing? –

He's .... a book. (read)

2 What's Linda doing? –

.... (swim)

3 What are Bob and Janet doing? –

.... a song. (write)

4 What's Mr Smith doing? –

.... a fridge. (buy)

5 What's the dog doing? –

It .... (sleep)

6 And Philip? –

.... into the room now. (come)

4 Vocabulary. Please match.

Welche Wörter passen zusammen?

1	☐ bank	a	agent
2	☐ central	b	class
3	☐ first	c	clerk
4	☐ for	d	costume
5	☐ oh	e	dear
6	☐ put	f	heating
7	☐ swimming	g	machine
8	☐ travel	h	sale
9	☐ washing	i	through

Jetzt setzen Sie diese Wendungen richtig ein.

10 Don't forget to take your ....

.... when you go to the beach.

11 If you're looking for a good ....

hotel, why don't you ask a .... to help you?

12 May I put these jeans in the ....

.... ?

13 Hold on just a moment, please, and I'll

.... you .... to Ms Riley.

14 ...., I'm afraid the .... didn't give me the right money.

15 This house is .... It's a modern

house with a balcony and ....

....

Test yourself 2

5 Pronunciation

Unterstreichen Sie die stummen Buchstaben, d.h. solche, die nicht ausgesprochen werden. In den vier Wörtern gibt es vier stumme Buchstaben.

climb cupboard knee know

6 Say it in English.

Schreiben Sie wieder eine Unterhaltung zwischen John und Sue. Die Redewendungen, die Sie dazu benötigen, haben Sie zum Teil in den Dialogen und Abschnitten *How to say it* kennengelernt. (Die in Klammern aufgeführten deutschen Hinweise sollen Sie nicht wörtlich übersetzen, sondern nur als Anhaltspunkt benutzen, um die jeweils passende Redewendung zu finden.)

(J = John, S = Sue)

J: Sue, ... ?
(John bittet Sue um Erlaubnis, ihre Fotos anzuschauen.)

S: Yes, ...
(Sie sagt ja, selbstverständlich.)

I ....
(Diese Fotos hat sie letztes Jahr in Griechenland aufgenommen.)

J: What ....
(John beglückwünscht Sue zu ihren großartigen Fotos.)

S: Thanks, ...
(Sue bedankt sich und sagt, daß sie im Sommer gern photographiert.)

J: Don't .... ?
(Er fragt, ob sie im Winter nicht gern photographiert.)

S: No, ...
(Sie sagt nein.)

It's ....
(Es sei zu kalt.)

And ....
(Und sie hat nicht genug Zeit im Winter.)

J: This ....
(Er sagt, dieses sei ein sehr schönes Foto.)

If ....
(Er gibt ihr den Rat, dieses Foto an eine Zeitschrift zu schicken.)

S: Well, ...
(Möglicherweise wird sie es an *Mega Magazines* schicken.)

They ....
(Sie brauchen immer viele Fotos.)

UNIT 5 *Step 1*

1 A complaint

Ein Kunde beschwert sich beim Manager eines Elektrofachhandels über einen defekten Video-Recorder. Hören Sie dem Gespräch zweimal zu und kreuzen Sie danach an, welche Aussagen richtig oder falsch sind.

	True	False
1 The customer is complaining about the shop assistant.		
2 He is complaining about the bad quality of the picture.		
3 The customer wants his money back.		
4 The manager offers the customer a new recorder.		
5 The customer does not want a new Japanese video recorder, he wants to buy a German one later.		
6 The customer says the recorder is too difficult for him.		
7 The manager does what the customer wants.		

2 A conversation in a shop

Die Unterhaltung zwischen einem Kunden und einem Verkäufer ist hier in einzelne Gesprächsanteile zerlegt worden. Bitte ordnen Sie sie den Sprechern richtig zu und bestimmen Sie auch die Reihenfolge.

1 We've got excellent Italian jackets. You will like them. What size do you take?
2 I'd prefer brown.
3 Good morning, sir. Can I help you?
4 50 or 52, I think.
5 And what colour would you like?
6 Can I try it on?
7 Yes, I'd like a jacket.
8 Certainly, sir. Over there, please.
9 Here's a brown one, size 50, sir.

Verkäufer	Kunde
....	....
....	....
....	....
....	....
....	

3 Odd man out

Teil 1: Ein Wort jeweils paßt nicht in die Reihe. Finden Sie es heraus.

1 rain spring winter summer
2 receptionist guest waitress teacher
3 ties trousers shirts sizes
4 kitchen dining room office bedroom
5 chips carrots steak vegetables
6 jogging climbing swimming sitting
7 television fridge lamp toilet
8 tonight last night yesterday two days ago
9 sofa table picture chair
10 fish cook orange apple

Teil 2: Nachstehend finden Sie Aussagen darüber, was die drei in den zehn Reihen verbleibenden Wörter gemeinsam haben. Ordnen Sie nun die Sätze den genannten Begriffen zu (z. B. 1 d).

☐ a They all stand on feet.
☐ b You can find them in private houses.
☐ c They are all clothes.
☐ d They are seasons of the year.
☐ e They are in the past.
☐ f They are people that you usually meet in a hotel.
☐ g You usually eat them with meat.
☐ h They are sports.
☐ i They need electricity.
☐ j You can eat them.

UNIT 5 *Step 2*

1 In a shop

Setzen Sie bitte die fehlenden Wörter in das Verkaufsgespräch ein, nachdem Sie den Text von der Cassette zweimal gehört haben.

(SA = Shop assistant, C = Customer)

SA: Good morning, madam. Can I .... (1) you?

C: Yes, I'd like a .... (2), please.

SA: .... (3) do you take?

C: 42, I think.

SA: And .... (4) would you .... (5)?

C: I like blue best. Oh, this one's .... (6). .... (7) is it?

SA: It's .... (8). It's .... (9) quality.

C: Oh, no, I'm sorry. That's far too .... (10). Haven't you got a .... (11) blouse than that?

SA: Of course, madam. What about this one?

C: Hm, yes. Can I .... (12), please?

SA: .... (13), madam. Follow me please.

C: It looks nice. I'll take it.

SA: Thank you, madam.

C: Do you take .... (14)?

SA: Yes, madam. We take ...

2 What happened when ...?

Vervollständigen Sie die begonnenen Sätze, indem Sie die Bildinhalte in Sprache umsetzen.

1

2

3

4

5

6

1 Mr Ryan ...., when the telephone rang.

2 She was working, when her boss ....

3 Mr and Mrs Selwood ...., when a man climbed in through the window.

4 The Jollys ...., when a camera team came to their house.

5 Sue and Tom .... the mountain, when suddenly it started to snow.

6 Mr Selby was driving much too fast, when he .... a police car behind him.

7 It ...., when Mr Drake ....

7

UNIT 5 *Step 2 / Step 3*

3 Clothes

Setzen Sie bitte die Ausdrücke für die Bilder in die entsprechenden Zeilen ein. Die beiden Lösungswörter senkrecht bezeichnen Kleidungsstücke, die viele Männer – so klagen sie zumindest häufig – viel zu oft geschenkt erhalten.

Across (→):

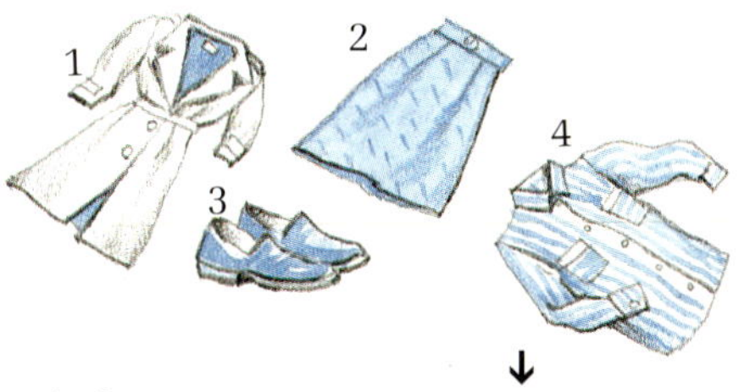

Down (↓):

1 Men get them for Christmas too often.

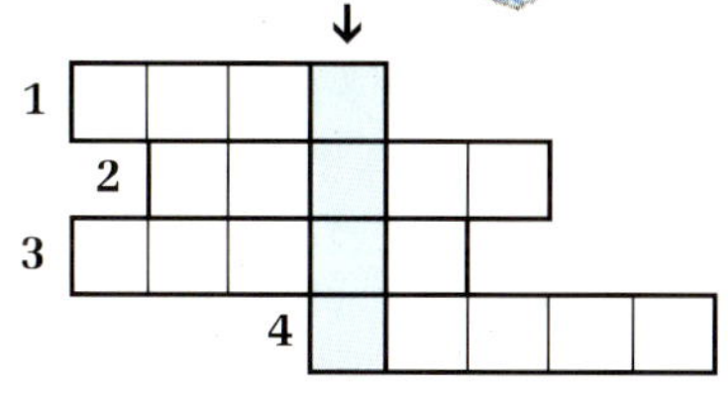

Across (→):

Down (↓):

1 Men get them for Christmas too often.

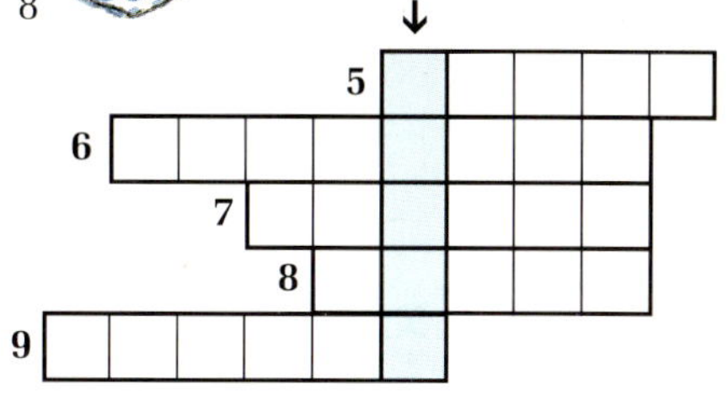

Step 3

1 Is that yours?

Hören Sie die Gespräche von der Cassette zweimal und ordnen Sie die Bilder den Wörtern der Liste zu.

- ☐ a mine
- ☐ b yours
- ☐ c his
- ☐ d hers
- ☐ e ours
- ☐ f theirs

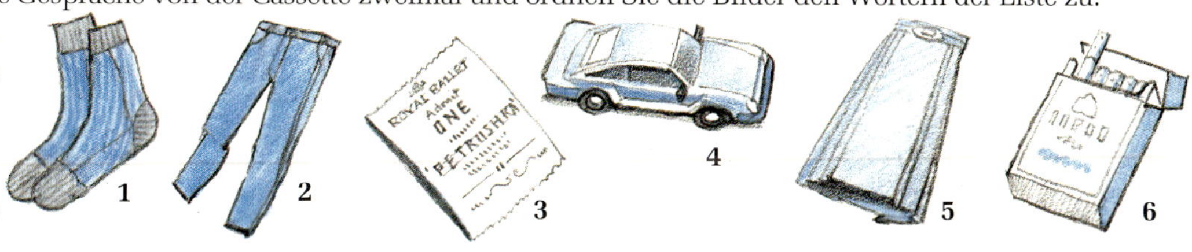

2 The city of York

Setzen Sie bitte in die Lücken des nachstehenden Textes die Wörter aus dem Kasten ein.

best, centre, famous, find, important, like, most, past, really, shops, tourists, will, years

York

York is a busy cultural .... (1) in the north of England, and one of the .... (2) beautiful cities in Britain.

Its .... (3) gothic cathedral and its old houses show how .... (4) the city was in the .... (5). Tourists .... (6) it for its beautiful old buildings, for its museums, but also for its .... (7).

Mulberry Hall in Stonegate is about 500 .... (8) old and is a big attraction for .... (9): it is one of the finest houses in York and one of the .... (10) shops in Europe for fine china.*

Like all .... (11) old cities, York is compact. It is not far from one place to another, and the buildings are not hard to .... (12).

Come and visit York, we know you .... (13) like it.

**china = Porzellan*

UNIT 5 *Step 3*

3 A time for a laugh!

Ordnen Sie bitte den Cartoons die vier passenden Texte zu.

1

2

3

4

a "I was having a shower when the music stopped."
b "What a lovely pullover!"
c "Why don't you sing in the bath like other men?"
d "Son, we think you should know now – we adopted you."
e "They all say that he loved talking to people."
f "When I saw you, I thought, there's a man who isn't married."

4 Oh, all these little words!

Setzen Sie bitte in die Lücken des nachstehenden Textes die passenden Verhältniswörter (Präpositionen) ein.

about for for for in in in in of of of on past to to to to with with with

A visit .... (1) London

When I first went .... (2) London, I wanted to buy a special souvenir. It was .... (3) a street full .... (4) exclusive and very expensive shops that I found a kilt*. I liked it very much, but it was too expensive. So I had to go shopping .... (5) a different souvenir. .... (6) Oxford Street you can find excellent department stores and specialist shops .... (7) books, clothes and shoes. There are lots .... (8) unusual things that you can buy like 3 D-sunglasses and robots. You'll have to come .... (9) me next time and bring two empty suitcases .... (10) you.
Ah, you want to know what I bought? Let me tell you. It was .... (11) the afternoon when I walked .... (12) the window .... (13) a very small shop. I do not really remember what I saw there, but I went in. I had to wait two or three minutes, because a customer was making a complaint .... (14) a swimming costume. Then I talked .... (15) the very friendly shop assistant, and he had a wonderful idea. He showed me some unusual towels .... (16) beautiful, big flowers on them, the right thing .... (17) our bathroom at home .... (18) Germany. And do you know what, my wife's first name was .... (19) them, Eve. We like them very much, and they are a fine souvenir of my visit .... (20) Great Britain.

**kilt = Schottenrock*

Lerntip 5

Grammatik – Spaß oder Büffelei?

1 Sie haben durch das Lehrwerk und durch den Kursbesuch die Grammatik als die Beschreibung des Regelwerks der englischen Sprache kennengelernt. Erfahrungsgemäß prägen sich Regeln besonders gut ein, wenn Sie sie selber entdeckt und für sich formuliert haben. Deshalb werden Ihnen zunächst Beispiele vermittelt, zu denen Sie die Regel(n) selbst ableiten können, bevor sie Ihnen vorgesetzt wird/werden. Wie wäre es, wenn Sie für sich ein grammatisches Merkheft anlegten? Dieses Heft ist im Unterricht mit Kindern weit verbreitet, erleichtert das Wiederholen, fördert das Behalten und ist eine nützliche Gedächtnisstütze, wenn Sie zu jeder Regel griffige und einprägsame Beispielsätze notieren. Denn grammatische Regeln zu wissen, ohne sie anwenden zu können, ist sinnlos.

2 Die Grammatik selbst ist kein Ziel, sondern nur Mittel zum Zweck. Und der Zweck ist unbestritten, die fremde Sprache anzuwenden, mit ihr Aussagen zu machen und nicht Aussagen über sie zu machen. Natürlich ist es verständlich, daß Sie begreifen wollen, was Sie lernen, doch sollten Sie folgendes wissen:

- Eine grammatische Aussage kann häufig nur beschreiben und nicht alles erklären.
- Nicht alles kann gleichzeitig vermittelt werden. Zügeln Sie deshalb Ihre Ungeduld. Vertrauen Sie darauf, daß nach manchem grammatischen Appetithäppchen auch noch das Hauptgericht mit dem vollständigen Speisenangebot auf Sie wartet und Sie bestimmt sättigen wird. Manche komplexeren grammatischen Probleme werden manchmal nur in einem Teilaspekt behandelt, später wieder aufgegriffen, ergänzt und vertieft.
- Lernen Sie ruhig bestimmte Ausdrücke als feste Einheiten, denn nicht alles kann grammatikalisch sinnvoll zergliedert werden. Sprachen verfahren nicht immer logisch und vernünftig: Wieso heißt es im Deutschen „ohne Dich“ aber „mit Dir“, während es im Englischen “*without you*” und viel vernünftiger auch “*with you*” heißt? Könnten Sie für Ihre Muttersprache hier eine logische Erklärung liefern? Und wenn nicht, was machen Sie dann? Am besten auswendig lernen.

3 Grammatische Bezeichnungen sind bisweilen noch willkürlich und nicht immer vereinheitlicht. Sie brauchen sie auch nicht zu lernen, es genügt eigentlich, genau zu wissen, wie und wann man eine Sprachstruktur verwendet und dies auch zu tun. Den Härtetest liefert die Praxis, und die ist auf jeden Fall aussagekräftiger als das begeisterte Nicken eines Lehrers/einer Lehrerin, wenn man ihnen sagen kann, daß es sich bei einer vorliegenden Form um die Zeit „Past tense progressive form“ handeln muß, weil ...

4 Sie werden in der Schule die Erfahrung gemacht haben, daß sich Regeln über Eselsbrücken oder Reime viel eher und dauerhafter einprägen: z.B.

> Der Engländer nimmt das Futur strikt,
> wenn er in die Zukunft blickt.
> Der Deutsche nimmt meist Gegenwart,
> das ist so seine Eigenart.[1]

Das macht Spaß, und die kleine Denksportaufgabe lohnt sich für Sie wirklich. Vergleichen Sie einmal Ihre Formulierungen mit denen Ihrer Mitlernenden, vielleicht kommt es unter Ihnen allen zu einem reizvollen Ideenwettbewerb. Etwas später dann können Sie es auf englisch versuchen (Ihr Kursleiter/Ihre Kursleiterin wird Ihnen sicher helfen!) und erhalten Ergebnisse wie die folgende nützliche Kommaregel für die englische Sprache:

> When in doubt leave it out.

frei übersetzt

> Das Komma im Englischen wird Dir nicht zur Plage, laß' es aus im Zweifel, das ist keine Frage.

oder auch

> Das Komma im Englischen wird Dir nicht zur Last, wenn Du es im Zweifel ausgelassen hast.

Sie sehen selbst, daß es in diesen Beispielen nicht auf dichterische Qualitäten ankommt. Jede(r) kann derartige Reime schmieden.

5 Der Grammatikanhang Ihres Lehrwerks bietet Ihnen Minitexte aus Alltagssituationen und Cartoons mit eben dem Quentchen Humor, das das Behalten zur Freude macht oder machen soll. Halten Sie also die Augen offen, reichern Sie Ihr Buch an, und bereichern Sie den Kurs dadurch, daß Sie Ihrerseits gefundene Witzzeichnungen, Ausschnitte aus Illustrierten, Verpackungen oder Bedienungsanleitungen mitbringen und für das gemeinsame Lernen zur Verfügung stellen.

[1] *Leicht verändert aus: Robert Kleinschroth und Dieter Maupai, La Grammaire en s'amusant. Wichtige Regeln zum Anlachen. Reinbek: Rowohlt 1990.*

UNIT 6 *Step 1*

1 Reading

Lesen Sie den Text ganz durch. Dann ergänzen Sie die nebenstehende Tabelle.

Doreen and Lynn are two American students who have just arrived at Frankfurt airport. They are going to travel round Europe by train this summer, and if they have time they might even go to Morocco for one or two days. They don't speak German, but Doreen learned some French at school and Lynn had two years of Spanish. They're going to walk round Frankfurt today, and tonight they'll probably sleep on the train on the way to Denmark. If they have time between trains, they'd like to visit Copenhagen tomorrow. Then they're going to travel to northern Norway to see the midnight sun.
After that, they're going to visit France and Spain. Doreen has a big book about Paris, and Lynn has maps of all the countries that they want to visit. They might go to the theatre in Madrid if they still have some clothes that are all right for that. At the end of the summer Lynn is going to leave Europe and go back to the United States, but Doreen hopes she will be able to stay in France until Christmas to learn some more French.

they have decided	they're not sure yet
They are going to travel round Europe by train.	*They might go to Morocco for one or two days.*
....	....
....	....
....	....
....	....

2 Count the words.

Hören Sie bitte den Einzelsätzen auf der Cassette mehrmals zu, und zählen Sie die einzelnen Wörter. Eine Kurzform wie z.B. *I'll* (= *I will*) zählt als zwei Wörter. Schreiben Sie die Kurz- und Langformen in die entsprechenden Spalten.

	Number of words	Short form	Long form
1	*7*	*she's*	*she has*
2			
3			
4			
5			
6			
7			

UNIT 6 *Step 1 / Step 2*

3 Crossword

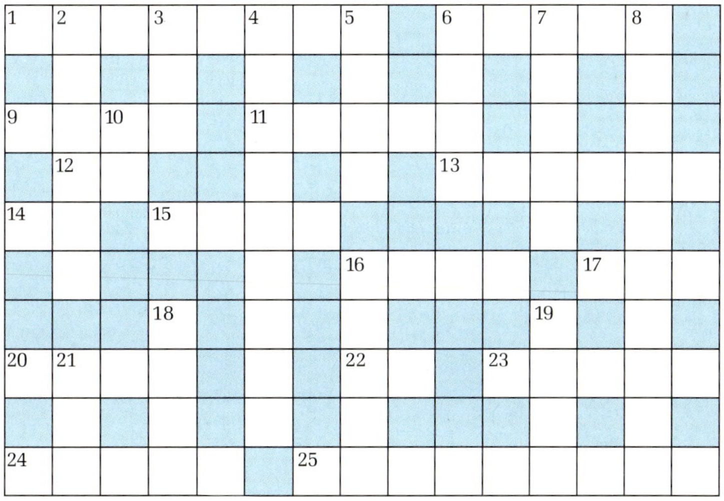

Across (➔):

1 They'll ... go to Australia next year.
6 He ... look for a job in a different town, but he isn't sure.
9 He'd prefer to ... here.
11 Our friends are going to come here ... next week.
12 That's a good idea, isn't ... ?
13 Can you stay for ... this evening?
14 I'd like to visit France ... Italy next summer.
15 Tim will probably live ... Kath's sister.
16 He is looking for a job to ... money for his holidays.
17 ... you going to swop homes with an Australian family?
20 I hope she'll be ... to find a more interesting job.
22 Tim's going ... start at university next year.
23 Oh, I'm afraid I don't ... agree with you.
24 Oh, I'm afraid I don't quite ... with you.
25 They have three sons and two ... .

Down (↓):

2 He's going to ... when he's sixty-five.
3 They'd like to go to Australia and ... a house there.
4 Your garden looks very nice. It's ... .
5 I'd like to change my job next ... .
6 Would you ... opening the window, please?
7 When are you ... to have a holiday?
8 He's writing a long letter on the electric ... .
10 Look ... this beautiful picture.
16 He needs some ... money for his holiday.
18 What ... you doing when the phone rang?
19 I'm sorry, I ... be home by six o'clock.
21 Her father lives in a ... house in the country.

Step 2

1 No, but I'm going to ...

Beantworten Sie die Fragen und benutzen Sie dabei die Zukunftsform mit *going to.*

1 Have you ever had a holiday in Madagascar?
No, but I'm going to have a holiday in Madagascar next year.

2 Have you ever bought a dress in Rome?

....

3 Have you ever climbed Mount Cook in New Zealand?

....

4 Have you ever bought a sports car in California?

....

5 Have you ever swum in the Pacific Ocean?

....

UNIT 6 *Step 2*

2 Question tags

Schreiben Sie nach jedem Satz die passende angehängte Kurzfrage mit der Bedeutung *nicht wahr?*

1 You've been to Chicago, ... ?

2 You're the man who sold me this car, ...
.... ?

3 The sun is shining, ... ?

4 He can't speak French, ... ?

5 She goes jogging every morning, ... ?

6 She went swimming this morning, ...
.... ?

7 They don't live here, ... ?

8 He works at a large bank in the city, ...
.... ?

3 Where's the stress?

Teil 1:
Welche Silbe wird besonders betont? Unterstreichen Sie sie, erst dann hören Sie der Cassette zu und vergleichen Ihre Lösung mit dem Schlüssel auf Seite 104.

1 specialist	5 every	9 hospital
2 probably	6 evening	10 immediately
3 advice	7 tomorrow	11 exclusive
4 vegetables	8 explanation	12 perfect

Teil 2:
Hören Sie den Sätzen zu und sprechen Sie sie nach. Achten Sie dabei auf die Satzmelodie und die korrekte Betonung.

- The specialist will probably give you some good advice.
- Eat some fresh vegetables every evening.
- Tomorrow you can ask your teacher for an explanation.
- Take him to the hospital immediately.
- In an exclusive shop the customer gets perfect service.

4 Times in her life

Ergänzen Sie die Sätze so, daß sie zu den Bildern passen. Die Wörter, die Sie dazu brauchen, haben Sie in Unit 6 schon gelernt, und zwar in *Before you go on* am Ende von Step 1.

1 When she was five years old she ....
....

2 Last year ....

3 Now she is .... as a ....

4 Next year she is going to .... some
....

5 Then she ....
....

UNIT 6 *Step 3*

1 What was the question?

Vervollständigen Sie die Fragen und überprüfen Sie Ihre Vorschläge durch die Cassette oder den Lösungsschlüssel.

1 How .... ?

I'm sixty-one. I'll be sixty-two next month.

2 When .... retire?

I'm going to retire when I'm sixty-five.

3 Do .... job?

Yes, I like my job very much.

4 What .... retire?

When I retire I'm going to write a book.

5 Oh, really? What ....

......................about?

I'm going to write about old cars.

6 Do ....

.... cars?

Yes, I know a lot about old cars. Old cars are my hobby.

2 Question tags

Hier geht es um die Zukunft. Schreiben Sie zu jedem Satz die passende angehängte Kurzfrage.

1 You're not going to get married in June,

.... ?

2 She's going to write a book about cats,

.... ?

3 We're going to finish this job quickly,

.... ?

4 He will agree with us, ... ?

5 He won't agree with us, ... ?

6 She'll write us a letter from London,

.... ?

3 Prepositions

Schreiben Sie in jede Lücke das passende Wort. Das längste Wort ist *between* und kommt nur einmal vor. Die anderen Wörter haben wir diesmal nicht aufgelistet.

I think there will probably be some changes .... (1) my life very soon. My brother-in-law has started a new company, and he has asked me to work .... (2) him. He told me all .... (3) it when he had dinner .... (4) our house last week. I get .... (5) very well .... (6) my brother-in-law, and I think the job will be interesting. He has asked me to start next month, but I can't leave my present job so soon. I have to stay there .... (7) six more months, and then I would like to have a holiday .... (8) jobs. I hope I will have enough money to pay .... (9) a long holiday .... (10) Greece. I think Greece is the most interesting country .... (11) the world, and I'd like to stay there .... (12) two or three months .... (13) I start my new job.

4 Listening

Hören Sie sich die Unterhaltung auf der Cassette ohne Unterbrechung mehrmals an und ordnen Sie die Zeitangaben den Bildern zu.

1 ☐ this afternoon — a

2 ☐ this evening — b

3 ☐ last year — c

4 ☐ next summer — d

5 ☐ next month — e

Erfolgserlebnisse

1 Wir möchten Ihr Augenmerk zunächst darauf richten, daß Sie als Erwachsene beim Lernen Kindern gegenüber nicht benachteiligt sind. Sie haben eine größere Ausdauer, die größere Lebenserfahrung, können Ihre Kräfte besser einteilen und haben auch in vielen Fällen schon ein trainiertes Gedächtnis und vor allem, Sie wissen, warum und wozu Sie die Fremdsprache (wieder) erlernen wollen. Sie sind besonders motiviert.

2 Der oft gehörte Stoßseufzer „Ich bin für das Lernen fremder Sprachen einfach nicht begabt genug" hält einer näheren wissenschaftlichen Überprüfung nicht stand. Jede(r) kann eine Fremdsprache erlernen, jede(r) kann die Sprachmodelle, die im Unterricht und im Lehrwerk vermittelt werden, nachahmen und sich einprägen.

3 „Heute gelernt und morgen schon wieder vergessen." Jawohl, das kennen wir alle. Vergessen gehört nun einmal zu unserer menschlichen Erfahrung und ist doch auch nicht nur negativ zu sehen. Schließlich vergessen wir unliebsame Erlebnisse, eigenes Fehlverhalten und Dummheiten nur allzu gern. Beim Lernen unseres Stoffs wollen wir dem Vergessen entgegenwirken, um das Behalten zu sichern, und das geht nur mit der Strategie des ständigen Wiederholens.

4 Beim Wiederholen ist es wichtig, ausreichende Pausen zu machen. Eine Lernphase sollte kurz sein und 20 bis 30 Minuten nicht überschreiten, ohne daß Sie eine Pause machen. Das Gelernte muß sich setzen. Am nächsten Tag dann können Sie mit erneuter Kraft und wiedergewonnenem Eifer durch nochmaliges fünf- bis zehnminütiges Wiederholen und Überlernen ein optimales Behalten erzielen. Massiertes, verbissenes Wiederholen unmittelbar nach dem einzelnen Lernvorgang kann dem Vergessen nicht entgegenwirken, es ist vergebliche Liebesmüh'. Wenn Sie sich dann, zum Beispiel eine Woche später, ein drittes Mal das zuvor Gelernte kurz anschauen, werden Sie mit Freude feststellen, daß (fast) der gesamte Stoff schon sitzt, d. h. im Langzeitgedächtnis gespeichert ist.

5 „Weniger ist oft mehr." In der Forschung hat man festgestellt, daß nur eine begrenzte Anzahl von Informationen zunächst im sogenannten Kurzzeitgedächtnis gespeichert werden kann, um danach in das Langzeitgedächtnis überführt zu werden. Und gerade das Langzeitgedächtnis brauchen wir, wenn wir z.B. nach Vokabeln suchen, die wir in der Fremdsprache verwenden wollen. Diesem Umstand trägt das Lehrbuch mit der Organisation des Lernstoffs in Einzelschritten (Steps) Rechnung. Auch Sie müssen Ihren Lernstoff in Häppchen einteilen und Ihre Lernarbeit über eine längere Zeit verteilen.

6 Verfahren Sie dabei so, daß das neu zu übende Sprachmaterial auf sinnvolle Art mit dem bisher Erlernten verknüpft ist. Ihr Lehrwerk macht Ihnen die Organisation der Stoffülle vor. Trichtern Sie sich nicht selbst etwas ein, sondern denken Sie mit, und strukturieren Sie Ihren Lernstoff in der soeben beschriebenen Weise. Und noch eins: Lernen Sie nicht nur aus dem Lehrbuch. Unterstützen Sie Ihr eigenes Lernen dadurch, daß Sie in englischsprachige Zeitschriften hineinschauen, im Radio englischsprachige Sender suchen und in die Programme hineinhören. Verbinden Sie die Dinge, die Ihnen Spaß machen, mit dem Lernen der Fremdsprache und Sie lernen mühelos etwas dazu.

7 Zum Schluß noch einige Sätze mehr zum Thema Pause. Pausen sind beim Lernen, wie schon oben gesagt wurde, keine Zeitverschwendung, sondern sollten als Belohnung für die Anstrengung und als Verstärkung zur Fortführung des Lernens gesehen werden. Sie müssen dieser Aussage eine konkrete Form geben, sei es durch eine Tasse Kaffee oder Tee, ein Stück Kuchen oder andere Kleinigkeiten. Machen Sie einerseits die Pause nicht zu kurz, andererseits aber auch nicht zu lang, damit die Lernphase nur unterbrochen, aber nicht abgebrochen wird. Eine konkrete Zeitempfehlung zu geben, ist nicht ganz einfach, doch haben Erfahrungen gezeigt, daß etwa eine Zigarettenlänge = sieben Minuten in der Regel ausreicht, die nötige geistige Frische und Aufnahmebereitschaft wiederzuerlangen.

Test yourself 3

1 Listening

Hören Sie dem gesprochenen Text mehrmals zu und ergänzen Sie die Sätze.

1 Susan's mother-in-law lives in ... .

☐ London ☐ Chicago
☐ New York ☐ Wisconsin

2 Susan hopes she'll ... Jim's parents.

☐ find ☐ meet
☐ like ☐ understand

3 Susan's parents weren't very ... at first.

☐ interesting ☐ friendly
☐ different ☐ careful

4 This will be Susan's ... visit to the USA.

☐ first ☐ second
☐ third ☐ fourth

5 Susan's father-in-law works on the ... floor.

☐ third ☐ twenty-third
☐ fifty-third ☐ one-hundred-and-third

6 Chicago is often called "The ... City".

☐ Sunny ☐ Rainy
☐ Windy ☐ Cloudy

7 Susan's sister-in-law lives in ... .

☐ London ☐ Chicago
☐ New York ☐ Wisconsin

2 You agree, don't you?

Schreiben Sie zu jedem Satz die passende angehängte Kurzfrage.

1 This book is yours, ... ?

2 You live in Germany, ... ?

3 You can't buy flowers at the baker's,

.... ?

4 You can buy a newspaper at the newsagent's,

.... ?

5 Paul doesn't live in Germany, ... ?

6 The train isn't going to be late, ... ?

3 What were they doing?

Ergänzen Sie die Sätze mit Hilfe der Bilder.

I was reading a book when the police arrived.

1 He ....

.... a cigarette when the doctor came in.

2 I ....

.... the piano when she said goodbye.

3 They ....

.... coffee when the boss came in to see them.

4 We ....

.... in the garden when we heard a car.

5 I was working in the kitchen when I

.... a wonderful idea.

Test yourself 3

4 British and American

Vervollständigen Sie die Tabelle, indem Sie die fehlende amerikanische bzw. britische Entsprechung einsetzen.

British	American
film	
cinema	
	color
	theater
chips	
	elevator
autumn	
	store

5 Please complete.

Achten Sie auf die Zeitangabe und setzen Sie die richtige Form ein.

We *are going to play* tennis tomorrow morning. (play)

1 I .... some meat at the butcher's yesterday. (buy)

2 They .... a long letter to their daughter next week. (write)

3 We .... an expensive holiday next year. (not take)

4 He .... his boss's daughter next spring. (marry)

5 She .... at the baker's yesterday afternoon on her way home from work. (stop)

6 We .... our friend Paul in York on our way up to Scotland next week. (visit)

6 Say it in English.

Schreiben Sie eine weitere Unterhaltung zwischen John und Sue. Die Redewendungen, die Sie dazu benötigen, haben Sie zum Teil in den Dialogen und Abschnitten *How to say it* kennengelernt. (Die in Klammern aufgeführten deutschen Hinweise sollen Sie nicht wörtlich übersetzen, sondern nur als Anhaltspunkt benutzen, um die jeweils passende Redewendung zu finden.)

(J = John, S = Sue)

J: I'm ....

....

(John entschuldigt sich dafür. daß er Sue gestern nachmittag nicht angerufen hat.)

S: That's ....

(Sue nimmt die Entschuldigung an.)

What ....

.... ?

(Sie fragt, was er für morgen früh vorhat.)

J: At ....

....

(Um zehn Uhr fährt er zum Flughafen: er muß bis elf dort sein.)

My ....

....

(Er sagt, daß seine Schwägerin aus Australien ankommen wird.)

S: How ....

.... ?

(Sue fragt, wie lang sie hier bleiben wird.)

J: She'll ....

....

(Er sagt, daß sie wahrscheinlich zwei oder drei Wochen bleiben wird.)

Then ....

(Danach wird sie möglicherweise Italien besuchen.)

S: Italy ....

....

(Sue sagt, Italien sei das interessanteste Land der Erde.)

J: ....

....

(John stimmt nicht zu. Nach seiner Meinung ist Australien interessanter als Italien.)

Schlüssel Homestudy

Unit 1 / Step 1

1a 1 playing, 2 being, 3 staying, 4 reading, 5 swimming, 6 walking, 7 taking

b 8 likes, 9 doesn't like, 10 likes/enjoys, 11 enjoys/likes, 12 like, 13 likes

2 1 I'd like to invite you to dinner next Thursday evening. Would you like to come to dinner next Thursday evening? Can I invite you to dinner next Thursday evening?
2 Would you like to go to the cinema tomorrow to see "Casablanca" again? Why don't we go to the cinema tomorrow to see "Casablanca" again? Let's go to the cinema tomorrow to see "Casablanca" again.
3 Would you like to go for a drink after work? I'd like to invite you to go for a drink after work. Let's go for a drink after work. Why don't we go for a drink after work?

3 1 wonderful, 2 mild, 3 friendly, 4 warm, 5 excellent, 6 fantastic, 7 great, 8 interesting, 9 attractive, 10 interesting, 11 excellent

Unit 1 / Step 2

1 1d, 2c, 3g, 4f, 5b, 6a, 7e, 8h

2 1 best, 2 most interesting, 3 oldest, 4 nicest, 5 most famous, 6 most beautiful, 7 fastest, 8 most expensive, 9 most wonderful, 10 happiest

3 1 Have you ever been to London? 2 Have you ever learned Spanish? 3 Have you ever met a film star? 4 Have they ever read an English book? 5 Have you ever seen "Rain Man"? 6 Has he ever driven a French/Italian/Japanese car? 7 Have you ever drunk French wine?

4 1 airport – plane– ticket, 2 France – Greece – Spain, 3 music – pop song – jazz, 4 summer – holiday – suntan, 5 room – flat – house, 6 museum – cinema – theatre, 7 week – month – year, 8 reading – learning – listening, 9 city – town – village, 10 small – big – large

Unit 1 / Step 3

1 Boat tours on the Thames to Hampton Court. £8.50 (children £4.25). Every day at 10.15 and 2.15 from April to September. Extra weekend tour at 12.15.

2 1 at/in, 2 for, 3 with, 4 on, 5 to ... for, 6 about/on, 7 by, 8 by, 9 on

3 1 smallest towns - largest/biggest cities, 2 feel unwelcome - feel welcome, 3 cheap - expensive, 4 have a terrible day - have a nice/wonderful/great day, 5 think of - forget, 6 country - city, 7 wrong - right

4 1 been, 2 did, 3 Have ... been, 4 When did you, 5 most, 6 cloudy, 7 didn't, 8 foggy, 9 sunny, 10 hot, 11 had, 12 did, 13 How long did you, 14 How did, 15 would, 16 love, 17 afraid

Unit 2 / Step 1

1 1 **What did you** do when you left school? 2 **How long did you** work as a telephonist? 3 **Why did you leave** that job? 4 Where **do you** work now? 5 **Do you like your job?**

2 Message for **Mr Brown**. Message from **Mary Walsh** of **Mega Magazines**. Telephone number **277 862**. She won't be in **this afternoon**. Please **ring** (call) her tomorrow between **nine** and **ten** o'clock.

3 2 Mr Brown might be about half an hour late. / Perhaps Mr Brown will be about half an hour late.
3 The others might arrive by two o'clock. / Perhaps the others will arrive by two o'clock. 4 Mrs Smith might leave by train at 11.42. / Perhaps Mrs Smith will leave by train at 11.42. 5 I might take an earlier train. / Perhaps I'll take an earlier train. 6 I might see you tomorrow afternoon. / Perhaps I'll see you tomorrow afternoon.

4 Der richtige Satz ist: It's the middle of the night and this is **not** the Apollo Hotel.

Unit 2 / Step 2

1 1 well, 2 slowly, 3 carefully, 4 nicely

2 Across (→): 1 student, 6 waitress, 10 policeman; Down (↓): 2 doctor, 3 boss, 4 farm, 5 teacher, 7 up, 8 old, 9 far

3 1 Always look, 2 Always write, 3 Always be, 4 Always say, 5 Always go, 6 Don't talk, 7 Always put, 8 Don't forget, 9 Don't call

4	She didn't say ...	She said ...
1	fast	slowly
2	most	not many
3	unfriendly	friendly
4	badly	carefully
5	Arizona	California
6	long	interesting
7	differently	again

Unit 2 / Step 3

1 2

2 Teil 1: 1 pre**fer**, 2 ho**tel**, 3 ex**pen**sive, 4 as**sis**tant, 5 **in**teresting, 6 infor**ma**tion, 7 **mo**ment, 8 **ex**cellent, 9 **stu**dent
Teil 2: I'd pre**fer** a cheaper ho**tel**. This one's too ex**pen**sive. My as**sis**tant can give you some **in**teresting infor**ma**tion. Just a **mo**ment, I'll put you through to Mr Smith. Your daughter is an **ex**cellent **stu**dent.

3 1 Bob used to be a student in Chicago. 2 He has always wanted to help people. 3 He used to live in a very big city in America. 4 He gets up very early every morning. 5 He doesn't speak their language very well.

4 1 desk, 2 pencil, 3 photocopier, 4 telephone, 5 assistant, 6 office, 7 pen, 8 salary, 9 work, 10 typewriter; key word: dictionary

Schlüssel Homestudy

Test yourself 1

1 1 true, 2 false, 3 true, 4 true, 5 true, 6 false, 7 true, 8 false, 9 true

2 1 Have, 2 never, 3 most, 4 did, 5 went, 6 used

3 chair, island, rain, doctor, policeman, toothbrush, comb, shoe; key word: congratulations

4 1 well, 2 badly, 3 hard, 4 slowly, 5 fast, 6 quickly

5 1 smallest, 2 better, 3 most expensive, 4 more interesting, 5 nicest, 6 worse

6 autum**n** [ˈɔːtəm], com**b** [kəʊm], i**s**land [ˈaɪlənd], wa**l**k [wɔːk]

7

J: Would you like to go/come to the cinema with me tomorrow evening?

S: I'd love to, but I'm afraid I can't. Why don't we go next Tuesday?

J: That's a good idea. Have you ever seen the film "Casablanca"?

S: Yes, I've seen it three times. I like old films, but I'd prefer to see a more modern film on Tuesday.

J: Okay, let's / why don't we / shall we go to the Apollo Cinema./? They always have the newest films there.

S: The cinema may/might be full. Let's try to be there early.

Unit 3 / Step 1

1 1e, 2c, 3b, 4a, 5g, 6d, 7f
1 helpful receptionist / single room, 2 terrible backache / famous specialist, 3 weekly magazine, 4 only child, 5 possible explanation

2 1 I were you, 2 Why don't you, 3 should, 4 don't you, 5 I were you

3 2, 4, 5, 1, 3

Unit 3 / Step 2

1 1 are playing, 2 is crying, 3 is reading a newspaper, 4 is cooking an, 5 are watching television, 6 is swimming

2 1 false, 2 false, 3 false, 4 true, 5 false, 6 false, 7 true, 8 false

3 1e, 2h, 3f, 4g, 5d, 6b, 7c, 8a

4 1 They **must** do their homework. 2 They **mustn't** watch TV all evening. 3 They **don't have to** work in the garden. 4 They **mustn't** forget to go for a walk with the dog. 5 They **must** phone Uncle Thomas. 6 They **mustn't** stay out too long. 7 They **must** remember their tennis lesson. 8 They **must** go shopping. 9 They **mustn't** smoke cigarettes and drink alcohol. 10 They **don't have to** make the beds.

Unit 3 / Step 3

1 1 must, 2 mustn't, 3 must, 4 don't have to, 5 mustn't, 6 mustn't, 7 must, 8 don't have to, 9 don't have to

2 1 ... machen mir den Mund wäßrig. / Da läuft mir das Wasser im Mund zusammen. 2 ... lebt von der Hand in den Mund. 3 ... nahm mir das Wort aus dem Mund. 4 ... die Füße hoch(zu)legen ... 5 ... versucht auf eigenen Füßen/Beinen zu stehen. 6 ... hat nur Augen für ... 7 ... unter den Augen ... 8 ... einen klaren/kühlen Kopf bewahren/behalten ... 9 ... in meinen Kopf bekommen. 10 ... steckte den Kopf in den Sand. 11 (Einige) Köpfe werden rollen. 12 ... rührte keinen Finger ...

3 a4, b1, c2, d3. 1 Why don't you go home? 2 I think we should buy a new bed. 3 You really must see the doctor. 4 If I were you I'd stop all that.

Unit 4 / Step 1

1 1 to, 2 of, 3 to, 4 for/on, 5 along/on, 6 On, 7 to, 8 On, 9 at (amerik. Engl.: on), 10 on, 11 for, 12 at, 13 of, 14 on, 15 for, 16 in, 17 at

2 Across (➔): 4 flat, 7 on, 8 idea, 10 eat, 12 bedroom, 14 Red, 16 stairs, 19 stand, 20 on, 23 rooms, 24 your; Down (↓): 2 address, 3 to, 5 like, 6 that, 9 doors, 11 are, 13 read, 15 did, 17 stay, 18 for, 21 No, 22 is

3 1 summer, 2 colour, 3 kitchen, 4 bedroom, 5 kitchen, 6 entrance hall, 7 living room, 8 stairs, 9 doors, 10 doors, 11 dining room, 12 interesting, 13 really, 14 holiday

4 1 May I use your telephone? 2 May I look at/see your dictionary? 3 May I open the/a window? 4 May I see/look at the kitchen? 5 May I bring you a drink? 6 May I go and have lunch?

Unit 4 / Step 2

1 1 the woman, 2 the daughter, 3 tomorrow morning, 4 four doors and is not more than two years old

2 1 If the weather is good, he'**ll** walk to work. 2 He'**ll** walk to work if the weather is good. 3 If the train isn't late, we'**ll** be able to go shopping. [future of *can*] 4 If she isn't here now, we'**ll** have to come back tomorrow morning. [future of *must*] 5 I'**ll** play the piano if you want to sing your new song. 6 You'**ll** feel better if you don't smoke so much. 7 If you come to Hanover, I'**ll** take you to a nice restaurant. 8 If you walk past the cinema and turn left, you'**ll** soon come to the supermarket.

3 1 dictionary, 2 Large, 3 terrible, 4 town, village, 5 Wine, 6 exercise, 7 north, 8 unfriendly, 9 irregular, 10 Meat, food, 11 Nice, lovely, 12 Start, stop

4 1 who, 2 which, 3 who, 4 who, 5 which, 6 who

Schlüssel Homestudy

Unit 4 / Step 3

1 1 on, 2 to, 3 in, 4 at, 5 at, 6 in, 7 at, 8 to, 9 In, 10 at, 11 with, 12 on, 13 to

2 Number of rooms: 4; Number of bathrooms: 1; Rent at the beginning: £50; Rent now: £105; Good things about this flat: 1. two balconies, 2. near the station

3 2 If you miss the bus, you **will have to** walk. 3 If you have a backache, you **will have to** see the doctor. 4 If you have a camera, you **will be able to** take some pictures. 5 If she gets a new job, she **will be able to** go on holiday this summer. 6 If the lift isn't working, we **will have to** walk up the stairs. 7 If you go to England, you **will be able to** practise your English. 8 You **will be able to** practise your English if you go to England.

Test yourself 2

1 1, 4, 5, 6, 11, 15, 16

2 1 you'll be able, 2 you'll have, 3 be able to, 4 you'll have to, 5 be able to, 6 have to

3 1 He's reading a book. 2 She's swimming. 3 They're writing a song. 4 She's buying a fridge. 5 It's sleeping. 6 He's coming into the room now.

4 1c, 2f, 3b, 4h, 5e, 6i, 7d, 8a, 9g, 10 swimming costume, 11 first-class, travel agent, 12 washing machine, 13 put you through, 14 Oh dear, bank clerk, 15 for sale, central heating

5 clim**b** [klaɪm], cu**p**board [ˈkʌbəd], **k**nee [niː], **k**now [nəʊ]

6

J: Sue, may I look at your photos?
S: Yes, of course. I took these photos in Greece last year.
J: What great/super/lovely photos!
S: Thanks, I like/love/enjoy taking photos in (the) summer.
J: Don't you like/love/enjoy taking photos in (the) winter?
S: No, I don't. It's too cold. And I haven't got enough time in (the) winter.
J: This is a very beautiful photo. If I were you, I'd send this photo to a magazine.
S: Well, perhaps I'll/I might/I may send it to *Mega Magazines*. They always need lots of/a lot of photos.

Unit 5 / Step 1

1 1 false, 2 false, 3 true, 4 false, 5 true, 6 true, 7 true

2 (V = Verkäufer, K = Kunde) V3, K7, V1, K4, V5, K2, V9, K6, V8

3 Teil 1: 1 rain, 2 teacher, 3 sizes, 4 office, 5 steak, 6 sitting, 7 toilet, 8 tonight, 9 picture, 10 cook

Teil 2: 1d, 2f, 3c, 4b, 5g, 6h, 7i, 8e, 9a, 10j

Unit 5 / Step 2

1 1 help, 2 blouse, 3 What size, 4 what colour, 5 like, 6 beautiful, 7 How much, 8 £68.95, 9 excellent, 10 expensive, 11 cheaper, 12 try it on, 13 Certainly, 14 credit cards

2 1 was having a shower/bath, 2 came in, 3 were reading (a/their newspaper), 4 were watching TV, 5 were climbing, 6 saw, 7 was raining ... left his flat/house

3 Across (→): 1 coat, 2 skirt, 3 shoes, 4 shirt; key word (↓): ties; 5 shirt, 6 pullover, 7 jacket, 8 skirt, 9 tights; key word (↓): socks

Unit 5 / Step 3

1 1c, 2a, 3f, 4e, 5d, 6b

2 1 centre, 2 most, 3 famous, 4 important, 5 past, 6 like, 7 shops, 8 years, 9 tourists, 10 best, 11 really, 12 find, 13 will

3 1c, 2f, 3e, 4d

4 1 to, 2 to, 3 in, 4 of, 5 for, 6 In, 7 for, 8 of, 9 with, 10 with, 11 in, 12 past, 13 of, 14 about, 15 to, 16 with, 17 for, 18 in, 19 on, 20 to

Unit 6 / Step 1

1 **they have decided:** They are going to travel round Europe by train. They're going to walk round Frankfurt today. They're going to travel to northern Norway. They're going to visit France and Spain. At the end of the summer Lynn is going to leave Europe.
they're not sure yet: They might go to Morocco for one or two days. They'll probably sleep on the train tonight. They'd like to see Copenhagen tomorrow. They might go to the theatre in Madrid. Doreen hopes she will be able to stay in France.

2

	Number of words	Short form	Long form
1	7	she's	she has
2	6	doesn't	does not
3	8	She'd	She would
4	7	What's	What is
5	4	don't	do not
6	5	We'll	We will
7	8	I'm	I am

3 Across (→): 1 probably, 6 might, 9 stay, 11 again, 12 it, 13 dinner, 14 or, 15 with, 16 earn, 17 Are, 20 able, 22 to, 23 quite, 24 agree, 25 daughters; Down (↓): 2 retire, 3 buy, 4 beautiful, 5 year, 6 mind, 7 going, 8 typewriter, 10 at, 16 extra, 18 were, 19 must, 21 big

Schlüssel Homestudy

Unit 6 / Step 2

1 1 No, but I'm going to have a holiday in Madagascar next year. 2 No, but I'm going to buy a dress in Rome next year. 3 No, but I'm going to climb Mount Cook in New Zealand next year. 4 No, but I'm going to buy a sports car in California next year. 5 No, but I'm going to swim in the Pacific Ocean next year.

2 1 haven't you? 2 aren't you? 3 isn't it? 4 can he? 5 doesn't she? 6 didn't she? 7 do they? 8 doesn't he?

3 Teil 1: 1 **spe**cialist, 2 **pro**bably, 3 ad**vice**, 4 **vege**tables (*nur drei Silben!*), 5 **eve**ry, 6 **eve**ning, 7 to**mor**row, 8 expla**na**tion, 9 **hos**pital, 10 im**me**diately, 11 ex**clu**sive, 12 **per**fect

Teil 2: The **spe**cialist will **pro**bably give you some good ad**vice**. Eat some fresh **vege**tables **eve**ry **eve**ning. To**mor**row you can ask your teacher for an expla**na**tion. Take him to the **hos**pital im**me**diately. In an ex**clu**sive shop the customer gets **per**fect service.

4 1 When she was five years old she started school. 2 Last year she left school. 3 Now she is training as a nurse. 4 Next year she is going to take some examinations. 5 Then she is going to get married.

Unit 6 / Step 3

1 1 How old are you? 2 When are you going to retire? 3 Do you like your job? 4 What are you going to do when you retire? 5 What are you going to write about? 6 Do you know a lot about old cars?

2 1 are you? 2 isn't she? 3 aren't we? 4 won't he? 5 will he? 6 won't she?

3 1 in, 2 for, 3 about, 4 at, 5 on, 6 with, 7 for, 8 between, 9 for, 10 in, 11 in, 12 for, 13 before

4 1b, 2d, 3c, 4e, 5a

Test yourself 3

1 1 Chicago, 2 like, 3 friendly, 4 first, 5 fifty-third, 6 Windy, 7 Wisconsin

2 1 isn't it? 2 don't you? 3 can you? 4 can't you? 5 does he? 6 is it?

3 1 was smoking, 2 was playing, 3 were drinking, 4 were sitting, 5 got/had

4 British/American: film/**movie**; cinema/**movie theater**; **colour**/color; **theatre**/theater; chips/**French fries**; **lift**/elevator; autumn/**fall**; **shop**/store

5 1 bought, 2 are going to/will write, 3 are not going to/won't take, 4 is going to/will marry, 5 stopped, 6 are going to/will visit

6

J: I'm sorry I didn't ring/call you yesterday afternoon.
S: That's all right. What are you going to do tomorrow morning?
J: At ten o'clock I'm going/going to drive to the airport. I must be there by eleven. My sister-in-law is going to arrive from Australia.
S: How long is she going to stay here?
J: She'll probably stay two or three weeks. Then she might/may/'ll perhaps visit/go to Italy.
S: Italy is the most interesting country in the world.
J: I'm afraid I don't quite agree with you (there). I think Australia is more interesting than Italy.

Höraufgabentexte Homestudy

Unit 1 / Step 1: Exercise 2 (page 65)
siehe Schlüssel Seite 101

Unit 1 / Step 2: Exercise 2 (page 66)
... And here are the winners of today's quiz, the Hamiltons. Mrs Hamilton will get one of the best Japanese cameras. She likes taking photos. And for her husband a very good book about one of the most interesting countries in the world - Italy. One of the oldest monuments there is the Colosseum in Rome, it's about 2000 years old. The Hamiltons will visit that beautiful country and meet the nicest people in the world. And for the children, what have we got? Video cassettes of one of the most famous pop singers of our time. And that's not all. Beautiful sunglasses, some say, the most beautiful sunglasses by our star designer Roberto Merlotti. People say he has got the fastest and most expensive car in Europe. And that's their extra prize. The Hamiltons will drive that wonderful car, they will have it for three weeks, the most wonderful weeks of their lives. I am sure the Hamiltons will be happy, not only happy, they will be the happiest people in the world.

Unit 1 / Step 3: Exercise 1 (page 67)
- How much is the boat tour to Hampton Court, please?
- It's £8.50 per person.
- And what time does it leave?
- The times are 10.15 and 2.15, that's every day from April to September. And on Saturdays and Sundays there is an extra tour at 12.15. It's the same price, of course.
- How long will it take?
- About two hours.
- Is it the same price for children?
- No, children are cheaper, they pay half price.
- Will there be someone with us on the tour?
- Yes, of course. There's a guide on every tour.
- Can he or she speak German?
- No, but you understand English. Your English is excellent.
- Oh, thank you. Will we have enough time to visit Hampton Court?
- Of course you will. It's really a beautiful place. The palace is one of the most interesting buildings on the river.

Unit 2 / Step 1: Exercise 1 (page 70)
- What did you do when you left school, Miss Smith?
- Well, the first thing I did was to take a long holiday, and then I worked as a telephonist.
- How long did you work as a telephonist?
- About three years.
- Why did you leave that job?
- I left because I wanted to take a computer course.
- Where do you work now?
- I work for a big company in London.
- Do you like your job?
- Yes, I like my job, but I don't earn enough money. That's why I'm here.

Unit 2 / Step 1: Exercise 2 (page 70)
Hello, I'd like to leave a message for Mr Brown. Oh, sorry, this is Mary Walsh, that is spelled W A L S H. Mary Walsh. I'm from *Mega Magazines*. I've got a new phone number. I don't know if Mr Brown's got it. It's 2 double 7 8 6 2, that's 2 double 7 8 6 2. Have you got that? Now, Mr Brown wanted to see me this afternoon, but I won't be here this afternoon, I'm afraid. So can he wait until tomorrow morning? Please ask him to ring me between nine and ten o'clock tomorrow morning, and I'll be happy to talk to him then. Okay? Thank you. Goodbye.

Unit 2 / Step 2: Exercise 1 (page 71)
- I think your friend Jim is a really good writer.
- Yes, he writes very well.
- But I've heard he's a slow worker.
- That's not true! He doesn't work slowly.
- But he is very careful about his work, I know.
- Yes, he works carefully, but he's not slow!
- Okay, okay. I'm sorry. I'll only say nice things about him next time.
- Yes, please talk nicely about him. He's a very nice person.

Unit 2 / Step 2: Exercise 4 (page 72)
My husband and I went to America last summer for a holiday. What I didn't know about America was that they all drive so slowly over there. The speed limit is 55 miles an hour, that's only about 88 kilometres. Not many Americans drive faster than that. They're all very friendly when you see them out on the roads, and they all drive very carefully, if you ask me. We got a car in New York and drove all the way to California. It was a very interesting journey, and I hope we can do it again next year.

Unit 2 / Step 3: Exercise 2 (page 73)
siehe Schlüssel Seite 101

Test yourself 1: Exercise 1 (page 75)
I've had some terrible jobs in my life, but the worst job I've ever had was in the summer when I left school. I saw an advert from a big hotel by the sea. They wanted young people to work in the restaurant all summer. They said their hotel was the nicest and most modern hotel in the area, and they said the weather was always warm and sunny there all summer.
I love swimming and I enjoy good food, so I took the job. I took my swimming costume with me, and my suntan cream, my sunglasses and beach shoes. Well, I didn't need any of those things. I was always inside, and worked very irregular hours. I didn't have much free time, and when I got any free time it was usually cloudy or it was raining.

Höraufgabentexte Homestudy

My boss was an unfriendly young man who didn't know much about hotel work or people, but he was the manager's son, and that's why he was our boss. I'm actually a very fast worker, but he always told me to work faster. "Do this, do that, take this, bring that." He used to tell me what to do all day. What he said made the work harder, because he didn't know the best way to do things.
He used to sit and drink gin all day. He had the biggest dog I've ever seen, and the dog used to sit around in the kitchen all day and do nothing.
There was one good thing about that job. I didn't eat too much that summer. It was a very expensive hotel, but the food was terrible. I used to give my food to the boss's dog. That dog was always hungry. He used to eat everything that we didn't want.

Unit 3 / Step 2: Exercise 2 (page 78)
- Can I ask you a few questions, Mrs Lamb. I'm writing an article on our neighbours for our school magazine.
- Yes, come in, Sue. I am busy at the moment, you know, I'm making dinner. Normally, we don't eat a lot in the evening, but my husband has invited his boss and some colleagues. So come into the kitchen and ask your questions here, I might need your help.
- Oh, I see. I'll hurry up then. – Your husband works at the bank in Grove Street, doesn't he?
- Yes, that's right.
- What time does he usually leave the house?
- At about 8.00 am. He usually takes the bus, but at the moment he is using his bike, because the weather is so good and cycling keeps him fit.
- And what about you? Have you got a job?
- Of course, I have. I am a housewife and a mother. That's a lot of work. I look after the children, do the housework and the garden and, as you can see, I do the cooking, too. I like working at home. But I know what you mean. When I was younger I worked at a hotel. I liked that very much, but I enjoy being a housewife now.
- And do you like cooking? I helped Mum with the lunch last Sunday; I don't do that very often, and I thought it was hard work.
- Well, I'm not enjoying it today. My husband's boss is coming to dinner and I don't know what he likes.

Unit 3 / Step 3: Exercise 3 (page 80)

1
- I feel awful.
- Well, why don't you go home?
- There's all this work still.
- Yes, but you can't do it if you've got a migraine.
- I don't think it's that. It's just a bad headache.
- Well, you go home. The work will still be here tomorrow.

2
- I've got a really good office chair, so it can't be that.
- Well, I think we should buy a new bed. I have backache, too, sometimes.
- It might be the bed, I suppose. The backache's never as bad when we're on holiday.

3
- The thermometer says 40.
- I know. I feel very hot. In fact I feel awful: sick and hot and ...
- You really must see the doctor. I'll go and telephone her now.

4
- Ouch!
- It's all right. I've finished now. The tooth is out.
- Thank you.
- Look, I know people don't like coming to the dentist, but why didn't you come when the toothache started?
- Well, I like sugar and chocolate, and I thought ...
- Well, if I were you I'd stop all that, and next time. ...

Unit 4 / Step 1: Exercise 3 (page 83)
- Hey, I've got a great idea. Why don't we paint the flat this summer?
- Okay. But what colour should we paint it?
- Well, the kitchen should be blue.
- Blue? Perhaps the bedroom could be blue, but not the kitchen!
- Here's a nice yellow for the entrance hall.
- That's not bad, but I'd prefer green for the living room and the stairs.
- Green? You know I can't stand green. But you can paint the doors green if you want to.
- I don't want to paint the doors green. That would be terrible.
- Well, the dining room has to be white, in any case.
- White isn't a very interesting colour. How about brown?
- Never!
- I've got a better idea. We don't really have to paint the flat. We can go on holiday instead.

Unit 4 / Step 2: Exercise 1 (page 84)
- 427 356, hello.
- Hello, are you the woman who has a car to sell?
- Yes, I am. Are you the man who spoke to my daughter this morning?
- That's right. She gave me your address. If the car is still there I'll come right over and look at it.
- You can't come now, I'm afraid, because I'm busy. But if you have time tomorrow morning I'll be able to show you the car then.
- Well, I have lots of things to do tomorrow morning. How about tomorrow afternoon?
- No, if you want to see the car you'll have to come over tomorrow morning. I can't stay home all day waiting for you.
- All right, then, I'll come over tomorrow morning. But tell me more about the car. I'm looking for a car which

Höraufgabentexte Homestudy

has got four doors and is not more than two years old.
- Well, my car only has two doors and it's four years old.
- Only two doors and four years old. Is that right?
- Of course that's right. I'm the person who drives this car every day.

Unit 4 / Step 3: Exercise 2 (page 85)
This is the flat that I've been living in for over eleven years now. There are four rooms, but three of them are very small. There's a kitchen, of course, and one bathroom, but the really nice thing about this flat is that there are two balconies. The rent has gone up three times altogether. When I took the flat I only paid 50 pounds a week, but after three years it went up to 65 pounds and two years later it went up to 75 pounds a week. Yes, here in Britain we often pay by the week, not by the month. Now I have to pay 105 pounds a week, and if I stay much longer, I'll have to pay more, I'm sure. But I like this flat because it's not far from the station and that's important to me.

Test yourself 2: Exercise 1 (page 87)
- I'm glad you came to visit me, son. I'd like to give you some advice.
- Well, that's very kind of you, Dad, but ...
- For one thing, I think you should buy a new car. You've been driving that car for several years now, and people might think ...
- But I don't need a new car, Dad, and what people might think isn't so important.
- Oh yes it is. If you don't buy a new car, they'll think you don't have enough money.
- Well, that's true. I don't have enough money for anything like that, because I still have to pay for the house every month.
- The house? Are you still paying for that house? If I were you, I'd sell that house and buy a smaller house. You don't really need such a big house any more.
- I know, but we love that house, and all our friends live nearby.
- Why don't you try to make some new friends? You should go to a country club and meet some important people.
- That's good advice, Dad, but I already know lots of important people. I'd prefer to meet some people who aren't so important. Important people talk too much and eat too much. I don't have enough time to listen to so many important people.
- Time ... You always say you don't have enough time. If I were you, son, I'd stop jogging. It's no good, and it takes too much of your time.
- Oh, I don't think I'll stop jogging. It's very good for me. And I hope I can find the time to go swimming once or twice a week.
- Well, I hope you can find the time to visit me more often, son. And think about my advice. Here, have another cup of coffee.

Unit 5 / Step 1: Exercise 1 (page 89)
- Can I help you, sir?
- Yes, you can. I bought this video recorder the day before yesterday, but something is wrong with it.
- Oh, I see. But it was okay here in the shop, wasn't it?
- Yes, that's right. The shop assistant was very kind, he told me how to use it and explained it all to me, because I'm not very good at these things. I'm sorry, but when I got home with the recorder there was a problem.
- I'm sorry to hear that. What was the problem then?
- I put a tape in, I got a picture, but heard nothing. I tried it out a lot of times, but I still couldn' t hear anything. The picture is all right, but there's no sound. I thought it was excellent Japanese quality when I bought it, but now we, that's my wife and I, are very unhappy.
- I can understand that. Let me have a look at the recorder. – Yes, you're right. There is something wrong. Can you leave the recorder here, so that we can have a look at it? We'll do it very quickly. It won't take long.
- Oh, no. I'd like my money back, please. And, you see, for us, this recorder, it's too complicated. We'd like to buy a German recorder, a cheaper one, a simpler one, that's not so difficult to use, but not now, later.
- All right. That's no problem. That's our policy, we want our customers to be happy. Have you got the receipt?

Unit 5 / Step 2: Exercise 1 (page 90)
- Good morning, madam. Can I help you?
- Yes, I'd like a blouse, please.
- What size do you take?
- 42, I think.
- And what colour would you like?
- I like blue best. Oh, this one is beautiful. How much is it?
- It's £68.95. It's excellent quality.
- Oh, no, I'm sorry. That's far too expensive. Haven't you got a cheaper blouse than that?
- Of course, madam. What about this one?
- Hm, yes. Can I try it on, please?
- Certainly, madam. Follow me please.
- It looks nice. I'll take it.
- Thank you, madam.
- Do you take credit cards?
- Yes, madam. We take ...

Unit 5 / Step 3: Exercise 1 (page 91)

1
- Whose socks are these?
- These brown socks? Jim's, I think. Yes, they're his.

2
- Whose trousers are these?
- They're mine.

Höraufgabentexte Homestudy

3
- Look, I've just found this ticket. Whose is it? Do you know?
- Yes. Those people over there with the dog, it's theirs.

4
- Whose car is this? It's a very expensive one.
- Well, actually, it's ours.

5
- What a beautiful skirt you've got.
- Yes, it's lovely, isn't it? But it's not mine. My sister let me try it for the day. It's hers.

6
- These cigarettes on the table. Are they yours or mine?
- They're yours.

Unit 6 / Step 1: Exercise 2 (page 94)
1 I hope she's got a car. 2 She probably doesn't like cars. 3 She'd like to buy a new bicycle. 4 What's wrong with her old bicycle? 5 I don't know. 6 We'll ask her tomorrow. 7 I'm going to ask her this afternoon.

Unit 6 / Step 2: Exercise 3 (page 96)
siehe Schlüssel Seite 104

Unit 6 / Step 3: Exercise 1 (page 97)
siehe Schlüssel Seite 104

Unit 6 / Step 3: Exercise 4 (page 97)
- Hi, Susan. How are you?
- Fine, and you?
- I'm fine, thanks. The weather's great today, isn't it?
- Yes, it is. I'm going to play tennis this afternoon right after work.
- You play tennis very well, don't you?
- Oh, ... well ..., thank you.
- What are you going to do this evening?
- I think I'll cook dinner for my husband.
- Your husband? Are you married? I didn't know that.
- Yes, I am. We got married last year.
- I didn't know that. Does your husband play tennis, too?
- No, but he's going to start next summer. I'm going to teach him.
- Where's your husband from?
- From Chicago. He's American. We're going to travel to Chicago next month so I can meet his family.
- Oh, really? I'm sure you'll like Chicago - some parts of it, anyway.

Test yourself 3: Exercise 1 (page 99)
My husband and I are going to visit Chicago next month so I can meet his family. Jim and I got married almost a year ago now, and I still haven't met his parents. I hope I'll like them. And I hope they'll like me. I don't think they really wanted their son to marry a foreigner.
My parents never liked Americans very much before they met Jim, and they weren't very friendly at first, but now they think he's super.
I've never been to the States before, so I'm sure it'll all be very different and interesting. Of course I've seen America lots of times in the cinema – I mean the movies – and on TV, but that's not the same, is it?
When we arrive in Chicago I'd like to take the lift – they call it the elevator over there – up to the top of the Sears Tower. When I go to a new city I always like to go up to the highest place and look at everything from there. Sears Tower used to be the highest building in the world. Perhaps it still is, I don't know. We can go up to the hundred-and-third floor and look out over the city. And on the way we can visit Jim's father. His office is in the Sears Tower, but only on the fifty-third floor, just a little more than halfway up.
If it isn't too windy we might borrow some bicycles and go for a ride along the lake. Jim says Chicago is called "The Windy City", and you really have to be careful on a bicycle on windy days.
We're going to stay in Chicago for a week and then drive to Wisconsin to meet Jim's sister and her family. I'd like to see New York, too, but I don't know if we'll have time.

Übersicht der wichtigsten grammatischen Bezeichnungen

Deutsch	Englisch	Lateinisch	Erläuterung
Bedingungssatz	conditional clause / *if*-clause	Konditionalsatz	gibt die Bedingung an, unter der etwas geschieht, z.B. ***If he comes in the morning,*** *he won't meet me.*
Befehlsform	imperative	Imperativ	z.B. ***Walk*** *straight on.*
Besitzfall	genitive	Genitiv	2. Fall; antwortet auf die Frage Wessen?
Bezugssatz	relative clause	Relativsatz	beschreibt Personen oder Dinge aus dem Hauptsatz näher, z.B. *The policeman* ***who stopped my car*** *is my brother.*
Bindewort	conjunction	Konjunktion	verbindet Sätze miteinander, z.B. *if, when*
Eigenschaftswort	adjective	Adjektiv	beschreibt, wie eine Person oder eine Sache ist, z.B. *nice, beautiful, okay*
Einzahl	singular	Singular	z.B. *dog, newspaper*
Frageanhängsel	question tag		z.B. *The weather is fine,* ***isn't it?***
Fragewort	question word	Interrogativ-pronomen	z.B. *Where? What? How?*
Fürwort	pronoun	Pronomen	steht für andere Wörter in Sätzen
bezügliches Fürwort	relative pronoun	Relativpronomen	steht als Verbindungswort zwischen Sätzen für eine Person oder Sache, z.B. *who, which, that. I'd like a car* ***which*** *isn't too expensive.*
persönliches Fürwort	personal pronoun	Personal-pronomen	steht für eine Person oder Sache, z.B. *he, him, we, us, it*
besitzanzeigendes Fürwort	possessive pronoun	Possessiv-pronomen	zeigt Besitz oder Zugehörigkeit an, z.B. ***my*** *book,* ***their*** *dog*
hinweisendes Fürwort	demonstrative pronoun	Demonstrativ-pronomen	weist auf eine Person oder Sache hin, z.B. ***this*** *town,* ***these*** *postcards*
Gegenwart	present	Präsens	z.B. ***I can whistle.*** *He* ***cooks*** *wonderful omelettes.*
vollendete Gegenwart	present perfect	Perfekt	macht Aussagen über Ereignisse und Tätigkeiten, die einen direkten Bezug zur Gegenwart (‚bis jetzt') haben, z.B. *I* ***have*** *always* ***helped*** *him.*
Geschlechtswort (Begleiter des Hauptworts)	article	Artikel	zeigt das grammatische Geschlecht von Hauptwörtern an, z.B. **der** *Tisch,* **die** *Lampe,* **das** *Buch*
bestimmtes Geschlechtswort	definite article	bestimmter Artikel	z.B. *der, die, das, the*
unbestimmtes Geschlechtswort	indefinite article	unbestimmter Artikel	z.B. *ein, eine, a/an*
Grundform	infinitive	Infinitiv	z.B. *do, eat*
Grundzahlen	cardinal numbers	Kardinalzahlen	z.B. *one, two, three*

Deutsch	Englisch	Lateinisch	Erläuterung
Hauptwort (Namenwort)	noun	Substantiv	wird benutzt, um Menschen, Tieren, Dingen und abstrakten Begriffen ihren Namen zu geben, z.B. *Peter, dog, love*
Hilfszeitwort	auxiliary verb	Hilfsverb	‚hilft' dem Hauptzeitwort; z.B. *He* ***can*** *cook. She* ***will*** *come.*
Mehrzahl	plural	Plural	z.B. *dog**s**, newspaper**s***
Mitlaut	consonant	Konsonant	z.B. *b, c, d, f* usw.
Mittelwort der Vergangenheit	past participle	Partizip Perfekt	Formen wie *gespielt, gegessen, gegangen;* engl. z.B. *played, eaten, gone*
Ordnungszahlen	ordinal numbers	Ordinalzahlen	z.B. *first, second, third*
Satzaussage	predicate		alle Satzteile, die nicht zum Satzgegenstand gehören, z.B. *Peter* ***reads the newspaper.***
Satzergänzung	object	Objekt	Satzglied, das das Zeitwort ergänzt (3.+4. Fall), z.B. *Peter reads* ***the newspaper.***
Satzgegenstand	subject	Subjekt	Person oder Sache, über die im Satz eine Aussage gemacht wird (1. Fall), z.B. ***Peter*** *reads the newspaper.*
Selbstlaut	vowel	Vokal	*a, e, i, o, u*
Steigerung	comparison		
1. Steigerungsstufe	comparative	Komparativ	z.B. *small**er**,* ***more*** *modern*
2. Steigerungsstufe	superlative	Superlativ	z.B. *(the) old**est**, (the)* ***most*** *expensive*
Umstandswort	adverb	Adverb	steht bei Zeit- oder Eigenschaftswörtern und drückt die Art und Weise aus, in der etwas geschieht *(**schnell** laufen)* oder den Grad einer Eigenschaft *(**sehr** alt); z.B. quickly, well, never*
Vergangenheit	past	Imperfekt/ Präteritum	Formen wie *kam, lachte;* engl. z.B. *stayed, did, ate*
Verhältniswort	preposition	Präposition	z.B. *in, on, between, at*
Verlaufsform	progressive form/ continuous form		drückt aus, daß eine Tätigkeit oder ein Geschehen gerade abläuft bzw. gerade im Gange war, als eine andere Handlung eintrat, z.B. *John* ***is watching*** *TV at the moment. Silvia* ***was reading*** *a book when the phone rang.*
Vollverb	full verb		das ‚Hauptzeitwort', das die eigentliche Bedeutung besitzt, z.B. *can* ***help,*** *will* ***come***
Zeitwort	verb	Verb	drückt Handlungen, Vorgänge und Zustände aus, z.B. *go, watch, be.*
Zukunft	future	Futur	macht Aussagen über Zukünftiges, Geplantes oder unmittelbar Bevorstehendes, z.B. *He* ***will stay.*** *I* ***will go*** *home.*

Grammar

Inhaltsverzeichnis

Die Ziffern G 1, G 2 etc. beziehen sich auf die Kapitelnummern in diesem Grammatikanhang.

0 Einleitung

In Band 1 des Lehrwerks *English Network* wurden Grundzüge der englischen Grammatik vermittelt. Diese Elemente werden nunmehr erweitert und vertieft, wobei selbstverständlich nicht Regeln um ihrer selbst willen zu lernen sind. Denken Sie einmal an die Regeln und Bestimmungen der Straßenverkehrsordnung, durch die – zumindest zeitweise – ein ‚geregeltes' Miteinander von Menschen im Verkehr ermöglicht und das absolute Chaos vermieden wird. So auch in der Sprache, wo die Verständigung untereinander erst auf der Grundlage von Regeln, die alle beachten, gewährleistet ist. Das bedeutet aber nicht, daß gleich jeder Fehler unverzeihlich ist und auf der Stelle geahndet wird. In der Alltagskommunikation machen viele – auch Muttersprachler – Fehler und werden trotzdem verstanden. Dies soll aber nicht bedeuten, daß wir uns nicht um eine möglichst korrekte Ausdrucksweise zu bemühen haben. Die nachstehenden Regeln sind dazu eine Anleitung und Hilfe.

1 Die Steigerung des Eigenschaftsworts / Comparison of adjectives

In *English Network 1* wurden Eigenschaftswörter und ihre Aufgaben in Sätzen vorgestellt (siehe dazu: *English Network 1, Grammar 4,* S.112). Eigenschaftswörter werden gesteigert, um Vergleiche anzustellen, z. B. zu sagen, daß ein Auto zwar *teurer* ist als das andere, dafür aber auch viel *schneller* und *bequemer.* Aber leider immer noch nicht unser Traumwagen, der *teuerste* aus dem ganzen Angebot, den sich kaum jemand leisten kann.

"You get lazier every day."*
**lazy = faul*

1.1 Komparativ- und Superlativformen / Comparative and superlative forms

Grundform	1. Steigerungsstufe (= Komparativ)	2. Steigerungsstufe (= Superlativ)
small	small**er**	(the) small**est**
new	new**er**	(the) new**est**
old	old**er**	(the) old**est**
sunny	sunn**ier**	(the) sunn**iest**
nice	nic**er**	(the) nic**est**

John is **older** than Sue, but Marge is the **oldest** in our class.
Which camera is **newer**?
Who is the **nicest** person in this class?

Einsilbige Eigenschaftswörter / (Adjektive) sowie zweisilbige Wörter, die auf *-y* enden, werden durch Anhängen von **-er** und **-est** gesteigert.

Haben Eigenschaftswörter in der Grundform als letzten Buchstaben ein **-e**, so werden nur noch ein **-r** in der ersten Steigerungsstufe und ein **-st** in der zweiten Steigerungsstufe angehängt (vgl. *nice*).

modern	**more** modern	(the) **most** modern
expensive	**more** expensive	(the) **most** expensive
interesting	**more** interesting	(the) **most** interesting

This French car is **more expensive** than that German car.
Which is **the most interesting** sport on TV?

Viele zweisilbige und alle drei- und mehrsilbigen Adjektive werden mit vorangestelltem **more** und (the) **most** gesteigert.

bad	**worse**	(the) **worst**	*schlecht*
good	**better**	(the) **best**	*gut*
much	**more**	(the) **most**	*viel*
many	**more**	(the) **most**	*viele*

That was **the worst** film that we have ever seen.
That is **the best** hotel in London.
I have had **more** jobs than my brother.

Einige Eigenschaftswörter haben besondere Steigerungsformen.

1.2 Der Gebrauch der Steigerung / Use of comparisons

as + (Grundform)+ as = so + (Grundform) + wie
I am **as old as** John. He is not **as nice as** his brother.

(Komparativ) + than = (Komparativ) + als
Our kitchen is **smaller than** your kitchen. I have got a **more interesting** job **than** Susan.

Vergleiche werden mit **as ... as** und **...-er than** ausgedrückt.

Wenn Sie dies alles begriffen und gelernt haben, können Sie mit Recht stolz auf sich sein und und in aller Bescheidenheit sagen: *I'm the greatest.*

2 Umstandswörter / Adverbs

In *Grammar 18* wurden auf den Seiten 123-124 von *English Network 1* verschiedene Kategorien von Umstandswörtern vermittelt und in Sätzen verwendet. Dieser Bereich soll hier etwas vertieft werden, indem gezeigt wird, wie Umstandswörter gebildet werden, oder noch genauer, wie aus Eigenschaftswörtern Umstandswörter gemacht werden.

2.1 Bildung der Umstandswörter / Formation of adverbs

Eigenschaftswort	+ -ly =	Umstandswort
bad	+ -ly =	**badly**
beautiful	+ -ly =	**beautifully**
quick	+ -ly =	**quickly**
slow	+ -ly =	**slowly**
He reads **slowly** but speaks **quickly**. They sing **beautifully**.		

In der Regel werden Umstandswörter durch Anhängen von **-ly** an das Eigenschaftswort gebildet.

"A room with a shower – but quickly, please."

Eigenschaftswort	Umstandswort	Bedeutung
fast	**fast**	*schnell*
good	**well**	*gut*
hard	**hard**	*hart, schwer*
He has got a fast car, and he drives too **fast**. Her English is good, she speaks English **well**. Their work is hard and they work very **hard**.		

Es gibt aber auch einige wenige Umstandswörter, die nicht so regelgerecht gebildet werden, sondern Ausnahmen bilden.

2.2 Gebrauch der Umstandswörter / Use of adverbs

He sings **badly**, but whistles **beautifully**.	*Er singt* ***schlecht****, pfeift aber* ***wunderbar****.*
You learn the new words **fast** and pronounce English **well**.	*Sie lernen die neuen Wörter* ***schnell*** *und sprechen Englisch* ***gut*** *aus.*
He can sing **badly**, but whistle **beautifully**.	*Er kann* ***schlecht*** *singen, aber* ***wunderbar*** *pfeifen.*
You can speak English **well**.	*Sie können* ***gut*** *Englisch sprechen.*

Umstandswörter werden wie im Deutschen den Verben nachgestellt.

Diese Stellungsregel gilt im Englischen auch dann noch, wenn in einem Satz ein Hilfs- und ein Vollverb vorkommen.

3 Besitzanzeigende Fürwörter / Possessive pronouns

In Abschnitt *5.2* des Grammatikanhangs von *English Network 1* (S. 114) wurden besitzanzeigende Fürwörter vorgestellt. Dieser Bereich soll hier nunmehr ergänzt werden.
Die in Band 1 behandelten Fürwörter können nur in Verbindung mit einem Hauptwort benutzt werden:
Your English *is fine.*
Our teacher *is excellent.*
Es gibt aber auch besitzanzeigende Fürwörter, die alleinstehend gebraucht werden. Sie werden wie Hauptwörter benutzt. Auch sie sind grundsätzlich unveränderlich, ihre Verwendung ist deshalb einfacher als im Deutschen.

mine	*meines (-er, -e)*
yours	*deines (-er, -e), Ihres usw.*
his	*seines usw.*
hers	*ihres usw.*
its	*seines, ihres usw. (selten!)*
ours	*unseres usw.*
yours	*eueres, Ihres usw.*
theirs	*ihres (Mehrzahl) usw.*

Is this your coat? - Yes, it's **mine**.
Are these your books? - No, they aren't. They're **hers**.

Their sentences and **mine** are different.
I have got my magazine, have you got **yours**?
We think it's **hers**.
Our teacher is German, **theirs** is British.

DENNIS THE MENACE

"THIS YOURS?"

4 Verneinte Aufforderungssätze / Negative Imperatives

In *Grammar 12* von *English Network 1* wurden Aufforderungssätze gebildet, mit denen Personen veranlaßt wurden, etwas zu tun. An dieser Stelle nun dienen die Aufforderungssätze dazu, Personen zu veranlassen, etwas *nicht* zu tun, z. B. nicht zu schnell zu fahren.

Don't/Do not phone too early.	*Ruf'/Rufen Sie nicht zu früh an.*
Don't/Do not drive too fast.	*Fahr'/Fahren Sie nicht zu schnell.*

Vor die Grundform der Verben ist stets **don't** oder (seltener) **do not** zu stellen. Die Kurzform werden Sie häufiger als die Langform antreffen, die oft auch besonders betont wird und wesentlich nachdrücklicher wirkt.

Please don't touch.
Don't park your car here, please.

Ein vor- oder nachgestelltes **please** kann in solchen Sätzen auch nicht schaden. Sie klingen dann viel höflicher und verbindlicher.

5 Die Verlaufsform der Gegenwart / The present progressive

In diesem Abschnitt wird eine Struktur behandelt, die in der englischen Grammatik noch häufig auftauchen wird, da die **progressive form** (oder auch **-ing-form**) verschiedene Aufgaben übernimmt und neben der Gegenwart auch in anderen Zeiten gebraucht wird.

– **Are** you **learning** new English words?
– No, I'm not. I'**m learning** the progressive form.

Bildung: Die Verlaufsform wird mit einer Form von **be** und einem Verb mit der Endung **-ing** gebildet.

* *look for = suchen*

Gebrauch: Die Verlaufsform wird im Englischen benutzt um auszudrücken, daß eine Tätigkeit *jetzt* ausgeübt wird und noch nicht abgeschlossen ist oder daß ein Geschehen *im Augenblick gerade verläuft*, deshalb auch der Begriff ‚Verlaufsform'.

5.1 Aussagesätze

I'**m (= am) working** very hard (at the moment).	*Ich arbeite (im Augenblick) sehr hart.*
You'**re (= are) singing** a nice song.	*Du singst / Sie singen (gerade) ein schönes Lied.*
He'**s (= is) living** in Belfast (now).	*Er wohnt (z. Z.) in Belfast.*
She'**s (= is) taking** a photo.	*Sie fotografiert (gerade).*
We'**re** / You'**re reading** a new book.	*Wir lesen / Ihr lest ein neues Buch.*
They '**re drinking** coffee.	*Sie trinken (gerade) Kaffee.*

Im Gegensatz zu Aussagesätzen des Musters *I work hard* und *He lives in Belfast*, die besagen, daß der Sprecher eine Arbeit ausübt, die ihn immer fordert und daß jemand seinen ständigen Wohnsitz in Belfast hat (vgl. auch *English Network 1, Grammar 11,* S. 118–119) wird hier über einen augenblicklichen Zustand, der nicht von Dauer ist, gesprochen.

5.2 Verneinung

I'**m not singing** a new pop song.
She **isn't driving** her taxi this morning.
They **aren't talking** to their teacher.

Die Verneinung von **be** ist aus *Grammar 7.2* von *English Network 1* (S. 116) bekannt. Die Verneinung der Verlaufsform folgt derselben Regel.

5.3 Fragen

Fragewort	Frage
	Is Dad **working?**
Where	**is** he **working?**
What	**are** they **doing** in our garden?

Die Form der Fragebildung mit dem Verb **be** *(English Network 1, Grammar 7.3,* S. 116) bleibt selbstverständlich weiterhin gültig.

5.4 Kurzantworten

Frage	Kurzantwort
Are you **cooking** an Italian meal?	Yes, I **am.** No, I'**m not.**
Is she **working** carefully?	Yes, she **is.** No, she **isn't.**

Auch die Regeln zur Kurzantwort (*English Network 1, Grammar 7.4,* S. 116) behalten ihre Gültigkeit.

6 Das Hilfsverb *must* / The auxiliary *must*

Englische Hilfsverben können mitunter zu einem Problem werden, da sie nicht immer den deutschen Hilfsverben in Bildung und Gebrauch entsprechen.

6.1 *must* / müssen

Must drückt eine starke, in der Regel unausweichliche Verpflichtung aus, die auch selbst auferlegt sein kann. In vielen Sätzen entspricht **must** dem deutschen *müssen,* so daß die Übersetzung eines Satzes wie *„Ich **muß** mit Dir/Ihnen sprechen"* keine Schwierigkeiten macht: *I **must** talk to you.*

I **must** go now.	*Ich **muß** jetzt gehen.*
You **must** learn your words.	*Du **mußt** deine Vokabeln lernen.*
We **must** work today.	*Wir **müssen** heute arbeiten.*
You **must** help me.	*Ihr **müßt** mir helfen.*

Wie auch das Hilfsverb **can** (vgl. *English Network 1, Grammar 9,* S. 117) verändert sich **must** nicht.

6.2 *mustn't, must not* / nicht dürfen

I **mustn't (= must not)** tell them.	*Ich darf es ihnen nicht erzählen.*
You **mustn't** eat ice cream here.	*Du darfst / Sie dürfen hier kein Eis essen.*
He / She **mustn't** go swimming today.	*Er / Sie darf heute nicht schwimmen gehen.*
We / You **mustn't** drive too fast.	*Wir dürfen / Ihr dürft nicht zu schnell fahren.*
Children **mustn't** smoke.	*Kinder dürfen nicht rauchen.*

Verneint wird **must** formal, indem man **n't** anhängt oder **not** hinter **must** als neues Wort schreibt. Doch Vorsicht, denn damit ändert sich die Bedeutung des Begriffs zu *‚nicht dürfen',* und es wird ein (ggf. auch selbst auferlegtes) Verbot ausgesprochen.

6.3 *don't have to* / nicht müssen

I **don't have to** go to my course today. It's tomorrow.
You **don't have to** stay at home all day. You can go out.
He / She **doesn't have to** see a doctor again. He's / She's fit now.
We / You **don't have to** finish the work today. We / You can do it tomorrow.
They **don't have to** go to Munich by car. They can go by train.

Will man im Englischen die Aussage machen, daß man etwas in der Gegenwart für *nicht notwendig* hält, es also momentan *nicht tun muß,* muß man auf eine Ersatzform zurückgreifen, die **have to** lautet, und sie – wie bei allen Vollverben schon gewohnt – verneinen.

6.4 *will have to* / werden müssen

We **will have to** speak English as often as possible.
Then we **won't (= will not) have to** start again.

Die Zukunft von **must** wird mit **will have to / won't have to** gebildet.

"He will have to learn a lot about computers."

7 Die Zeitform des Perfekts / The present perfect

Sprechen wir im Englischen über etwas Vergangenes, seien es Ereignisse oder Tätigkeiten, die einen direkten Bezug zur Gegenwart haben („jetzt" oder „bis jetzt"), müssen wir die Zeitform des Perfekts (vollendete Gegenwart; **present perfect**) verwenden. Die Vergangenheitsform (**past simple**) ist nicht möglich. Das ist eine Vorstellung, an die wir uns erst gewöhnen müssen, da in unserer Muttersprache dieser Unterschied nicht gemacht wird (vgl. *English Network 1,* S. 120).
Wenn es heißt: *I **have** always **helped** him,* wird ausgedrückt, daß jemand immer, d. h. bis jetzt, bis zum gegenwärtigen Zeitpunkt geholfen hat. Wichtig ist jetzt (in der Gegenwart), daß ich geholfen habe, nicht wann bzw. zu welchem bestimmten Zeitpunkt (in der Vergangenheit) geholfen wurde.
Der Unterschied zwischen **present perfect** und **past simple** läßt sich anhand des folgenden Beispiels aufzeigen: *Have you ever been to America?*
Das Wort **ever** (= jemals) zeigt, daß der/die Fragende wissen möchte, ob jemand schon einmal in seinem Leben (d. h. zu einem beliebigen Zeitpunkt bis zum heutigen Tage) in Amerika gewesen ist. Die bejahende Antwort auf diese Frage lautet: *Yes, I have.*
Und dann könnte weiter ausgeführt werden: *I was there three years ago,* womit bei Zeitangaben der Vergangenheit konsequent auch die Zeitform der Vergangenheit benutzt wird (vgl. dazu *English Network 1, Grammar 13,* S. 120–121).

7.1 Die Bildung des Perfekts / The formation of the present perfect

I **have** ask**ed** him.	*Ich **habe** ihn **gefragt**.*
You **have** sav**ed** some money.	*Du **hast** etwas Geld **gespart**.*
He **has** always play**ed** football.	*Er **hat** immer Fußball **gespielt**.*
She **has** work**ed** a lot.	*Sie **hat** viel **gearbeitet**.*
We **have** often listen**ed** to this song.	*Wir **haben** dieses Lied oft **gehört**.*
You / They **have** cook**ed** wonderful omelettes.	*Ihr **habt** / Sie **haben** wunderbare Omelettes **gekocht**.*

Zur Bildung des Perfekts wird immer **have/has** gebraucht, das vor das Mittelwort der Vergangenheit eines Verbs, auch das Partizip Perfekt genannt, gestellt wird.
Die Partizipform regelmäßiger Verben wird durch das Anhängen von **-ed** an die Grundform gebildet. Im Deutschen verfahren wir im Prinzip ähnlich, nur benötigen wir dafür bei unseren Verben in der Regel eine Vorsilbe *‚ge-'* und eine Endung *‚t'* (*gefragt* usw.).

He has **gone** home.
You have **been** to Chicago three times.

Bei unregelmäßigen Verben müssen wir die Partizipform auswendig lernen.

I **have** often been to Scotland.	*Ich **bin** oft in Schottland gewesen.*
He **has** gone away.	*Er **ist** fortgegangen.*
They **have** arrived early.	*Sie **sind** früh angekommen.*

Zur Bildung des Perfekts wird bei allen Verben **have/has** verwendet, also auch bei den Verben, die im Deutschen mit *sein* benutzt werden.

7.2 Das Verb *be* im Perfekt / The verb *be* in the present perfect

Aussage	I **have been** to New York. She **has been** to San Francisco. We all **have been** to America very often.
Verneinung	I **haven't been** to New York. She **hasn't been** to San Francisco. We **haven't been** to America.
Frage	**Have** you ever **been** to America? **Has** she ever **been** to Dallas?
Kurzantwort	Yes, I **have.** / No, I **haven't.** Yes, she **has.** / No, she **hasn't.**

Die in *English Network 1* aufgeführten Hinweise für Aussagen, Fragen und Kurzantworten mit **have/has got** gelten auch für die Bildung des **present perfect.**

7.3 Vollverben im Perfekt / Full verbs in the present perfect

Aussage	I **have** always **worked** part-time. She **has listened** to the dialogue now. They **have** often **used** regular verbs.
Verneinung	I **haven't** ever **visited** my friends in Greece. He **hasn't** ever **climbed** in the mountains. They **haven't played** tennis before.
Frage	**Have** you ever **watched** French TV? **Has** she **finished** her work? **Have** they ever **cooked** an Italian meal?
Kurzantwort	Yes, I **have.** / No, I **haven't.** Yes, she **has.** / No, she **hasn't.** Yes, they **have.** / No, they **haven't.**

ANDY CAPP

7.4 Unregelmäßige Verben / Irregular verbs

(Siehe dazu auch: Kapitel 16)

Grundform	Partizip	Grundform	Partizip
bring	**brought**	give	**given**
buy	**bought**	go	**gone**
come	**come**	have	**had**
do	**done**	meet	**met**
drink	**drunk**	read	**read**
drive	**driven**	see	**seen**
eat	**eaten**	speak	**spoken**
get	**got**	take	**taken**

Die Formen aller in diesem Band auftretenden unregelmäßigen Verben (sogenannte ‚Stammformen') finden Sie in einer Übersichtstabelle auf Seite 123.

8 *used to*

Aussage
I **used to** play football when I was younger. We **used to** smoke, but we don't smoke now.

Der Ausdruck **used to** bezeichnet eine Gewohnheit, die man in der Vergangenheit hatte und die man nicht länger pflegt. Damit entspricht er dem deutschen ‚pflegte früher zu...'

"We used to come here when it really was private."

Verneinung	
I **didn't use to** go on holiday when I was a child.	*Ich fuhr* ***gewöhnlich*** *nicht in Ferien, als ich ein Kind war.*
He **didn't use to** stay long.	*Er blieb* ***in der Regel*** *nicht sehr lange.*
They **didn't use to** drink wine when they visited friends.	*Früher tranken sie* ***gewöhnlich / in der Regel*** *keinen Wein, wenn sie Freunde besuchten.*

Die verneinte Form findet sich in Unterhaltungen relativ selten. Auch im Deutschen ziehen wir Ausdrücke mit der einfachen Vergangenheit und **‚gewöhnlich'** oder **‚immer'** dem schwerfällig wirkenden **‚pflegte (nicht) zu tun'** vor.

Frage
Did you **use to** smoke?
Where **did** he/she **use to** work?
What **did** they **use to** do?

Gefragt wird nach Gewohnheiten der Vergangenheit, indem für alle Personen **did** benutzt wird. Dieses Verfahren der Bildung von Fragesätzen ist schon aus *Grammar 14.4* von *English Network 1* (S. 122) bekannt.

9 Die einfache Form und die Verlaufsform der Vergangenheit / The past simple and the past progressive

9.1 Die Bildung der Verlaufsform der Vergangenheit / The formation of the past progressive

I **was waiting** for a bus yesterday when it started to rain.
You **were speaking** on the phone when I rang you.

Diese Form wird aus **was/were + -ing-**Form von Verben gebildet.

9.2 Verwendung der Verlaufsform der Vergangenheit / Use of the past progressive

I **was reading** a book when I heard someone on the first floor.
The children **were playing** with their train when I entered their room.
– What **were** you **doing** when I met you at the travel agency?
– I **was booking** our holidays when you saw me.

Gern erscheinen die einfache Form und die Verlaufsform der Vergangenheit zusammen in einem Satz. Für die in der Vergangenheit neu eintretende Handlung wird die einfache Form und für die bereits ablaufende Handlung die Verlaufsform benutzt.

10 Das Frageanhängsel „nicht wahr?" / Question tags

Satz (+)	Anhängsel (–)
The weather **is** fine,	**isn't** it?
He **works** flexi-time,	**doesn't** he?
They **have** got 4 brothers,	**haven't** they?
He **went** to Switzerland,	**didn't** he?
Satz (–)	**Anhängsel (+)**
He **isn't** very careful,	**is** he?
He **doesn't** live here,	**does** he?
She **didn't** meet you,	**did** she?

An Aussagesätze wird im Deutschen häufig **‚nicht wahr?'** angehängt. Ein Frageanhängsel gibt es auch im Englischen, das aber aus der zuvor benutzten Verbform gebildet wird. Nach einer bejahenden (+) Aussage steht es in der Form einer verneinten Frage (–), nach einer verneinenden Feststellung (–) in Form einer Frage (+).

You liked the film, didn't you? *Du hast den Film doch wohl gemocht, nicht wahr? Wie fandest du ihn?*

You liked the film, didn't you? *Du hast den Film schon gemocht, nicht wahr? Er gefiel dir ja.*

Die Aussprache ist in solchen Sätzen bedeutsam: Wird die Stimme am Satzende gehoben (steigende Intonation), möchte der Sprecher die Meinung des Gesprächspartners erfahren. Sinkt die Stimme (fallende Intonation), erwartet der Sprecher in der Regel die Zustimmung der angesprochenen Person.

11 Bezugs- oder Relativsätze / Relative clauses

We're good friends of an American woman.
She lives at number 10.

We're good friends of an American woman **who** lives at number 10.

Sätze können miteinander verbunden werden, um Personen oder Dinge näher zu beschreiben. Wie im Deutschen verwendet man im Englischen dazu Verbindungswörter, die Relativpronomen genannt werden.

11.1 Relativpronomen / Relative pronouns

who, that für Personen	I know a woman **who/that** speaks five languages.
which, that für Sachen und Gegenstände	I'd prefer a car **which/that** isn't too expensive.

11.2 Die Wortfolge in Relativsätzen / Word order in relative clauses

The policeman **who stopped my car** was one of my friends.	*Der Polizist, **der meinen Wagen anhielt,** war einer meiner Freunde.*
The car **that I liked most** was too expensive for me.	*Das Auto, **das ich am meisten mochte,** war mir zu teuer.*
I'd like a flat **which has got central heating.**	*Ich möchte eine Wohnung, **die Zentralheizung hat.***

Die Bildung der Relativsätze in der Subjektform (Sie fragen: Wer? oder Was?, 1. Fall) ist wie im Deutschen, jedoch mit einem kleinen Unterschied: Die Wortfolge und Stellung der Satzglieder im Relativ- oder Nebensatz folgt der Grundregel *Subjekt – Zeitwort – Ergänzung* (vgl. *English Network 1, Grammar 6.1,* S. 115).

That's a nice bag you've got.
Those are beautiful shoes you've got.
Is this the only blue shirt you've got?

Bei weiteren Relativsätzen kann das Relativpronomen ausgelassen werden. Diese werden Sie in Band 3 von *English Network* noch näher kennenlernen. Im Augenblick genügt es, sie als ‚verkürzte' Relativsätze zu erkennen und zu verstehen.

12 Bedingungs- oder Konditionalsätze (*if*-Sätze) / *if*-clauses

Vieles in unserem Leben ist von Bedingungen oder besser der Erfüllung von Bedingungen abhängig: Wenn/Falls A geschieht, tun wir B, oder B wird ohne unser Zutun dann eintreten.
Solche Satzarten werden Bedingungs- oder Konditionalsätze genannt. Da sie im Englischen mit dem Wort **if** beginnen, auch häufig ***if****-Sätze (****if****-clauses).*

if-Satz (Nebensatz)	Hauptsatz
If I **arrive** on time, **If** you **don't stay** at home, **If** he **comes** before lunch,	I **will meet** him in town. you **won't finish** your work. he **won't see** me.
If she **doesn't drink** coffee, **If** we **meet** our friends, **If** they **don't get** the job,	she **will sleep** very well. we **will go** to the pub. they **will be** very unhappy.

Im Englischen wird die **einfache Gegenwart** im *if*-Satz verwendet und im Hauptsatz in der Regel die Zukunft mit **will.** Damit wird ausgedrückt, daß man ein Ereignis oder eine Tätigkeit für möglich hält (im *if*-Satz) und daß sich daraus bestimmte Folgen ergeben/ergeben werden (deshalb *will-future* im Hauptsatz).
Weitere Typen von Bedingungssätzen werden Sie im dritten Band von *English Network* kennenlernen.

13 Die Zukunft von *can* / The future of *can*

Gegenwart	Zukunft
can cannot/can't	**will / 'll be able to** **will not / won't be able to**
If the sun shines, we'**ll be able to** go for a walk. If my boss is in, I **won't be able to** leave the office early.	

Die Zukunft von **can** wird mit **will / won't be able to** gebildet. Diese Form können Sie auch in Bedingungssätzen (s. Abschnitt 12 oben) verwenden.
Und *falls/wenn* Sie dies *tun, werden* Sie Englisch gut sprechen *können.*
*And **if** you **do** this, you'**ll be able to** speak English well.*

14 Die Zukunft mit *going to* / *going to*-future

In Abschnitt *16* des Grammatikanhangs zu *English Network 1* wurde schon angedeutet, daß es neben **will** noch weitere sprachliche Möglichkeiten gibt, über die Zukunft zu sprechen.

Aussage	I'**m going to travel** by train. He'**s going to stay** with us. They'**re going to complain** about me.
Verneinung	She **isn't going to cook** lunch. They **aren't going to stay** in France.
Frage	**Are** you **going to watch** TV tonight? Where **are** they **going to sleep** tonight?

Im Englischen wird eine Form von **be** in Verbindung mit **going to** und der **Grundform eines Verbs** benutzt, wenn man sagen will, daß man etwas vorhat und daß man dieses Vorhaben auch in die Tat umsetzen wird oder will. Man hat sich etwas überlegt und sich dazu entschlossen, etwas in Zukunft zu tun.

Our friend's going to buy the tickets for us.

Going to wird auch benutzt, wenn von einer unmittelbar bevorstehenden Handlung gesprochen wird. Der Sprecher ist also sicher, daß sie gleich eintreten wird. Hier z. B., wenn der Freund an der Theaterkasse ansteht und die Karten gleich kaufen wird.

DENNIS THE MENACE

"Carrots again?"

"I'm going to send myself to bed without any supper."

⚠ Vermeiden Sie bitte die Verbindungen *going to go* und *going to come.* Zwar sind sie grammatikalisch richtig, klingen jedoch holprig und schwerfällig.

15 *like* / *hate ...-ing*

Aussage	I **like** watch**ing** TV. He **enjoys** read**ing** magazines. They **hate** garden**ing.**
Verneinung	I **don't like** walk**ing.** He **doesn't enjoy** read**ing** books.
Frage	**Do** you **like** listen**ing** to modern jazz? **Does** he **hate** visit**ing** his sisters?

Will man im Englischen über Hobbies und Freizeitbeschäftigungen sprechen, die man gern / nicht gern betreibt, verwendet man **like / enjoy / love / hate** und hängt an das nachfolgende Verb oft **-ing** an.
Diese Struktur wird in Band 3 von *English Network* detailliert behandelt. Im Augenblick genügt es, sie in diesem Sinnzusammenhang zu verwenden.

16 Stammformen unregelmäßiger Verben / Principal parts of irregular verbs

Grundform	Vergangenheit	Perfekt	
be	was/were	have (has) been	sein
become	became	have become	werden
begin	began	have begun	beginnen
break	broke	have broken	brechen
bring	brought	have brought	bringen
build	built	have built	bauen
buy	bought	have bought	kaufen
choose	chose	have chosen	(aus-)wählen
come	came	have come	kommen
cost	cost	have cost	kosten
do	did	have done	tun, machen
drink	drank	have drunk	trinken
drive	drove	have driven	(Auto) fahren
eat	ate	have eaten	essen
feel	felt	have felt	(sich) fühlen
fall	fell	have fallen	fallen
find	found	have found	finden
forget	forgot	have forgotten	vergessen
get	got	have got	bekommen
give	gave	have given	geben
go	went	have gone	gehen, fahren
have	had	have had	haben
hear	heard	have heard	hören
know	knew	have known	wissen, kennen
leave	left	have left	verlassen, abfahren
let	let	have let	lassen
lose	lost	have lost	verlieren
make	made	have made	machen
mean	meant	have meant	meinen, bedeuten
meet	met	have met	treffen, begegnen
pay	paid	have paid	(be-)zahlen
put	put	have put	stellen, legen
read	read	have read	lesen
ring	rang	have rung	anrufen, klingeln
say	said	have said	sagen
see	saw	have seen	sehen
sell	sold	have sold	verkaufen
send	sent	have sent	schicken
show	showed	have shown	zeigen
sing	sang	have sung	singen
sit	sat	have sat	sitzen
sleep	slept	have slept	schlafen
speak	spoke	have spoken	sprechen
spend	spent	have spent	verbringen, ausgeben
stand	stood	have stood	stehen
strike	struck	have struck	schlagen
swim	swam	have swum	schwimmen
take	took	have taken	nehmen
tell	told	have told	sagen, erzählen
think	thought	have thought	denken
understand	understood	have understood	verstehen
wear	wore	have worn	tragen
win	won	have won	gewinnen
write	wrote	have written	schreiben

Leitfaden Aussprache

In den nachfolgenden Wortschatzanhängen *Vocabulary* und *Dictionary* wird die Aussprache in eckigen Klammern nach jedem Eintrag angegeben. Dazu wird eine spezielle Lautschrift verwendet, deren wichtigste Symbole hier erläutert werden.

Symbol	Beispielwort	Aussprache
ə	numb**er**	wie *e* in deutsch *singe*
ɪ	**i**n	wie *i* in deutsch *in*
ɪə	**here**	wie *ie* in deutsch *hier*
iː	m**ee**t	wie *ie* in deutsch *Knie*
e	y**e**s	etwa wie *e* in deutsch *fett*
eɪ	d**ay**	nicht wie deutsch *ei*, sondern [e] + [ɪ]
eə	wh**ere**	wie *air* in deutsch *fair*
æ	th**a**nks	zwischen deutschem *a* und *ä*
aɪ	n**i**ce	wie *ei* in deutsch *Eile*
aʊ	h**ow**	wie *au* in deutsch *flau*
ɑː	f**a**ther	wie *ah* in deutsch *Kahn*
ɒ	c**o**ffee	wie *o* in deutsch *Motte*
ɔɪ	b**oy**	wie *eu* in *deutsch*
ɔː	f**our**	wie *o* in deutsch *Borke*
ʌ	c**o**me	wie *a* in deutsch *Klatsch*
ʊ	l**oo**k	wie *u* in deutsch *Butter*
ʊə	t**ou**rist	[ʊ] + [ə]
əʊ	n**o**	[ə] + [ʊ]
uː	t**oo**	etwa wie *u* in deutsch *Tuch*
ɜː	**ear**ly	etwa wie *ö* in deutsch *Segeltörn*
v	ha**v**e	wie *v* in deutsch *Virus*
θ	**th**anks	wie ein gelispeltes *ß* in deutsch *Biß*
ð	**th**is	wie ein gelispeltes *s* in deutsch *Sand*
s	**s**eat	wie *ß* in deutsch *Muße*
z	plea**s**e	wie *s* in deutsch *Museum*
ʃ	**sh**e	wie *sch* in deutsch *fesch*
ʒ	televi**s**ion	wie *g* in deutsch *Regie*
tʃ	**ch**eers	wie *tsch* in deutsch *Klatsch*
dʒ	**G**erman	[d] + [ʒ]
ŋ	so**ng**	wie *ng* in deutsch *singen*
r	**r**epeat	nicht wie ein deutsches r, sondern vorn im Munde gesprochen
w	**w**e	nicht wie ein deutsches w, sondern durch die Lippen wie [uː]

Der hochgestellte Strich ˈ steht in Wörtern mit mehr als einer Silbe vor dem Teil des Wortes, der am stärksten betont wird. Der tiefgestellte Strich ˌ bedeutet, daß die folgende Silbe auch etwas betont wird.
Bei Sätzen werden im *Vocabulary* nur die Hauptbetonungen angegeben, nicht aber alle Betonungen im Einzelwort angeführt.

Vocabulary

Hier finden Sie eine Auflistung aller englischen Wörter und Wendungen, die Sie in diesem Buch kennenlernen. Sie erscheinen in derselben Reihenfolge, wie sie vorne im Buch vorkommen.

In der linken Spalte steht jeweils das englische Wort oder die Wendung und dahinter in eckigen Klammern die Aussprache. Einen Leitfaden zur Aussprache finden Sie auf der Vorseite. In der mittleren Spalte erscheint die deutsche Übersetzung und in der rechten Spalte ein Satzbeispiel, in dem das englische Wort stehen könnte. Wenn Sie die Vokabeln einmal gelernt haben, können Sie diese rechte Spalte benutzen, um sich selbst abzufragen. Sie decken dabei die linke Spalte zu und versuchen, die durch das Zeichen ~ markierte Lücke mit dem richtigen Wort zu füllen.

Die **fettgedruckten** Wörter und Wendungen sind besonders nützlich. Sie werden sie öfter brauchen und sollten sie deshalb vorrangig lernen. Die Wörter in normalem Druck sind in diesem Buch noch nicht so wichtig.

Alle Wörter und Wendungen sind in dieser Wortliste nur dort aufgeführt, wo sie zum ersten Mal vorkommen. Wenn Sie ein Wort zu einem späteren Zeitpunkt nochmals nachschlagen möchten, finden Sie die Aussprache und Übersetzung in der alphabetischen Wortschatzliste ab Seite 147.

Im Anschluß an die alphabetische Wortschatzliste finden Sie eine Liste von Wörtern und Wendungen, die besonders häufig in den Übungsanweisungen und Überschriften vorkommen. Diese Wörter sind nicht noch einmal im *Vocabulary* aufgeführt, sondern nur in die alphabetische Liste aufgenommen.

UNIT 1

I	**free time** [fri: taɪm]	Freizeit	At weekends I have a lot of ~.
	irregular [ɪ'regjʊlə]	unregelmäßig	

UNIT 1 *Step 1*

1	**for …** [fɔ:]	… lang (*zeitlich*)	I'll stay in Italy ~ two weeks.
	Greek [gri:k]	griechisch(-e, -er, -es); Grieche, Griechin	
	island ['aɪlənd]	Insel	Great Britain is an ~.
	both … and [bəʊθ ænd]	sowohl … als auch	~ Paris ~ London are big cities.
	part-time [ˌpɑ:t 'taɪm]	Teilzeit-	I work ~, from 9 to 12.
	hobby ['hɒbɪ]	Hobby	His ~ is playing football.
	camera ['kæmrə]	Kamera	I can take photos with a ~.
	enjoy, ~ doing [ɪn'dʒɔɪ]	genießen, Gefallen finden; gern tun	Sue ~s travelling.
	take up ['teɪk ʌp]	aufnehmen, beginnen	
	like, ~ doing [laɪk 'du:ɪŋ]	gern tun	John ~s cooking.
	ever ['evə]	jemals, schon einmal	Have you ~ been to Greece?
	weather ['weðə]	Wetter	Usually the ~ is fine in Greece.
1a	write in [raɪt ɪn]	einsetzen	
	cook [kʊk]	Koch, Köchin	My mother is a good ~.
	mean [mi:n]	bedeuten	
	something ['sʌmθɪŋ]	etwas	Next week we'll learn ~ new.
1b	text [tekst]	Text	
	question mark ['kwestʃən mɑ:k]	Fragezeichen	
1d	possible ['pɒsəbl]	möglich	
	reaction [rɪ'ækʃn]	Reaktion	
	someone ['sʌmwʌn]	jemand	

2	**plan** [plæn]	Plan	What ~s have you got for tomorrow?
	travel agent ['trævl ˌeɪdʒənt]	Reisebürokaufmann	A ~ can tell you many things about holidays.
	than [ðæn, ðən]	als (*Vergleich*)	Germany is bigger ~ Austria.
	at all [æt ɔːl, ət ɔːl]	überhaupt	I don't like wine ~.
	brochure ['brəʊʃə]	Broschüre	Our Greece ~ will give you all the information that you need.
	page [peɪdʒ]	Seite	There are some new words on this ~.
	example [ɪg'zɑːmpl]	Beispiel	Can you give an ~?
	for example [fər‿ɪg'zɑːmpl]	zum Beispiel	
	paradise ['pærədaɪs]	Paradies	
	beach [biːtʃ]	Strand	Greece has got nice ~es.
	cheap [tʃiːp]	billig, preiswert	This hotel is ~; that one is expensive.
	oh dear [əʊ dɪə]	oh jeh, meine Güte	
2b	before [bɪ'fɔː]	ehe, bevor	
	activity [æk'tɪvətɪ]	Aktivität, Tätigkeit	
	find out [faɪnd aʊt]	herausfinden	
	missing ['mɪsɪŋ]	fehlend	
	like this [laɪk ðɪs]	wie dies(-e, -es, -er)	
	palace ['pælɪs]	Palast, Schloß	
	airport ['eəpɔːt]	Flughafen	One of London's ~s is called Heathrow.
	flight [flaɪt]	Flug	You can book a ~ at the travel agent's.
	extra cost ['ekstrə kɒst]	Aufpreis	The ~ for a single room is £ 20.
2c	suggestion [sə'dʒestʃən]	Vorschlag	
	shall we ...? [ʃæl wiː]	sollen wir	~ go out tonight?
	this time [ðɪs taɪm]	dieses Mal	~ we'd like to go to Greece, next time we'll go to Italy.
	let's (= let us) [lets]	laß' uns (+ *Vorschlag*)	
B	most [məʊst]	meiste(-r, -s)	
	picture ['pɪktʃə]	Bild	
	towel ['taʊəl]	Handtuch	
	comb [kəʊm]	Kamm	
	shoe [ʃuː]	Schuh	
	beach shoe [biːtʃ ʃuː]	Strandschuh, Badeschuh	
	sunglasses ['sʌnglɑːsɪz]	Sonnenbrille	When the weather is fine, you need ~.
	suntan ['sʌntæn]	(Sonnen)Bräune	
	cream [kriːm]	Creme	
	suntan cream ['sʌntæn kriːm]	Bräunungscreme	On the beach you need sunglasses and ~.
	swimming costume ['swɪmɪŋ ˌkɒstjuːm]	Badeanzug	
	tooth (teeth) [tuːθ, tiːθ]	Zahn (Zähne)	
	toothbrush ['tuːθbrʌʃ]	Zahnbürste	
	toothpaste ['tuːθpeɪst]	Zahnpasta	

UNIT 1 *Step 2*

S	sit [sɪt]	sitzen	
	circle ['sɜːkl]	Kreis	
	if [ɪf]	wenn, falls; ob	

	passport ['pɑ:spɔ:t]	(Reise)Paß	I need a ~ when I go to America.
	get [get]	*hier*: werden	
1	comparative [kəm'pærətɪv]	Komparativ (*1. Steigerungsstufe*)	
	superlative [su:'pɜ:lətɪv]	Superlativ (*2. Steigerungsstufe*)	
	sunny ['sʌnɪ]	sonnig	Summers are very ~ in Corfu.
	most [məʊst]	meiste(-r, -s)	~ children like ice cream.
	better ['betə]	besser	The weather in Greece is ~ than in Germany.
	worse [wɜ:s]	schlechter, schlimmer	The weather in Germany is ~ than in Greece.
	best [best]	beste(-r, -s)	Mum is the ~ cook in our family.
	worst [wɜ:st]	schlechteste(-r, -s), schlimmste(-r, -s)	Monday is the ~ day of the week.
	as … as [əz … əz]	so … wie (*Vergleich*)	Marge isn't ~ old ~ Sue.
1a	grammar table ['græmə teɪbl]	Grammatiktafel	
	above [ə'bʌv]	oben	
	should [ʃʊd]	sollen	
	mixed [mɪkst]	gemischt	
	order ['ɔ:də]	Reihenfolge, Ordnung	
	student ['stju:dnt]	Student(-in), *auch*: Kursteilnehmer(-in)	~s learn English best in an English-speaking country.
	sort into [sɔ:t 'ɪntʊ]	sortieren in	
2	present perfect [ˌpreznt 'pɜ:fɪkt]	Perfekt, vollendete Gegenwart	
2a	report [rɪ'pɔ:t]	berichten, melden	
	negative ['negətɪv]	negativ	
	positive ['pɒzətɪv]	positiv	
2b	participle ['pɑ:tɪsɪpl]	Partizip, Mittelwort	
	verb [vɜ:b]	Verb, Zeitwort	
	past [pɑ:st]	Imperfekt, Vergangenheit	
	use [ju:z]	benutzen	
	film star ['fɪlm stɑ:]	Filmstar	Marlene Dietrich was a great ~.
B	**rain** [reɪn]	regnen	In Greece it doesn't ~ as often as in Germany.
	hot [hɒt]	heiß	The summers in Greece are ~.
	snow [snəʊ]	schneien	It ~s more often in Germany than in Greece.
	windy ['wɪndɪ]	windig	It is very ~ in autumn.
	cloudy ['klaʊdɪ]	bewölkt	In England it's often very ~.
	cold [kəʊld]	kalt	The winters in Germany are ~.
	fog [fɒg]	Nebel	
	foggy ['fɒgɪ]	neblig	It's often ~ by the sea.
	expression [ɪk'spreʃn]	Ausdruck	

UNIT 1 *Step 3*

S	associate [ə'səʊsɪeɪt]	assoziieren, verbinden	
	sun [sʌn]	Sonne	The afternoon ~ is too hot for me.
	rain [reɪn]	Regen	Some people like walking in the ~.
	snow [snəʊ]	Schnee	Children like playing in the ~.
1	remember [rɪ'membə]	sich erinnern an	
	win (won) [wɪn, wʌn]	gewinnen (gewann, gewonnen)	
	competition [ˌkɒmpɪ'tɪʃn]	Wettbewerb	The best one will win the ~.
	prize [praɪz]	(Sieger)Preis	
	congratulations [kənˌgrætʃʊ'leɪʃnz]	Glückwunsch	~! You won the competition.
	hear (heard) [hɪə, hɜ:d]	hören (hörte, gehört)	Can you ~ me?

	before [bɪ'fɔː]	vorher, zuvor	I've never seen him ~.
	before [bɪ'fɔː]	ehe, bevor	I have breakfast ~ I go to work.
	interested in ['ɪntrəstɪd ɪn]	interessiert an	Are you ~ art?
1a	send [send]	senden, schicken	
	compare [kəm'peə]	vergleichen	
1b	conversation [ˌkɒnvə'seɪʃn]	Unterhaltung, Gespräch	
	past [pɑːst]	vergangen	

Panorama

apart from [ə'pɑːt frəm] außer, abgesehen von
beginner [bɪ'gɪnə] Anfänger(-in)
business ['bɪznɪs] Geschäft, Beruf, Handel
cathedral [kə'θiːdrəl] Kathedrale
class [klɑːs] *hier*: Unterricht, Kurs
commercial [kə'mɜːʃl] kaufmännisch, Handels-, Geschäfts-
commercial and business studies [kə'mɜːʃl ənd 'bɪznɪs 'stʌdɪz] Handels- und Wirtschaftskurs
description [dɪ'skrɪpʃn] Beschreibung
diagnose ['daɪəgnəʊz] Diagnose
draw [drɔː] zeichnen
education [ˌedʒʊ'keɪʃn] Bildung, Erziehung, Ausbildung
enjoyable [ɪn'dʒɔɪəbl] vergnüglich, erfreulich
fault [fɔːlt] Fehler, Mangel
fit [fɪt] fit, in guter Form
flexibility [ˌfleksə'bɪlətɪ] Flexibilität; *hier*: Gelenkigkeit
form [fɔːm] Form
future ['fjuːtʃə] Zukunft
general ['dʒenrəl] allgemein
get around [get ə'raʊnd] herumlaufen in, seinen Weg finden in/durch
guide [gaɪd] Führer
library ['laɪbrərɪ] Bibliothek, Bücherei
lively ['laɪvlɪ] lebhaft, lebendig
lovely ['lʌvlɪ] wunderschön, reizend
meal [miːl] Essen, Mahlzeit
muscle ['mʌsl] Muskel
on offer [ɒn 'ɒfə] im Angebot
paint [peɪnt] malen
practical ['præktɪkl] praktisch
public ['pʌblɪk] öffentlich
repair [rɪ'peə] reparieren
return [rɪ'tɜːn] zurückkehren
Russian ['rʌʃən] russisch(-e, -er, -es); Russe, Russin
section ['sekʃn] Abschnitt, Ausschnitt
shorthand ['ʃɔːthænd] Kurzschrift
stamina ['stæmɪnə] Lebenskraft; *hier*: Ausdauer
study ['stʌdɪ] Studium
survival [sə'vaɪvl] Überleben
talent ['tælənt] Talent, Begabung
technique [tek'niːk] Technik
teeline ['tiːlaɪn] (*moderne Form der Kurzschrift*)
tone [təʊn] *hier*: Spannung, Spannkraft
translator [træns'leɪtə] Übersetzer
trip [trɪp] Ausflug, Reise
various ['veərɪəs] verschieden
well [wel] *hier*: gesund
without [wɪ'ðaʊt] ohne
yourself [jɔː'self] (du, ihr, Sie) selbst

UNIT 1 *Revision activities*

S	alphabet ['ælfəbet]	Alphabet	
	letter ['letə]	Buchstabe	
	nobody ['nəʊbədɪ]	niemand	
	end [end]	Ende	
	teacher ['tiːtʃə]	Lehrer(-in), Kursleiter(-in)	Good students listen to their ~.
	serious ['sɪərɪəs]	ernst(haft)	
	goldfish ['gəʊldfɪʃ]	Goldfisch	Have you got a ~ at home?
1	complete [kəm'pliːt]	vervollständigen, beenden	
	invitation [ˌɪnvɪ'teɪʃn]	Einladung	
2	list [lɪst]	Liste	
	Russian ['rʌʃən]	russisch(-e, -er, -es); Russe, Russin	

3	choose [tʃu:z]	wählen	
	topic ['tɒpɪk]	Thema, Gegenstand	
	way [weɪ]	Art, Weise	
	forget [fə'get]	vergessen	
4	wordfield ['wɜ:dfi:ld]	Wortgruppe, Wortfeld	
	put [pʊt]	legen, stellen, setzen	
	ride [raɪd]	reiten; fahren	

UNIT 2

I	**situation** [ˌsɪtjʊ'eɪʃn]	Situation	
	outside [ˌaʊt'saɪd]	außerhalb	Children like to play ~ the house.
	apprentice [ə'prentɪs]	Lehrling, Auszubildende(-r)	He is an ~ in a car company.
	retired [rɪ'taɪəd]	pensioniert, im Ruhestand	My father is ~. He is 65 years old now.

UNIT 2 *Step 1*

1	**advertisement** [əd'vɜ:tɪsmənt]	Anzeige, Inserat; Reklame, Werbung	On Saturdays you can find many ~s in the newspaper.
	advert, ad (= advertisement) [əd'vɜ:t, æd]	(*Abkürzung*)	
	assistant [ə'sɪstənt]	Assistent(-in), Gehilfe, Gehilfin, Mitarbeiter(-in)	An ~ usually helps the boss.
	office assistant ['ɒfɪs əˌsɪstənt]	Bürogehilfe, Bürogehilfin	
	publish ['pʌblɪʃ]	veröffentlichen	This book company ~es many English books.
	flexi-time (= flexible time) ['fleksɪ taɪm]	Gleitzeit, flexible Arbeitszeit	~ means you can start work at different times.
	pay [peɪ]	Bezahlung, Gehalt	An apprentice's ~ isn't very good.
	decide [dɪ'saɪd]	beschließen	Angela ~d to take the job.
	Ms [mɪz]	Frau (*Anrede*)	
	telephonist [tɪ'lefənɪst]	Telefonist(-in)	Our ~ always answers the telephone.
	hold on [həʊld ɒn]	*hier*: dranbleiben, am Apparat bleiben, warten	~, you can speak to her in a minute.
	put through [pʊt θru:]	*hier*: durchstellen	
	busy ['bɪzɪ]	beschäftigt	I am too ~ to have lunch now.
	try [traɪ]	versuchen	I'll ~ to come later.
	ring [rɪŋ]	anrufen	Don't ~ before four o'clock.
	out, be ~ [bi: aʊt]	*hier*: ausgegangen sein	
	early ['ɜ:lɪ]	früh	We arrived too ~. The train wasn't there.
1a	short [ʃɔ:t]	kurz	
1b	correct [kə'rekt]	korrekt, richtig	
	correct [kə'rekt]	korrigieren	
1c	number ['nʌmbə]	(durch)numerieren, zählen	
2	**interview** ['ɪntəvju:]	Interview, Vorstellungsgespräch	She had an ~ for a new job.
	arrange [ə'reɪndʒ]	arrangieren, ausmachen	He ~d a dinner for tonight.
	leave (left) [li:v, left]	verlassen (verließ, verlassen), zurücklassen; (weg)gehen, (weg)fahren	Why did you ~ so early?
	train [treɪn]	(sich) ausbilden, trainieren, eine Ausbildung machen	I'm ~ing as an apprentice in a big company.

used to [ju:st tə]	früher (etw. [regelmäßig] getan haben); pflegte(-n, -st, -t) zu	I ~ get up very early in the morning, but I don't now.
use [ju:z]	benutzen	If we don't know a word, we can ~ a dictionary.
quickly ['kwɪklɪ]	schnell	Some people talk too ~.
might, ~ do sth. [maɪt]	vielleicht etwas tun	I ~ have dinner with you.
2a exchange [ɪks'tʃeɪndʒ]	(aus)tauschen	
paper ['peɪpə]	Papier, Blatt	
2b express [ɪk'spres]	ausdrücken	
possibility [ˌpɒsə'bɪlətɪ]	Möglichkeit	
may, ~ do sth. [meɪ]	vielleicht etwas tun	I ~ come to see you later, if I have time.
probably ['prɒbəblɪ]	wahrscheinlich	
B **waitress** ['weɪtrɪs]	Kellnerin	Jane works as a ~ in a Spanish restaurant.
shop assistant ['ʃɒp əˌsɪstənt]	Verkäufer(-in), Ladengehilfe, Ladengehilfin	Susan works as a ~ at the boutique.
farm [fɑ:m]	Bauernhof, Farm	It's nice for children to have a holiday on a ~.
worker ['wɜ:kə]	Arbeiter(-in)	
farm worker ['fɑ:m ˌwɜ:kə]	Landarbeiter(-in)	A ~ usually starts his work early in the morning.
policeman [pə'li:smən]	Polizist	
engineer [ˌendʒɪ'nɪə]	Ingenieur(-in), Techniker(-in)	
clerk [klɑ:k]	Sekretär(-in), Büroangestellte(-r)	
bank clerk ['bæŋk klɑ:k]	Bankangestellte(-r)	A ~ sees a lot of money every day.
driver ['draɪvə]	Fahrer(-in)	A good taxi ~ always knows the way.

UNIT 2 *Step 2*

S pair [peə]	Paar	
in pairs [ɪn 'peəz]	paarweise, zu zweit	
park [pɑ:k]	parken	May I ~ my car here?
1a **young** [jʌŋ]	jung	He's too ~, he's only 15.
2 adverb ['ædvɜ:b]	Adverb, Umstandswort	
singer ['sɪŋə]	Sänger(-in)	Elvis Presley was a famous ~.
sing [sɪŋ]	singen	Elvis used to ~ very well.
quick [kwɪk]	schnell	He is a ~ worker.
learner ['lɜ:nə]	Lerner(-in)	Sue is a good ~.
careful ['keəfʊl]	vorsichtig	Many people drive too fast. They aren't ~.
hard [hɑ:d]	hart, schwer, fleißig	A policeman's job is a ~ job.
2a **type** [taɪp]	tippen, mit der Maschine schreiben	I'll ~ the letter for you.
slow [sləʊ]	langsam	My boss doesn't like ~ workers.
stop [stɒp]	anhalten, aufhören	Can you ~ the car on the corner, please?
police [pə'li:s]	Polizei	If you drive too fast, the ~ will stop you.
marry ['mærɪ]	heiraten	When did your parents ~?
3 imperative [ɪm'perətɪv]	Imperativ, Befehlssatz	
3a **put** [pʊt]	setzen, stellen, legen	Please, ~ the sunglasses back.
sit [sɪt]	sitzen, setzen	Can I ~ next to you?
smoke [sməʊk]	rauchen; Rauch	Please don't ~ in this room.

3b	rule [ruːl]	Regel, Vorschrift	
	jeans [dʒiːnz]	Jeans	Young people like ~.
	photocopy [ˈfəʊtəʊˌkɒpɪ]	(Foto)Kopie	
B	**pen** [pen]	Feder(halter), Füller	May I use your ~ for a moment?
	pencil [ˈpensl]	(Blei)Stift	Can I have your ~, please?
	photocopier [ˈfəʊtəʊˌkɒpɪə]	Fotokopiergerät	This ~ makes good photocopies.
	calculator [ˈkælkjʊleɪtə]	Taschenrechner	
	typewriter [ˈtaɪpˌraɪtə]	Schreibmaschine	Did you write the letter on a ~?
	desk [desk]	Schreibtisch	There's one pen and some pencils on my ~.
	chair [tʃeə]	Stuhl	This is a comfortable ~.

UNIT 2 *Step 3*

S	object [ˈɒbdʒɪkt]	Gegenstand	
	over, be ~ [biː ˈəʊvə]	vorbei sein	
	after [ˈɑːftə]	nachdem	
	understand [ʌndəˈstænd]	verstehen	Do you ~ all the words in this unit?
	problem [ˈprɒbləm]	Problem	A good teacher understands the ~s of the students.
	full-time [ˌfʊlˈtaɪm]	ganztägig	In a ~ job you work about 8 hours a day.
	working hours [ˈwɜːkɪŋ ˈaʊəz]	Arbeitszeit, -stunden	
	normal [ˈnɔːml]	normal	It is ~ to work about 8 hours a day in a full-time job.
	must [mʌst]	müssen	You ~ be careful when you drive in the city.
	salary [ˈsælərɪ]	Lohn, Gehalt	Students work hard, but they don't get a ~.
	more again [mɔː əˈgen]	noch(mals) mehr	
	employer [ɪmˈplɔɪə]	Arbeitgeber	I work for him. He's my ~.
	eye [aɪ]	Auge	
	describe [dɪˈskraɪb]	beschreiben	
	underline [ˈʌndəlaɪn]	unterstreichen	
1a	present [ˈpreznt]	gegenwärtig, momentan	
	paragraph [ˈpærəgrɑːf]	Absatz, Abschnitt, Paragraph	
2	**inside** [ˌɪnˈsaɪd]	innerhalb, drinnen	Most of the time he works ~ the house.
	outside [ˌaʊtˈsaɪd]	außerhalb, draußen	
	regular [ˈregjʊlə]	regelmäßig	Angela works ~ hours, from 9 to 5 every day.

Panorama

Africa [ˈæfrɪkə]	Afrika
abroad [əˈbrɔːd]	nach/in Übersee
age [eɪdʒ]	Alter
agriculture [ˈægrɪkʌltʃə]	Landwirtschaft
alive [əˈlaɪv]	lebend(-ig)
at first [ət ˈfɜːst]	zuerst
back home [bæk ˈhəʊm]	daheim, zuhause
change [tʃeɪndʒ]	sich verändern
contact [ˈkɒntækt]	Kontakt
could [kʊd]	konnte(-t, -st, -n)
countryside [ˈkʌntrɪsaɪd]	Landschaft
critical of, be ~ [ˈkrɪtɪkl əv]	kritisieren, beanstanden
difficult [ˈdɪfɪkəlt]	schwierig, schwer
earth [ɜːθ]	Erde
egg [eg]	Ei
electricity [ˌɪlekˈtrɪsətɪ]	Elektrizität
else [els]	*hier*: andere(-r, -s)
European [ˌjʊərəˈpiːən]	europäisch(-e, -er, -es); Europäer(-in)

flat [flæt]	flach
girl [gɜːl]	Mädchen
go for [gəʊ fɔː]	sich bemühen um, mitmachen bei
have to [hæv tə]	müssen
homesick, be ~ ['həʊmsɪk]	Heimweh haben
hut [hʌt]	Hütte
kill [kɪl]	töten
kind [kaɪnd]	Art, Weise
live on [lɪv ɒn]	leben von
make friends [meɪk frendz]	Freundschaft schließen, anfreunden
many more ['mænɪ mɔː]	viele andere
market ['mɑːkɪt]	Markt
miss [mɪs]	vermissen
Nigerian [naɪ'dʒɪərɪən]	nigerianisch(-e, -er, -es); Nigerianer(-in)
only ['əʊnlɪ]	nur
ourselves [aʊə'selvz]	uns (selbst)
overseas [ˌəʊvə'siːz]	nach/in Übersee
powdered milk ['paʊdəd mɪlk]	Trockenmilch
sardine [sɑː'diːn]	Sardine
secondary school ['sekəndrɪ skuːl]	weiterführende Schule
service ['sɜːvɪs]	Dienst
soon [suːn]	bald
story ['stɔːrɪ]	Geschichte
such as [sʌtʃ əz]	*hier*: wie (zum Beispiel)
teach [tiːtʃ]	unterrichten, lehren
technology [ˌtek'nɒlədʒɪ]	Technologie, Technik
tin [tɪn]	Blech, Dose
uninteresting [ˌʌn'ɪntrəstɪŋ]	uninteressant
university [ˌjuːnɪ'vɜːsətɪ]	Universität
voluntary ['vɒləntrɪ]	freiwillig
volunteer [ˌvɒlən'tɪə]	Freiwillige(-r)
way of life [ˌweɪ əv 'laɪf]	Lebensweise, Lebensstil

UNIT 2 *Revision activities*

S	even ['iːvn]	selbst, sogar	
	continue [kən'tɪnjuː]	fortfahren, weitermachen	
	and so on [ənd səʊ ɒn]	usw.	
1	**lunchtime** ['lʌntʃtaɪm]	Mittagszeit, -pause	My ~ is one hour, from 12 to 1.
2	reserve [rɪ'zɜːv]	reservieren	
5	across [ə'krɒs]	*hier*: waagrecht	
	down [daʊn]	*hier*: senkrecht	

THE ENGLISH GAZETTE 1

adult ['ædʌlt]	Erwachsene(-r)
alcohol ['ælkəhɒl]	Alkohol
average; on ~ ['ævrɪdʒ]	Durchschnitt(s-), durchschnittlich; im Durchschnitt
call [kɔːl]	nennen
click [klɪk]	klicken, (zu)schnappen
difference ['dɪfrəns]	Unterschied
door [dɔː]	Tür, Tor
do well [duː wel]	*hier*: gut daran sein
editor ['edɪtə]	Herausgeber(-in), Redakteur(-in)
er [ɜː]	*etwa*: äh, eh
etc. (= et cetera) [ɪt 'setərə]	und so weiter
fact [fækt]	Faktum, Tatsache
favourite ['feɪvrɪt]	Lieblings-
figure ['fɪgə]	Zahl
garden ['gɑːdn]	gärtnern, Gartenbau betreiben
gazette [gə'zet]	Zeitung, Zeitschrift
inside [ˌɪn'saɪd]	drinnen
inside [ˌɪn'saɪd]	(der, die, das) Innere
interest ['ɪntrəst]	Interesse
in there [ɪn ðeə]	da drinnen
later ['leɪtə]	später
machine [mə'ʃiːn]	Maschine
Miss [mɪs]	Fräulein (*Anrede*)
Mr ['mɪstə]	Herr (*Anrede*)
official [ə'fɪʃl]	offiziell, amtlich
popular ['pɒpjʊlə]	beliebt, populär
professor [prə'fesə]	Professor(-in)
reader ['riːdə]	Leser(-in)
research [rɪ'sɜːtʃ]	Forschungs-
side [saɪd]	Seite
statistics [stə'tɪstɪks]	Statistik
still [stɪl]	noch (immer)
the other day [ðɪ 'ʌðə deɪ]	kürzlich, neulich
typical ['tɪpɪkl]	typisch
vacation [və'keɪʃn]	Urlaub
wish [wɪʃ]	(Glück)Wunsch
yours sincerely [jɔːz sɪn'sɪəlɪ]	mit freundlichen Grüßen (*am Briefschluß*)

UNIT 3

I	**fitness** ['fɪtnəs]	Fitneß	
	seldom ['seldəm]	selten	She goes out very ~.
	get exercise [get 'eksəsaɪz]	Sport treiben, Übungen machen	It's good for your health to ~ every day.
	jogging ['dʒɒgɪŋ]	Jogging	~ is good for your health, too.
	feel [fi:l]	(sich) fühlen	Do you ~ well today?
	stressed [strest]	gestreßt, unter Druck	Many people feel ~ after work.

UNIT 3 *Step 1*

1	**Dr** ['dɒktə]	(*Abkürzung für Doktor*)	
	family doctor ['fæməlɪ 'dɒktə]	Hausarzt, Hausärztin	How often do you see your ~?
	terrible ['terəbl]	schrecklich	The food was really ~.
	back [bæk]	Rücken; Rückseite	
	backache ['bækeɪk]	Rückenschmerz(en)	She can't go out tonight, because she's got ~.
	nothing ['nʌθɪŋ]	nichts	There's ~ I can do. We must call a doctor.
	ill [ɪl]	krank	He's very ~.
	advice [əd'vaɪs]	Rat(schlag)	Can you give me some good ~?
	soon [su:n]	bald	The doctor will come very ~.
	if [ɪf]	wenn, falls	~ I were you, I'd go to work.
	were [wɜ:]	wäre(-st, -t, -n)	
	should [ʃʊd]	sollte(-st, -t, -n)	You ~ go to the doctor.
	serious ['sɪərɪəs]	ernst(haft)	This is a ~ problem.
	send [send]	senden, schicken	Will you ~ me a letter from Italy?
	explanation [ˌekspləˈneɪʃn]	Erklärung	The doctor had no ~ for her backache.
1a	meaning ['mi:nɪŋ]	Bedeutung	
	under ['ʌndə]	unter	The dog is sitting ~ the table.
	under the weather, feel ~ ['ʌndə ðə 'weðə]	nicht in Form sein	I don't feel good; I'm a bit ~.
	on top of [ɒn tɒp əv]	(oben) auf	Please put the red book ~ the others.
	on top of the world [ɒn tɒp əv ðə wɜ:ld]	obenauf, rundum glücklich	I'm feeling ~ today.
1c	**flat** [flæt]	Wohnung	Do you live in a ~ or in a house?
	make friends [meɪk frendz]	Freundschaft(en) schließen	It's a good idea to ~ with the other students.
	fit [fɪt]	fit, in Form	He has been ill and is not ~ for work yet.
	rich [rɪtʃ]	reich	
2	**appointment** [ə'pɔɪntmənt]	Verabredung, Termin	When is your ~? – At 3 o'clock.
	make an appointment [meɪk ən ə'pɔɪntmənt]	eine Verabredung treffen, einen Termin ausmachen	Shall we ~ for tomorrow?
	someone ['sʌmwʌn]	jemand(-em, -en)	~ called yesterday, but I don't know who.
	how about …? [haʊ ə'baʊt]	wie wäre es mit …? wie wäre es, wenn …?	~ some ice cream now?
	possible ['pɒsəbl]	möglich	Please, ask him as soon as ~.
	possibly ['pɒsəblɪ]	vielleicht, möglicherweise	
	sleep [sli:p]	schlafen	How did you ~ last night?

2c	dentist ['dentɪst]	Zahnarzt	
	ouch [aʊtʃ]	*etwa*: au, aua	
	offer ['ɒfə]	anbieten	
B	body ['bɒdɪ]	Körper	
	arm [ɑ:m]	Arm	
	ear [ɪə]	Ohr	
	finger ['fɪŋgə]	Finger	
	hand [hænd]	Hand	
	head [hed]	Kopf	
	knee [ni:]	Knie	
	leg [leg]	Bein	
	mouth [maʊθ]	Mund	
	nose [nəʊz]	Nase	
	shoulder ['ʃəʊldə]	Schulter	

UNIT 3 *Step 2*

S	game [geɪm]	Spiel	
	instruction [ɪn'strʌkʃn]	Instruktion, Anweisung	
	out, be ~ [bi: aʊt]	*hier*: ausscheiden	
1	present progressive ['preznt prə'gresɪv]	Verlaufsform der Gegenwart	
	song [sɒŋ]	Lied	Can you sing an English ~?
1a	discuss [dɪ'skʌs]	diskutieren	
1b	careful ['keəfʊl]	vorsichtig, *hier*: genau, gründlich	
	shine [ʃaɪn]	scheinen	In Greece the sun ~s more often than in Germany.
	garden ['gɑ:dn]	Garten	Sue's parents have got a big ~.
	instead [ɪn'sted]	statt dessen	I can't come. I'd like to see my friend ~.
2	**mustn't (= must not)** ['mʌsnt]	nicht dürfen	You ~ smoke in here.
	have to, don't ~ [dəʊnt hæv tə]	nicht müssen	I feel fine. I ~ go to the doctor again.
	order ['ɔ:də]	Befehl, Anordnung	
	necessary ['nesəsərɪ]	nötig, notwendig	I feel fine. It's not ~ to see the doctor again.
2a	**change** [tʃeɪndʒ]	Veränderung, Wechsel	Let's hope there will be a ~ in the weather.
	life (lives) [laɪf, laɪvz]	Leben	Some people take ~ too seriously.
	once [wʌns]	einmal, einst	To get some exercise ~ a day is enough.
2b	**sign** [saɪn]	Zeichen, Schild	
B	**headache** ['hedeɪk]	Kopfschmerzen	He's got a very bad ~. I hope he'll feel better soon.
	migraine ['mi:greɪn]	Migräne	
	toothache ['tu:θeɪk]	Zahnschmerzen	When I get ~ I get migraine, too.
	dentist ['dentɪst]	Zahnarzt	I've got terrible toothache. I must see the ~.
	temperature ['temprətʃə]	Temperatur	
	have a temperature [hæv ə 'temprətʃə]	Temperatur/Fieber haben	When you ~, you should not go to work.
	sore [sɔ:]	weh, wund, entzündet	
	throat [θrəʊt]	Hals, Kehle	
	sore throat [sɔ: θrəʊt]	Halsentzündung	During the winter people often get a ~.

	sick [sɪk]	krank	When you are ~, you should stay in bed.
	feel sick [fiːl sɪk]	übel, schlecht sein	I've eaten too much. Now I ~.
	cold [kəʊld]	Erkältung	I've got a ~ and a sore throat.

UNIT 3 *Step 3*

S	**body** ['bɒdɪ]	Körper	You should be kind to your ~.
	square [skweə]	Quadrat, Viereck	
	below [bɪ'ləʊ]	unten	
1	**healthy** ['helθɪ]	gesund	If you get some exercise every day you will stay ~.
	believe [bɪ'liːv]	glauben	~ me, it's true!
	secret ['siːkrɪt]	Geheimnis	Is there a ~ to good health?
	whisky ['wɪskɪ]	Whisky	
	cigarette [ˌsɪgə'ret]	Zigarette	How many ~s do you smoke a day?
	diet ['daɪət]	Ernährung; Diät	Your ~ is what you eat and drink.
	sugar ['ʃʊgə]	Zucker	Sue never eats ~, because it is bad for her health.
	accident ['æksɪdənt]	Unfall	If you don't drive carefully, you might have an ~.
	worry ['wʌrɪ]	sich sorgen, sich Sorgen machen	Do you all know the song: "Don't ~, be happy"?
	gardener ['gɑːdnə]	Gärtner(-in)	My uncle used to be a ~.
1a	article ['ɑːtɪkl]	Artikel	
	illness ['ɪlnɪs]	Krankheit	
	lady ['leɪdɪ]	Frau, Dame, Lady	
1c	in general [ɪn 'dʒenrəl]	im allgemeinen	

Panorama

acupuncture ['ækjʊˌpʌŋktʃə]	Akupunktur
acupuncturist ['ækjʊˌpʌŋktʃərɪst]	Akupunkteur
alternative [ɔːl'tɜːnətɪv]	alternativ
anaemia [ə'niːmjə]	Anämie, Blutarmut
asleep [ə'sliːp]	schlafend, eingeschlafen
become (became, become) [bɪ'kʌm, bɪ'keɪm]	werden (wurde, geworden)
blood [blʌd]	Blut
cure [kjʊə]	heilen, kurieren
diabetic [ˌdaɪə'betɪk]	diabetisch, zuckerkrank; Diabetiker(-in)
dose [dəʊs]	Dosis
explain [ɪk'spleɪn]	erklären
fine [faɪn]	dünn, fein
first finger [fɜːst 'fɪŋgə]	Zeigefinger
heavy ['hevɪ]	schwer, stark
homeopath ['həʊmjəʊpæθ]	Homöopath
homeopathy [ˌhəʊmɪ'ɒpəθɪ]	Homöopathie
into ['ɪntʊ]	in, in … hinein
invent [ɪn'vent]	erfinden
less [les]	weniger
light [laɪt]	leicht
medicine ['medsɪn]	Medizin
method ['meθəd]	Methode
mistake [mɪ'steɪk]	Fehler
needle ['niːdl]	Nadel
operation [ˌɒpə'reɪʃn]	Operation
pain [peɪn]	Schmerz
painful ['peɪnfʊl]	schmerzhaft
patient ['peɪʃnt]	Patient
point [pɔɪnt]	Punkt, Stelle
produce [prə'djuːs]	produzieren, herstellen
side-effect ['saɪdɪˌfekt]	Nebenwirkung
smoker ['sməʊkə]	Raucher
successful [sək'sesfʊl]	erfolgreich
symptom ['sɪmptəm]	Symptom
thumb [θʌm]	Daumen
traditional [trə'dɪʃnl]	traditionell, herkömmlich
treat [triːt]	behandeln

UNIT 3 *Revision activities*

S	piece [piːs]	Stück	
	collect [kəˈlekt]	(ein)sammeln	
	give out [gɪv aʊt]	ausgeben, austeilen	
4	crossword [ˈkrɒswɜːd]	Kreuzworträtsel	
	cry (cried) [kraɪ, kraɪd]	weinen (weinte, geweint), schreien	
	cat [kæt]	Katze	
	coloured [ˈkʌləd]	farbig	
	box [bɒks]	*hier*: Kästchen	

UNIT 4

UNIT 4 *Step 1*

1	**that** [ðæt, ðət]	der, die, das; welche(-r, -s) *(Relativpronomen)*	
	bathroom [ˈbɑːθrʊm]	Bad, Badezimmer	Big houses have sometimes got two ~s.
	kitchen [ˈkɪtʃɪn]	Küche	I love cooking in our new ~.
	central [ˈsentrəl]	zentral, Zentral-	
	heating [ˈhiːtɪŋ]	Heizung	Do you have central ~ in your flat?
	furnished [ˈfɜːnɪʃt]	möbliert	Doris needs a ~ room.
	able to, be ~ [ˈeɪbl tə]	können	Are you ~ go to work today?
	while [waɪl]	während	~ I'm in England, I'll be able to learn English very well.
	have to [ˈhæv tə]	müssen	Do you ~ learn English? Is it really necessary?
	rent [rent]	Miete	
	high [haɪ]	hoch	I have to pay a ~ rent for my new flat.
	two-roomed flat [ˈtuːruːmd ˈflæt]	2-Zimmer-Wohnung	My friend lives in a ~.
1b	**bedroom** [ˈbedrʊm]	Schlafzimmer	The ~ is the room where you sleep.
	dining room [ˈdaɪnɪŋrʊm]	Eßzimmer	The ~ is the room where you eat.
	door [dɔː]	Tür	Please come in and close the ~.
	entrance [ˈentrəns]	Eingang	The ~ to the museum was closed.
	hall [hɔːl]	Halle; Flur	
	entrance hall [ˈentrəns hɔːl]	Eingangshalle, Hausflur	Does your house have an ~?
	living room [ˈlɪvɪŋrʊm]	Wohnzimmer	I sleep in the ~ because I haven't got a bedroom.
	stairs [steəz]	Treppe, Treppenhaus	
	toilet [ˈtɔɪlɪt]	Toilette, WC	Do you know where the ~ is?
	window [ˈwɪndəʊ]	Fenster	It's cold in here. Please close the ~.
1c	need [niːd]	Bedürfnis, Bedarf	
	wish [wɪʃ]	Wunsch	
	rent [rent]	mieten	
2	**lovely** [ˈlʌvlɪ]	wunderschön, entzückend	I like the garden. It is really ~.
	face [feɪs]	schauen, blicken, liegen	The kitchen ~s north.
	may [meɪ]	dürfen	
	super [ˈsuːpə]	herrlich, prima, super	This balcony is ~. I really like it.

	perfect ['pɜ:fɪkt]	perfekt, vollkommen, genau richtig	The flat is furnished? That's ~ for me.
	agree [ə'gri:]	zustimmen, übereinstimmen, einverstanden sein	I asked him to help me and he ~d.
2b	compliment ['kɒmplɪmənt]	Kompliment, Lob	
2c	label ['leɪbl]	beschriften	
2d	permission [pə'mɪʃn]	Erlaubnis	
	borrow ['bɒrəʊ]	(aus)borgen, (aus)leihen	
B	**attic** ['ætɪk]	Dachstube, Mansarde	Students sometimes have to live in an ~.
	basement ['beɪsmənt]	Kellergeschoß	The ground floor is on top of the ~.
	downstairs [ˌdaʊn'steəz]	unten, (die Treppe) hinunter/herunter	The kitchen is ~, on the ground floor.
	garage ['gærɑ:dʒ]	Garage; Tankstelle, (Auto)Werkstatt	Please, drive my car into the ~.
	lift [lɪft]	Lift, Aufzug	Houses with more than four floors usually have a ~.
	upstairs [ˌʌp'steəz]	oben, (die Treppe) hinauf/herauf	We've got one bathroom ~, and another one downstairs.

UNIT 4 *Step 2*

S	line [laɪn]	Linie, Zeile, Strich	
1a	**princess** [prɪn'ses]	Prinzessin	
	climb [klaɪm]	klettern, besteigen	We ~ed the mountain in 6 hours.
	moon [mu:n]	Mond	You can see the sun in the day and the ~ in the night.
	prince [prɪns]	Prinz	
1b	**robot** ['rəʊbɒt]	Roboter	
2	first conditional [fɜ:st kən'dɪʃənl]	Bedingungssatz (Typ 1): die offene Bedingung	
2a	**tonight** [tə'naɪt]	heute abend, heute nacht	Shall we go to a restaurant ~?
2b	add [æd]	hinzufügen	
	first class [fɜ:st klɑ:s]	erste(-r) Klasse	You should send the letter ~.
2c	**lose** [lu:z]	verlieren	Where did you ~ your key?
	bankrupt ['bæŋkrʌpt]	bankrott	Last week my boss went ~. Now I have to find a new job.
	go bankrupt [gəʊ 'bæŋkrʌpt]	bankrott machen	
B	**sofa** ['səʊfə]	Sofa	Do you like my new ~?
	lamp [læmp]	Lampe	
	stereo ['sterɪəʊ]	Stereo(anlage)	Have you seen his new ~?
	fridge (= refrigerator) [frɪdʒ, rɪ'frɪdʒəreɪtə]	Kühlschrank	Please, put the milk in the ~.
	cooker ['kʊkə]	Herd	You cook your food on a ~.
	cupboard ['kʌbəd]	(Küchen)Schrank	Can you put the cups in the ~, please.
	washing machine ['wɒʃɪŋ məˌʃi:n]	Waschmaschine	

UNIT 4 *Step 3*

1	**let** [let]	*hier*: vermieten	I saw the advertisement. Have you got a room to ~?
	share [ʃeə]	teilen	There is only one apple. Shall we ~ it?

	sale [seɪl]	Verkauf	He was happy about the ~ of his old car.
	for sale [fə 'seɪl]	verkäuflich, zum Verkauf	Is this flat ~? Do you want to sell it?
	party ['pɑ:tɪ]	Party	Let's have a ~ tonight!
	abbreviation [əˌbri:vɪ'eɪʃn]	Abkürzung	
1a	also ['ɔ:lsəʊ]	auch	
1c	**neighbour** ['neɪbə]	Nachbar(-in)	

Panorama

a few [ə 'fju:] – einige
air [eə] – Luft
business centre ['bɪznɪs 'sentə] – Geschäftszentrum
catch [kætʃ] – fangen
catch a train [kætʃ ə 'treɪn] – einen Zug erreichen
choose (chose, chosen) [tʃu:z, tʃəʊz, tʃəʊzn] – wählen; *hier*: vorziehen
commuter [kə'mju:tə] – Pendler
compact [kəm'pækt] – kompakt, dicht, gedrängt
directly [dɪ'rektlɪ] – direkt
for weeks and weeks [fə 'wi:ks ən 'wi:ks] – wochenlang
freezing ['fri:zɪŋ] – eisig
fresh [freʃ] – frisch
get [get] – holen
go up [gəʊ 'ʌp] – hinaufgehen
hostel ['hɒstl] – Herberge, Heim
in fact [ɪn 'fækt] – in der Tat, tatsächlich
metre ['mi:tə] – Meter
monthly ['mʌnθlɪ] – monatlich, Monats-
nearly ['nɪəlɪ] – fast, beinahe
outside [ˌaʊt'saɪd] – hinaus, nach draußen
photographer [fə'tɒgrəfə] – Fotograf(-in)
poor [pɔ:] – (der, die, das) Arme, (die) Armen
report [rɪ'pɔ:t] – Bericht
return [rɪ'tɜ:n] – Rück-
shock [ʃɒk] – schockieren
shopping ['ʃɒpɪŋ] – Einkauf, Einkaufen
do the shopping [dʊ ðə 'ʃɒpɪŋ] – Einkäufe machen
spend [spend] – verbringen
stand [stænd] – stehen
stop [stɒp] – Aufenthalt, Pause
thousand ['θaʊznd] – Tausend
ticket ['tɪkɪt] – Ticket, Fahrkarte
twice [twaɪs] – zweimal
underground garage ['ʌndəgraʊnd 'gærɑ:dʒ] – Tiefgarage
underground station ['ʌndəgraʊnd 'steɪʃn] – U-Bahn-Station, U-Bahn-Haltestelle
warm [wɔ:m] – warm
have a wash [hæv ə 'wɒʃ] – sich waschen
wash basin ['wɔ:ʃ ˌbeɪsn] – Waschbecken
wide [waɪd] – breit, weit
workplace ['wɜ:kpleɪs] – Arbeitsplatz

UNIT 4 *Revision activities*

S	realistic [ˌrɪə'lɪstɪk]	realistisch
	ideal [aɪ'dɪəl]	ideal
1	read out [ri:d aʊt]	vorlesen
	column ['kɒləm]	Spalte
2	beginning [bɪ'gɪnɪŋ]	Anfang, Beginn
5	already [ɔ:l'redɪ]	schon, bereits

THE ENGLISH GAZETTE 2

bungalow ['bʌŋgələʊ] – Bungalow
cost [kɒst] – kosten
cost an arm and a leg [kɒst ən 'ɑ:m ənd ə 'leg] – sehr viel kosten, ein Vermögen kosten
cycling ['saɪklɪŋ] – Radfahren
dancing ['dɑ:nsɪŋ] – Tanzen
effective [ɪ'fektɪv] – effektiv, wirkungsvoll
gentleman (gentlemen) ['dʒentlmən, 'dʒentlmən] – Gentleman, Herr (Herren)

Gents (= gentlemen) [dʒents]	*hier*: Herrentoilette
gymnastics [dʒɪm'næstɪks]	Gymnastik, Turnen
Hindu ['hɪndu:]	hinduistisch(-e, -er, -es); Hindu; Hindu-
judo ['dʒu:dəʊ]	Judo
keep [ki:p]	*hier*: bleiben
Ladies ['leɪdɪz]	*hier*: Damentoilette
loo [lu:]	Toilette, Klo
Lord [lɔ:d]	Herr
meeting ['mi:tɪŋ]	Treffen, Versammlung, Konferenz
private ['praɪvɪt]	privat
put (your) foot in it [pʊt jɔ: 'fʊt ɪn ɪt]	ins Fettnäpfchen treten
right, be ~ [bi: 'raɪt]	recht haben
rowing ['rəʊɪŋ]	Rudern
show [ʃəʊ]	zeigen
squash [skwɒʃ]	Squash
thanks, with ~ [wɪð 'θæŋks]	dankend, mit Dank
traveller ['trævlə]	Reisende(-r)
Turkish ['tɜ:kɪʃ]	türkisch(-e, -er, -es)
up to (my) eyes in work [ʌp tə (maɪ) aɪz ɪn wɜ:k]	bis zum Hals in Arbeit, bis über beide Ohren in Arbeit
veranda [və'rændə]	Veranda
wrong [rɒŋ]	falsch, verkehrt

UNIT 5

I	**clothes** [kləʊðz]	Kleider, Kleidung	T-shirts and jeans are examples of ~.
	present ['preznt]	Geschenk	Tomorrow is his birthday. Have you got a ~ for him?

UNIT 5 *Step 1*

1	**complaint** [kəm'pleɪnt]	Beschwerde	I have a ~ about room service.
	matter ['mætə]	Sache, Angelegenheit	
	what's the matter [ˌwɒts ðə 'mætə]	worum geht es? was ist los?	~? – There's a problem with my room.
	sir [sɜ:]	(mein) Herr (*höfliche Anrede*)	Waiter! – Yes, ~.
	have/take a shower [hæv/teɪk ə 'ʃaʊə]	(sich) duschen, eine Dusche nehmen	I usually ~ every morning.
	get dressed [get 'drest]	sich anziehen, sich ankleiden	Where are my shoes? I want to ~.
	lady ['leɪdɪ]	Lady, Dame	She is not just a woman, but a real ~.
	hers [hɜ:z]	ihre(-r, -s), der (die, das) ihre	It's her bicycle. I know it's ~.
	mine [maɪn]	mein(-e, -er, -es), der (die, das) mein(ig)e	The key is ~, give it to me.
	look [lʊk]	Blick	
	have a look [hæv ə 'lʊk]	(sich) etw. ansehen	Your camera doesn't work? I'll ~ at it.
	happen ['hæpən]	passieren, geschehen, sich ereignen	When did the accident ~?
	also ['ɔ:lsəʊ]	auch	He got a present, she ~ got one.
	mistake [mɪ'steɪk]	Fehler	I made a ~. I'm sorry.
	it doesn't matter [ɪt 'dʌznt 'mætə]	es macht nichts	~ if we arrive a little too late.
	by the way [baɪ ðə 'weɪ]	übrigens	~, I won't be here tomorrow night.
1a	**Mr** ['mɪstə]	Herr *(Anrede)*	
1b	**complain** [kəm'pleɪn]	sich beschweren	I want to ~ about room service. It's terribly slow.
1c	listener ['lɪsnə]	Hörer, Zuhörer, Horcher	
1d	apologize [ə'pɒlədʒaɪz]	sich entschuldigen	

	react [rɪ'ækt]	reagieren	
	apology [ə'pɒlədʒɪ]	Entschuldigung	
2	**pants** [pænts]	(lange) Hose(n) (*amerik.*)	I need some new summer ~.
	stupid ['stju:pɪd]	dumm, töricht	Did you lose your money? How ~ of you.
	pair [peə]	Paar	
	trousers ['traʊzəz]	(lange) Hose(n)	
	a pair of trousers [ə peər‿əv 'traʊzəz]	eine lange Hose	I'd like to buy ~.
	size [saɪz]	Größe	I usually take ~ ten.
	try on [traɪ 'ɒn]	anprobieren	I like these trousers. Can I ~ them ~?
	jacket ['dʒækɪt]	Jacke, Jakett	Do you like my new ~?
	shirt [ʃɜ:t]	Hemd	Do you prefer the green or the red ~?
	tie [taɪ]	Krawatte	I've got my shirt, but where's my ~?
3	spelling ['spelɪŋ]	Schreibweise, Rechtschreibung, Buchstabierung	
	movie ['mu:vɪ]	Film (*amerik.*)	Did you see the ~ last night?
	fall [fɔ:l]	Herbst (*amerik.*)	I started my new job in the ~ of 1990.
	check [tʃek]	Rechnung (*amerik.*)	We must go now. I'll ask for the ~.
	bill [bɪl]	Banknote, Geldschein (*amerik.*)	
	store [stɔ:]	Laden, Geschäft (*amerik.*)	Have you ever bought anything in this ~?
	movie theater ['mu:vɪ 'θɪətə]	Kino (*amerik.*)	Would you like to go to the ~ tonight to see the new film?
	French fries ['frentʃ fraɪz]	Pommes frites (*amerik.*)	~ is the American word for chips.
	elevator ['elɪveɪtə]	Lift, Fahrstuhl (*amerik.*)	~ is the American word for lift.
	apartment [ə'pɑ:tmənt]	Wohnung, Apartment (*amerik.*)	My ~ has got two rooms.
	first floor ['fɜ:st 'flɔ:]	Erdgeschoß (*amerik.*)	The ground floor in England is the ~ in America.
	cab [kæb]	Taxi (*amerik.*)	
B	**coat** [kəʊt]	Mantel, Jacke	
	skirt [skɜ:t]	Rock	
	pullover ['pʊl,əʊvə]	Pullover	
	blouse [blaʊz]	Bluse	A "shirt" for a woman is a ~.
	tights [taɪts]	Strumpfhose	
	sock [sɒk]	Socke, Strumpf	
	dress [dres]	Kleid	

UNIT 5 *Step 2*

1	past progressive [pɑ:st prə'gresɪv]	Verlaufsform der Vergangenheit	
1a	**midnight** ['mɪdnaɪt]	Mitternacht	Not 12 o'clock in the day, but 12 o'clock in the night, ~.
1b	**gun** [gʌn]	Gewehr, Pistole	He had a ~. So I had to give him the money.
	robber ['rɒbə]	Räuber	I had to do what the ~ said because he had a gun.

2	possessive pronoun [pə'zesɪv 'prəʊnaʊn]	Possessivpronomen, besitzanzeigendes Fürwort	
	whose [hu:z]	wessen	~ book is this?
	ticket ['tɪkɪt]	Ticket, (Fahr)Karte	Have you got our theatre ~s?
	ours ['aʊəz]	unsere(-r, -s), der (die, das) unsere	
	yours [jɔ:z]	Ihre/eure/deine(-r, -s), der (die, das) Ihr/euer/dein(ig)e	
	his [hɪz]	seine(-r, -s), der (die, das) sein(ig)e	
	theirs [ðeəz]	ihre(-r, -s) der (die, das) ihr(ig)e	
2b	individual [ˌɪndɪ'vɪdʒʊəl]	Individuum, Einzelne(-r)	
B	**baker's** ['beɪkəz]	Bäcker(laden)	Please, go to the ~, and buy some bread.
	butcher's ['bʊtʃəz]	Metzger, Fleischer(laden)	Buy some meat at the ~, too.
	chemist's ['kemɪsts]	Apotheke, Drogerie	You should go to the doctor, and not to the ~.
	department store [dɪ'pɑ:tmənt ˌstɔ:]	Kaufhaus, Warenhaus	The new ~ is really big. It sells everything.
	florist's ['flɒrɪsts]	Blumenladen, Blumengeschäft	Yesterday I talked to the shop assistant of the ~. She's very nice.
	newsagent's ['nju:zˌeɪdʒənts]	Zeitungsladen, Zeitungsgeschäft	Every morning I buy a newspaper from the ~ on the corner.
	market ['mɑ:kɪt]	Markt	There is a ~ every Saturday.

UNIT 5 *Step 3*

1	**well-known** ['welnəʊn]	berühmt, wohlbekannt	Covent Garden is a ~ place in London.
	they say [ðeɪ 'seɪ]	man sagt	~ it is often foggy in London.
	traditional [trə'dɪʃnl]	traditionell, herkömmlich	Harrods is a ~ department store in London.
	exclusive [ɪk'sklu:sɪv]	exklusiv	In London you can find many ~ shops.
	specialist ['speʃəlɪst]	Fach-, Spezial-	
	department [dɪ'pɑ:tmənt]	Abteilung	There are many different ~s in Harrods.
	even ['i:vn]	selbst, sogar	It was cold there ~ in July.
	elephant ['elɪfənt]	Elefant	
	chain [tʃeɪn]	Kette	~s have shops in lots of different towns.
	chain stores ['tʃeɪn stɔ:z]	*(Läden, die zu einer Kette gehören)*	
	unusual [ʌn'ju:ʒl]	ungewöhnlich	If I get up at 4 o'clock, that's very ~.
	musician [mju:'zɪʃn]	Musiker(-in), Musikant(-in)	My friend is an excellent ~.
	empty ['emptɪ]	leer	My glass is ~. I'll order another beer.
	suitcase ['su:tkeɪs]	Koffer	We took four ~s and six bags on holiday.
	sight seeing ['saɪt ˌsi:ɪŋ]	Besichtigung von Sehenswürdigkeiten	I want to do a lot of ~ because it's my first holiday in London.
	adjective ['ædʒɪktɪv]	Adjektiv, Eigenschaftswort	

Panorama

African ['æfrɪkən]	afrikanisch(-e, -er, -es); Afrikaner(-in)
anywhere ['enɪweə]	irgendwo(hin)
arrival, on ~ [ɒn ə'raɪvl]	bei der Ankunft
baby ['beɪbɪ]	Baby, Säugling
baby elephant ['beɪbɪ 'elɪfənt]	Elefantenbaby
born, was ~ [wəz bɔ:n]	wurde geboren
carpet ['kɑ:pɪt]	Teppich
cognac ['kɒnjæk]	Kognak
cost [kɒst]	Preis, Kosten
enter ['entə]	betreten, eintreten
escalator ['eskəleɪtə]	Rolltreppe
export ['ekspɔ:t]	Export-, Ausfuhr-
fossil ['fɒsl]	Fossil, Versteinerung
free [fri:]	gratis, kostenlos
handkerchief ['hæŋkətʃɪf]	Taschentuch
history ['hɪstrɪ]	Geschichte
immediate [ɪ'mi:djət]	sofortig, unmittelbar
introduce [ˌɪntrə'dju:s]	einführen
itself [ɪt'self]	(sich) selbst
legend ['ledʒənd]	Legende
midnight ['mɪdnaɪt]	mitternächtlich, Mitternachts-
motto ['mɒtəʊ]	Motto, Wahlspruch
move [mu:v]	(sich) bewegen
nervous ['nɜ:vəs]	nervös
one night [wʌn naɪt]	eines Nachts
order ['ɔ:də]	Bestellung
Persian ['pɜ:ʃn]	persisch(-e, -er, -es); Perser(-in)
president ['prezɪdənt]	Präsident
re-export ['ri:ˌɪkspɔ:t]	wieder ausführen
shopper ['ʃɒpə]	(Ein)Käufer(-in)
strange [streɪndʒ]	seltsam, komisch
Texan ['teksən]	texanisch(-e, -er, -es); Texaner(-in)
top, at the ~ [ət ðə 'tɒp]	oben
unique [ju:'ni:k]	einzigartig
value ['vælju:]	Wert

UNIT 5 *Revision activities*

S	follow ['fɒləʊ]	folgen	
1	together [tə'geðə]	zusammen	
	act [ækt]	*hier*: (vor)spielen	
	forget [fə'get]	vergessen	Don't ~ your key when you go out.
	time [taɪm]	*hier*: Mal	It's the first ~ I've been to this pub.
	good [gʊd]	der (die, das) Gute, Gutes	We should all try to do a lot of ~.
	what good does that do? [wɒt gʊd dʌz 'ðæt du:]	wozu soll das gut sein?	
2	**in black and white** [ɪn ˌblæk ən 'waɪt]	schwarz auf weiß	
	role [rəʊl]	Rolle	
	not … anymore [nɒt … ˌenɪ'mɔ:]	nicht mehr, nicht länger	

UNIT 6

I	**future** ['fju:tʃə]	Zukunft; Futur	Do you have any plans for the near ~?
	replace [rɪ'pleɪs]	ersetzen	

UNIT 6 *Step 1*

1	be in the late forties [bi: ɪn ðə leɪt 'fɔ:tɪz]	Ende vierzig sein
	aged ['eɪdʒd]	… Jahre alt, im Alter von …

	friend of hers, a [ə 'frend əv hɜːz]	eine(-r) ihrer Freunde (Freundinnen), ein(-e) Freund(-in) von ihr	
	going to ['gəʊɪŋ tə]	werden (*Form der Zukunft*)	She is ~ travel to Italy.
	university [juːnɪ'vɜːsətɪ]	Universität	My brother has left school and will start at ~ next year.
	sister-in-law ['sɪstərɪnlɔː]	Schwägerin	My brother's wife is my ~.
	get on well with [get ɒn 'wel wɪð]	gut auskommen mit	Do you ~ your parents?
	training ['treɪnɪŋ]	Ausbildung, Training	Why did you stop your ~ as a teacher and learn another job?
	nurse [nɜːs]	Krankenschwester	A ~ usually works in a hospital.
	yet [jet]	schon	Has Kath arrived ~?
	not yet [nɒt jet]	noch nicht	No, she has ~ arrived ~.
	crisis ['kraɪsɪs]	Krise	Things are very bad. This is a ~.
	spend [spend]	verbringen	I'm going to ~ my next holiday in London.
1b	in-laws ['ɪnlɔːz]	angeheiratete Verwandte	
1c	**certain** ['sɜːtn]	bestimmt, gewiß, sicher	
1d	**crazy** ['kreɪzɪ]	verrückt	Yesterday I had a ~ idea.
2	**round** [raʊnd]	(rund) um, um … (herum)	She likes travelling ~ the world.
	retire [rɪ'taɪə]	in Pension gehen, in den Ruhestand treten	Some people ~ when they are 63, others when they are 65.
	quite [kwaɪt]	ganz, völlig, ziemlich	He's 99, not ~ 100 yet.
	impossible [ɪm'pɒsəbl]	unmöglich	It is ~ to know what will happen in the future.
	right, be ~ [biː 'raɪt]	recht haben	Some people always want to ~.
	swop [swɒp]	tauschen, austauschen	You can't drive this car? Shall we ~ cars?
	Australian [ɒ'streɪljən]	australisch(-e, -er, -es); Australier(-in)	
2b	disagree [ˌdɪsə'griː]	nicht übereinstimmen	
	statement ['steɪtmənt]	Aussage, Behauptung	
B	**become (became, become)** [bɪ'kʌm, bɪ'keɪm, bɪ'kʌm]	werden (wurde, geworden)	After his training at university he'll ~ a doctor.
	get married [get 'mærɪd]	heiraten, sich verheiraten	When people ~ they become husband and wife.
	examination [ɪgˌzæmɪ'neɪʃn]	Examen, Prüfung	He has learned a lot for his ~.
	take an examination [teɪk ən ɪgˌzæmɪ'neɪʃn]	eine Prüfung machen, sich einer Prüfung unterziehen	Before he becomes a doctor he has to ~.
	while [waɪl]	Weile	
	for a while [fər‿ə 'waɪl]	eine Zeitlang, einige Zeit	First I watched TV ~, and then I read a newspaper.
	bring up ['brɪŋ ʌp]	erziehen	It's hard work to ~ children.
	grandmother ['grænˌmʌðə]	Großmutter, Oma	

UNIT 6 *Step 2*

S	present ['preznt]	Gegenwart	
	comment ['kɒment]	Kommentar, Be-, Anmerkung	
	aged [eɪdʒd]	… Jahre alt, im Alter von …	He's got one brother ~ twenty.

1c	poem ['pəʊɪm]	Gedicht	
	pilot ['paɪlət]	Pilot, Flieger	He's a ~ with British Airways.
	proud of [praʊd əv]	stolz auf	All parents are ~ their children.
	look after [lʊk 'ɑ:ftə]	sich kümmern um, sorgen für	Can you ~ my children today?
	gran (= grandmother) [græn, 'græn,mʌðə]	Großmutter, Oma	I've got two ~s. They are 80 and 82.
	writer ['raɪtə]	Autor, Schriftsteller, Verfasser	
2	question tag ['kwestʃən tæg]	Frageanhängsel	
B	**the day before yesterday** [ðə deɪ bɪ'fɔ: 'jestədɪ]	vorgestern	Today is Tuesday. ~ was Sunday.
	the day after tomorrow [ðə deɪ 'ɑ:ftə tə'mɒrəʊ]	übermorgen	Today is Tuesday. ~ is Thursday.

UNIT 6 *Step 3*

1	dream [dri:m]	Traum	
	one day [wʌn 'deɪ]	eines Tages	
	handsome ['hænsəm]	schön (*bei Männern*)	Kath always wanted to marry a ~ man.
	hair [heə]	Haar(e)	She wanted to marry a handsome man with black ~.
	cat [kæt]	Katze	Not a dog, but a ~.
	horse [hɔ:s]	Pferd	Can you ride a ~?
	Queen [kwi:n]	Königin (von England)	Did you see the ~ when you were in London?
	come true [kʌm 'tru:]	wahr werden, sich verwirklichen	Do your plans ever ~?
1a	detail ['di:teɪl]	Detail, Einzelheit	

Panorama

arrive [ə'raɪv]	*hier*: kommen
away [ə'weɪ]	weg, fort
come 6th [kʌm 'sɪksθ]	an 6. Stelle kommen
contact ['kɒntækt]	erreichen, kontaktieren, sich in Verbindung setzen
daytime, in the ~ [ɪn ðə 'deɪtaɪm]	tagsüber, bei Tag
demonstrate ['demənstreɪt]	zeigen, demonstrieren, vorführen
dial ['daɪəl]	wählen
dial telephone ['daɪəl 'telɪfəʊn]	Selbstanschlußtelefon, Wähltelefon
distance ['dɪstəns]	Distanz, Entfernung
document ['dɒkjʊmənt]	Dokument, Schriftstück
enthusiast [ɪn'θju:zɪæst]	Enthusiast(-in), Schwärmer(-in)
everyday ['evrɪdeɪ]	alltäglich, Alltags-
inventor [ɪn'ventə]	Erfinder(-in)
operator ['ɒpəreɪtə]	*hier*: Vermittlung
picture phone ['pɪktʃə fəʊn]	Bildtelefon
pyjama(s) [pə'dʒɑ:mə(z)]	Schlafanzug, Pyjama
screen [skri:n]	Bildschirm
stand [stænd]	stellen
switch off [swɪtʃ 'ɒf]	ausschalten, abstellen
telephone answering machine [,telɪfəʊn 'ɑ:nsərɪŋ mə,ʃi:n]	Telefonanrufbeantworter
wonder ['wʌndə]	sich fragen

UNIT 6 *Revision activities*

1	speech bubble ['spi:tʃ ,bʌbl]	Sprechblase
2	interview ['ɪntəvju:]	befragen, interviewen
	full [fʊl]	*hier*: ganz

	photography [fə'tɒgrəfɪ]	Fotografie	When did you take your course in ~?
	cooking ['kʊkɪŋ]	Kochen	I want to learn to cook. I'm going to take ~ lessons.
3	**match** [mætʃ]	Spiel (*Sport*)	
4	member ['membə]	Mitglied	

THE ENGLISH GAZETTE 3

bell [bel]	Glocke, Klingel
budget ['bʌdʒɪt]	Budget, (Haushalts)Plan
capital ['kæpɪtl]	Hauptstadt
capital letter [ˌkæpɪtl 'letə]	Großbuchstabe
communication [kəˌmju:nɪ'keɪʃn]	Kommunikation, Verbindung, Verkehr
complicated ['kɒmplɪkeɪtɪd]	kompliziert, schwierig
deserted [dɪ'zɜ:tɪd]	verlassen, ausgestorben
energy ['enədʒɪ]	Energie
exactly [ɪg'zæktlɪ]	genau
foot (feet) [fʊt, fi:t]	Fuß (Fuß) (*Maßeinheit*)
gallon ['gælən]	Gallone (*Maßeinheit*)
get home [get 'həʊm]	heimgehen, -fahren, -kommen
get on [get 'ɒn]	einsteigen, aufsteigen
household ['haʊshəʊld]	Haushalt
inch [ɪntʃ]	Zoll (*Maßeinheit*)
item ['aɪtəm]	Gegenstand, Artikel
linear measure ['lɪnɪə 'meʒə]	Längenmaß
liquid measure ['lɪkwɪd 'meʒə]	Flüssigkeitsmaß
litre ['li:tə]	Liter
measure ['meʒə]	Maß, Maßeinheit
middle, in the ~ [ɪn ðə 'mɪdl]	in der Mitte, mitten
mile [maɪl]	Meile
motor-bike ['məʊtəbaɪk]	Motorrad, Kraftrad
ounce [aʊns]	Unze
petrol ['petrəl]	Benzin
pint [paɪnt]	(*engl. Maßeinheit*)
pound [paʊnd]	Pfund (*Maßeinheit*)
quart [kwɔ:t]	Quart (*Maßeinheit*)
start [stɑ:t]	*hier*: losfahren
stone [stəʊn]	Stein (*Maßeinheit*)
through [θru:]	durch
transport ['trænspɔ:t]	Transport, Verkehr
tunnel ['tʌnl]	Tunnel
weight [weɪt]	Gewicht
what is he like? [ˌwɒt ɪz hɪ 'laɪk]	wie sieht er aus?
worried ['wʌrɪd]	besorgt, beunruhigt
yard [jɑ:d]	Yard, Elle (*Maßeinheit*)

Dictionary

Hier finden Sie sämtliche Wörter und Wendungen des Buches in alphabetischer Reihenfolge. Darüber hinaus enthält das *Dictionary* die wichtigen Wörter aus *English Network 1*. Neben dem englischen Stichwort, der Aussprache und der deutschen Übersetzung sehen Sie auch, wo das betreffende englische Wort im *Vocabulary* zu finden ist. Viele der Wörter (mit Fundstelle in *Schrägdruck*) brauchen Sie nur zu verstehen. Die übrigen Wörter (Fundstelle in normalem Druck) sollten Sie lernen. Möchten Sie mehr über ein Wort wissen, können Sie es mit Hilfe der Fundortangabe im *Vocabulary* nachschlagen.

Die erste Ziffer der Fundortangabe weist auf den Band hin, in dem das Wort vorkommt, die zweite auf die Unit, die dritte (nach dem Punkt) auf den Step. I/3.2 heißt also Band 1, Unit 3, Step 2; II/6.1 heißt Band 2, Unit 6, Step 1. Die anderen Abkürzungen bedeuten:

G = Gazette
I = Introduction (= Wortschatz, der auf der Auftaktseite zu einer Unit erscheint)
P = Panorama
R = Revision activities

A

a, an [ə, æn, ən] ein(-e) I/1.1: **three days a week** dreimal pro Woche I/2.3
a bit [ə 'bɪt] ein bißchen, ein wenig I/1.1
a few [ə 'fjuː] einige *II/4.3P*
abbreviation [əˌbriːvɪ'eɪʃn] Abkürzung *II/4.3*
able ['eɪbl]: **be able to** können II/4.1
about [ə'baʊt] über I/2.1; ungefähr I/3.1: **what about ...?** wie ist es mit ...? I/2.1
above [ə'bʌv] oben *II/1.2*
abroad [ə'brɔːd] nach/in Übersee *II/2.3P*
accident ['æksɪdənt] Unfall II/3.3
account [ə'kaʊnt] Konto I/5.2
across [ə'krɒs] *hier*: waagrecht *II/2.R*
act [ækt] *hier*: (vor)spielen *II/5.R*
action ['ækʃn] Handlung *II/1.2*: **in action** *hier*: in der Anwendung *II/1.2*
activity [æk'tɪvətɪ] Aktivität, Tätigkeit *II/1.1*
actually ['æktʃʊəlɪ] eigentlich, wirklich I/1.1
acupuncture ['ækjʊˌpʌŋktʃə] Akupunktur *II/3.3P*
acupuncturist ['ækjʊˌpʌŋktʃərɪst] Akupunkteur *II/3.3P*
add [æd] hinzufügen *II/4.2*
address [ə'dres] Adresse I/1.3
adjective ['ædʒɪktɪv] Adjektiv, Eigenschaftswort *II/5.3*
adult ['ædʌlt] Erwachsene(-r) *II/G1*
adverb ['ædvɜːb] Adverb, Umstandswort *II/2.2*
advert, ad (= advertisement) [əd'vɜːt, æd] (*Abkürzung*) II/2.1
advertisement [əd'vɜːtɪsmənt] Anzeige, Inserat; Reklame, Werbung II/2.1
advice [əd'vaɪs] Rat(schlag) II/3.1
afraid [ə'freɪd]: **I'm afraid** ich bedaure, leider I/1.1; **I'm afraid I can't** nein, leider nicht I/1.1
Africa ['æfrɪkə] Afrika *II/2.3P*
African ['æfrɪkən] afrikanisch(-e, -er, -es); Afrikaner(-in) *II/5.3P*
after ['ɑːftə] nach I/2.2; nachdem *II/2.3*; hinter I/3.1: **after that** danach I/6.1
afternoon [ˌɑːftə'nuːn] Nachmittag I/2.2
again [ə'gen] noch einmal, wieder I/2.1
age [eɪdʒ] Alter *II/2.3P*
aged ['eɪdʒd] ... Jahre alt, im Alter von ... *II/6.1*, II/6.2
... ago [ə'gəʊ] vor (+*Zeitraum*) I/5.2: **a long time ago** vor längerer Zeit I/5.2
agree [ə'griː] zustimmen, übereinstimmen, einverstanden sein II/4.1
agriculture ['ægrɪkʌltʃə] Landwirtschaft *II/2.3P*
air [eə] Luft *II/4.3P*: **airport** Flughafen II/1.1
alcohol ['ælkəhɒl] Alkohol *II/G1*
alive [ə'laɪv] lebend(-ig) *II/2.3P*
all [ɔːl] alle(-s) I/2.R: **at all** überhaupt II/1.1; **not at all** bitte, nichts zu danken I/3.1; **all day** den ganzen Tag I/5.R; **all his work** seine ganze Arbeit I/5.2; **all right** in Ordnung I/3.1; **all the best** alles Gute I/3.3
alone [ə'ləʊn] allein I/2.1
along [ə'lɒŋ] entlang I/3.2
alphabet ['ælfəbet] Alphabet *II/1.R*
already [ɔːl'redɪ] schon, bereits *II/4.R*
also ['ɔːlsəʊ] auch *II/4.3*, II/5.1
alternative [ɔːl'tɜːnətɪv] alternativ *II/3.3P*
altogether [ˌɔːltə'geðə] zusammen, insgesamt I/5.1
always ['ɔːlweɪz] immer I/1.3
am [æm, m] bin: **I'm** ich bin I/1.1
America [ə'merɪkə] Amerika I/5.1
American [ə'merɪkən] amerikanisch(-e, -er, -es); Amerikaner(-in) I/1.1
anaemia [ə'niːmjə] Anämie, Blutarmut *II/3.3P*
and [ænd, ənd] und I/1.1: **and so on** usw. *II/2.R*

another [ə'nʌðə] ein(-e) andere(-r, -s) I/5.3
answer ['ɑːnsə] Antwort I/2.1
answer ['ɑːnsə] antworten I/2.1
any ['enɪ] welche, irgendwelche I/2.1
anymore ['enɪmɔː]: **not … anymore** nicht mehr, nicht länger *II/5.R*
anything else? ['enɪθɪŋ els] noch etwas? (*in Fragen*) I/5.1
anywhere ['enɪweə] irgendwo(hin) *II/5.3P*
apart from [ə'pɑːt frəm] außer, abgesehen von *II/1.3P*
apartment [ə'pɑːtmənt] Wohnung, Apartment (*amerik.*) II/5.1
apologize [ə'pɒlədʒaɪz] sich entschuldigen *II/5.1*
apology [ə'pɒlədʒɪ] Entschuldigung *II/5.1*
apple ['æpl] Apfel I/6.1
appointment [ə'pɔɪntmənt] Verabredung, Termin II/3.1: **make an appointment** eine Verabredung treffen, einen Termin ausmachen II/3.1
apprentice [ə'prentɪs] Lehrling, Auszubildende(-r) II/2.I
April ['eɪprəl] April I/2.2
are [ɑː, ə] sind, bist, seid I/1.I
area ['eərɪə] Gebiet I/3.1
arm [ɑːm] Arm II/3.1
arrange [ə'reɪndʒ] arrangieren, ausmachen II/2.1
arrival [ə'raɪvl]: **on arrival** bei der Ankunft *II/5.3P*
arrive [ə'raɪv] ankommen I/5.3, *II/6.3P*
art [ɑːt] Kunst I/2.3
article ['ɑːtɪkl] Artikel *II/3.3*
as [æz, əz] wie I/6.3; als I/4.3: **as … as** so … wie (*Vergleich*) II/1.2
ask [ɑːsk] fragen, (eine Frage) stellen I/2.1: **ask for** bitten um I/6.1
asleep [ə'sliːp] schlafend, eingeschlafen *II/3.3P*
assistant [ə'sɪstənt] Assistent(-in), Gehilfe, Gehilfin, Mitarbeiter(-in) II/2.1
associate [ə'səʊsɪeɪt] assoziieren, verbinden *II/1.3*
at [æt, ət] *hier*: auf I/1.1; an I/3.1: **at 7 o'clock** um 7 Uhr I/2.2; **at all** überhaupt II/1.1; **at first** zuerst *II/2.3P*; **at home** zuhause I/1.2; **at work** bei der Arbeit I/1.2
attic ['ætɪk] Dachstube, Mansarde II/4.1
August ['ɔːgəst] August I/2.2
aunt [ɑːnt] Tante I/2.1
Australia [ɒ'streɪljə] Australien I/5.3
Australian [ɒ'streɪljən] australisch(-e, -er, -es); Australier(-in) II/6.1
Austria ['ɒstrɪə] Österreich I/1.1
Austrian ['ɒstrɪən] österreichisch(-e, -er, -es); Österreicher(-in) I/1.1
autumn ['ɔːtəm] Herbst I/2.2
average; on ~ ['ævrɪdʒ] Durchschnitt(s-), durchschnittlich; im Durchschnitt *II/G1*
away [ə'weɪ] weg, fort *II/6.3P*

B

baby ['beɪbɪ] Baby, Säugling *II/5.3P*: **baby elephant** Elefantenbaby *II/5.3P*
back [bæk] Rücken; Rückseite II/3.1
back [bæk] zurück I/6.1: **back home** daheim, zuhause *II/2.3P*
backache ['bækeɪk] Rückenschmerz(en) II/3.1
bad [bæd] schlecht, schlimm I/4.3
bag [bæg] Tasche I/4.1
baker's ['beɪkəz] Bäcker(laden) II/5.2
balcony ['bælkənɪ] Balkon I/4.1
bank [bæŋk] Bank I/2.3: **bank clerk** Bankangestellte(-r) II/2.1; **bank note** Banknote I/5.I
bankrupt ['bæŋkrʌpt] bankrott II/4.2: **go bankrupt** bankrott machen II/4.2
bar [bɑː] Bar, Kneipe, Schnellimbiß usw. I/6.2: **coffee bar** Café I/6.2; **snack bar** Schnellimbiß I/6.2
basement ['beɪsmənt] Kellergeschoß II/4.1
bath [bɑːθ] Bad(ewanne) I/4.1
bathroom ['bɑːθrʊm] Bad, Badezimmer II/4.1
be (was/were, been) [biː, wɒz/wɜː, biːn] sein (war/waren, gewesen) I/4.1, I/5.1, II/1.1: **be in the late forties** Ende vierzig sein *II/6.1*
beach [biːtʃ] Strand II/1.1: **beach shoe** Strandschuh, Badeschuh II/1.1
beautiful ['bjuːtəfʊl] schön I/3.3
because [bɪ'kɒz] weil I/3.3
become (became, become) [bɪ'kʌm, bɪ'keɪm] werden (wurde, geworden) *II/3.3P*, II/6.1
bed [bed] Bett I/4.2: **in bed** im Bett I/4.2; **bed and breakfast** Zimmer mit Frühstück (*in Privatunterkunft*) I/6.R
bedroom ['bedrʊm] Schlafzimmer II/4.1
beer [bɪə] Bier I/5.3
before [bɪ'fɔː] vor (*zeitlich*) I/6.2; ehe, bevor *II/1.1*, II/1.3; vorher, zuvor II/1.3
begin (began, begun) [bɪ'gɪn, bɪ'gæn, bɪ'gʌn] beginnen (begann, begonnen), anfangen I/2.2, II/4.3P
beginner [bɪ'gɪnə] Anfänger(-in) *II/1.3P*
beginning [bɪ'gɪnɪŋ] Anfang, Beginn *II/4.R*
behind [bɪ'haɪnd] hinter I/5.1
believe [bɪ'liːv] glauben II/3.3
bell [bel] Glocke, Klingel *II/G3*
below [bɪ'ləʊ] unten *II/3.3*
best [best] beste(-r, -s) II/1.2: **all the best** alles Gute I/3.3; **best** am besten I/5.3
better ['betə] besser II/1.2
between [bɪ'twiːn] zwischen I/5.1
bicycle ['baɪsɪkl] Fahrrad I/2.2
big [bɪg] groß I/3.1
bill [bɪl] Rechnung I/6.1; Banknote, Geldschein (*amerik.*) II/5.1
birthday ['bɜːθdeɪ] Geburtstag I/3.2
black [blæk] schwarz I/5.1: **in black and white** schwarz auf weiß II/5.R
blood [blʌd] Blut *II/3.3P*
blouse [blaʊz] Bluse II/5.1
blue [bluː] blau I/5.1
body ['bɒdɪ] Körper *II/3.1*, II/3.3

book [bʊk] Buch I/2.R
book [bʊk] buchen, reservieren I/4.1
bookshop ['bʊkʃɒp] Buchladen I/2.R
border ['bɔːdə] Grenze I/3.1
born [bɔːn]: **was born** wurde geboren *II/5.3P*
borrow ['bɒrəʊ] (aus)borgen, (aus)leihen II/4.1
boss [bɒs] Chef(-in) I/2.1
both [bəʊθ] beide(-s) I/4.R: **both … and** sowohl … als auch II/1.1
bottle ['bɒtl] Flasche I/6.1
boutique [buː'tiːk] Boutique I/3.3
box [bɒks] *hier*: Kästchen *II/3.R*
bread [bred] Brot I/6.1
break [breɪk] Pause I/2.2: **have a break** Pause machen I/2.2
breakfast ['brekfəst] Frühstück I/4.1: **a full breakfast** ein englisches Frühstück I/4.1; **bed and breakfast** Zimmer mit Frühstück (*in Privatunterkunft*) I/6.R
bridge [brɪdʒ] Brücke I/3.2
bring (brought) [brɪŋ, brɔːt] bringen (brachte) I/5.3, I/6.1: **bring up** erziehen II/6.1
Britain ['brɪtn] Großbritannien I/3.1
British ['brɪtɪʃ] britisch(-e, -er, -es); Brite, Britin I/1.1
brochure ['brəʊʃə] Broschüre II/1.1
brother ['brʌðə] Bruder I/2.1: **brother-in-law** Schwager II/6.1
brown [braʊn] braun I/5.1
bubble ['bʌbl]: **speech bubble** Sprechblase *II/6.R*
budget ['bʌdʒɪt] Budget, (Haushalts)Plan *II/G3*
building ['bɪldɪŋ] Gebäude I/3.2
bungalow ['bʌŋgələʊ] Bungalow *II/G2*
bus [bʌs] Bus I/4.2: **bus stop** Bushaltestelle I/5.2
business ['bɪznɪs] Geschäft, Beruf, Handel *II/1.3P*: **business centre** Geschäftszentrum *II/4.3P*
busy ['bɪzɪ] beschäftigt II/2.1
but [bʌt, bət] aber I/1.2
butcher's ['bʊtʃəz] Metzger, Fleischer(laden) II/5.2
butter ['bʌtə] Butter I/6.1
buy (bought) [baɪ, bɔːt] kaufen (kaufte) I/5.1, I/5.2
by [baɪ] *hier*: mit I/4.I; (*geschrieben*) von I/5.2; **by plane/train** mit dem Flugzeug/Zug I/4.I; **by the sea** am Meer I/3.3; **by the way** übrigens II/5.1
bye [baɪ] tschüs I/2.1: **bye-bye** tschüs I/2.1

C

cab [kæb] Taxi (*amerik.*) II/5.1
calculator ['kælkjʊleɪtə] Taschenrechner II/2.2
Californian [ˌkælə'fɔːnɪən] kalifornisch(-e, -er, -es); Kalifornier(-in) I/1.3
call [kɔːl] Anruf I/4.1
call [kɔːl] anrufen I/6.1; nennen *II/G1*: **called** genannt I/1.1
camera ['kæmrə] Kamera II/1.1
campsite ['kæmpsaɪt] Zeltplatz I/6.R
can [kæn, kən] können, kann(-st), könnt I/1.1: **can't stand** nicht ausstehen können I/6.1
capital ['kæpɪtl] Hauptstadt *II/G3*
capital letter [ˌkæpɪtl 'letə] Großbuchstabe *II/G3*
car [kɑː] Auto I/2.2: **car park** Parkplatz I/3.2
card [kɑːd] Karte I/5.1: **credit card** Kreditkarte I/5.2
careful ['keəfʊl] vorsichtig II/2.2; *hier*: genau, gründlich *II/3.2*
carpet ['kɑːpɪt] Teppich *II/5.3P*
carrot ['kærət] Möhre, Mohrrübe I/6.1
cash [kæʃ] bar, Bargeld I/5.2
cassette [kə'set] Tonbandkassette I/2.2
castle ['kɑːsl] Burg I/4.1
cat [kæt] Katze *II/3.R*, II/6.3
catch [kætʃ] fangen *II/4.3P*: **catch a train** einen Zug erreichen *II/4.3P*
cathedral [kə'θiːdrəl] Kathedrale *II/1.3P*
central ['sentrəl] zentral, Zentral- II/4.1
centre ['sentə] Mitte, Zentrum I/3.1: **city centre** Stadtmitte, City I/3.1
certain ['sɜːtn] bestimmt, gewiß, sicher II/6.1
certainly ['sɜːtnlɪ] gewiß, natürlich I/6.1
chain [tʃeɪn] Kette II/5.3: **chain stores** (*Läden, die zu einer Kette gehören*) II/5.3
chair [tʃeə] Stuhl II/2.2
change [tʃeɪndʒ] Wechselgeld I/5.1; Veränderung, Wechsel II/3.2
change [tʃeɪndʒ] wechseln I/5.1; sich verändern *II/2.3P*
cheap [tʃiːp] billig, preiswert II/1.1
check [tʃek] Rechnung (*amerik.*) II/5.1
check [tʃek] überprüfen *II/1.1*
cheese [tʃiːz] Käse I/6.1
chemist's ['kemɪsts] Apotheke, Drogerie II/5.2
cheque [tʃek] Scheck I/5.2: **traveller's cheque** Reisescheck I/5.2
chicken ['tʃɪkɪn] Hähnchen I/6.1
child (children) [tʃaɪld, 'tʃɪldrən] Kind (Kinder) I/1.3
Chinese [ˌtʃaɪ'niːz] chinesisch(-e, -er, -es); Chinese, Chinesin I/3.3
chips [tʃɪps] Pommes frites I/6.1
choose (chose, chosen) [tʃuːz, tʃəʊz, tʃəʊzn] wählen (wählte, gewählt) *II/1.R*; *hier*: vorziehen *II/4.3P*
Christmas ['krɪsməs] Weihnachten I/6.2: **Christmas Day** Erster Weihnachtstag I/6.2
cigarette [ˌsɪgə'ret] Zigarette II/3.3
cinema ['sɪnəmə] Kino I/3.2
circle ['sɜːkl] Kreis *II/1.2*
city ['sɪtɪ] Großstadt, Weltstadt I/3.1: **city centre** Stadtmitte, City I/3.1
class [klɑːs] Klasse I/3.2; *hier*: Unterricht, Kurs *II/1.3P*: **first class** erste(-r) Klasse II/4.2
classroom ['klɑːsrʊm] Klassenzimmer I/3.2
clerk [klɑːk] Sekretär(-in), Büroangestellte(-r) II/2.1
click [klɪk] klicken, (zu)schnappen *II/G1*

climb [klaɪm] klettern, besteigen II/4.2
clock [klɒk]: **o'clock** Uhr (*bei Zeitangabe*) I/2.2: **at 7 o'clock** um 7 Uhr I/2.2
close [kləʊz] schließen I/4.R
clothes [kləʊðz] Kleider, Kleidung II/5.I
cloudy ['klaʊdɪ] bewölkt II/1.2
club [klʌb] Club I/2.3
coat [kəʊt] Mantel, Jacke II/5.1
cod [kɒd] Kabeljau I/6.1
coffee ['kɒfɪ] Kaffee I/2.2: **coffee bar** Café I/6.2
cognac ['kɒnjæk] Kognak *II/5.3P*
coin [kɔɪn] Münze I/5.1
cold [kəʊld] Erkältung II/3.2
cold [kəʊld] kalt II/1.2
collect [kə'lekt] (ein)sammeln *II/3.R*
colour ['kʌlə] Farbe I/5.2
coloured ['kʌləd] farbig *II/3.R*
column ['kɒləm] Spalte *II/4.R*
comb [kəʊm] Kamm II/1.1
come [kʌm] kommen I/1.3: **come 6th** an 6. Stelle kommen *II/6.3P*; **come true** wahr werden, sich verwirklichen II/6.3
comfortable ['kʌmfətəbl] bequem I/4.3
comment ['kɒment] Kommentar, Be-, Anmerkung *II/6.2*
commercial [kə'mɜːʃl] kaufmännisch, Handels-, Geschäfts- *II/1.3P*: **commercial and business studies** Handels- und Wirtschaftskurs *II/1.3P*
communication [kə,mjuːnɪ'keɪʃn] Kommunikation, Verbindung, Verkehr *II/G3*
commuter [kə'mjuːtə] Pendler *II/4.3P*
compact [kəm'pækt] kompakt, dicht, gedrängt *II/4.3P*
company ['kʌmpənɪ] Unternehmen I/1.3
comparative [kəm'pærətɪv] Komparativ (*1. Steigerungsstufe*) *II/1.2*
compare [kəm'peə] vergleichen *II/1.3*
competition [,kɒmpɪ'tɪʃn] Wettbewerb II/1.3
complain [kəm'pleɪn] sich beschweren II/5.1
complaint [kəm'pleɪnt] Beschwerde II/5.1
complete [kəm'pliːt] vervollständigen, beenden *II/1.R*
complicated ['kɒmplɪkeɪtɪd] kompliziert, schwierig *II/G3*
compliment ['kɒmplɪmənt] Kompliment, Lob *II/4.1*
comprehension [,kɒmprɪ'henʃn] Verständnis(übung) *II/1.1*
computer [kəm'pjuːtə] Computer I/3.2
conditional [kən'dɪʃənl]: **first conditional** Bedingungssatz (Typ 1): die offene Bedingung *II/4.2*
congratulations [kən,grætʃʊ'leɪʃnz] Glückwunsch II/1.3
contact ['kɒntækt] Kontakt *II/2.3P*
contact ['kɒntækt] erreichen, kontaktieren, sich in Verbindung setzen *II/6.3P*
continue [kən'tɪnjuː] fortfahren, weitermachen *II/2.R*
conversation [,kɒnvə'seɪʃn] Unterhaltung, Gespräch *II/1.3*
cook [kʊk] Koch, Köchin II/1.1
cook [kʊk] kochen, zubereiten I/1.2
cooker ['kʊkə] Herd II/4.2
cooking ['kʊkɪŋ] Kochen II/6.R
corner ['kɔːnə] Ecke I/3.2
correct [kə'rekt] korrigieren *II/2.1*
correct [kə'rekt] korrekt, richtig *II/2.1*
cost [kɒst] Preis, Kosten *II/5.3P*: **extra cost** Aufpreis II/1.1
cost [kɒst] kosten *II/G2*: **cost an arm and a leg** sehr viel kosten, ein Vermögen kosten *II/G2*
could [kʊd] könnte(-st, -t, -n) I/4.1; konnte(-t, -st, -n) *II/2.3P*
country ['kʌntrɪ] Land I/3.1: **in the country** auf dem Land I/3.1
countryside ['kʌntrɪsaɪd] Landschaft *II/2.3P*
course [kɔːs] Kurs I/2.2; Gang (*einer Mahlzeit*) I/6.1: **main course** Hauptgericht I/6.1
course [kɔːs]: **of course** selbstverständlich I/5.1
cousin ['kʌzn] Cousin(-e) I/2.1
crazy ['kreɪzɪ] verrückt II/6.1
cream [kriːm] Creme II/1.1: **suntan cream** Bräunungscreme II/1.1
credit card ['kredɪt kɑːd] Kreditkarte I/5.2
crisis ['kraɪsɪs] Krise II/6.1
critical ['krɪtɪkl]: **be critical of** kritisieren, beanstanden *II/2.3P*
crossroads ['krɒsrəʊdz] Kreuzung I/3.1
crossword ['krɒswɜːd] Kreuzworträtsel *II/3.R*
cry (cried) [kraɪ, kraɪd] weinen (weinte, geweint), schreien *II/3.R*
cup [kʌp] Tasse I/6.2
cupboard ['kʌbəd] (Küchen)Schrank II/4.2
cure [kjʊə] heilen, kurieren *II/3.3P*
currency ['kʌrənsɪ] Währung I/5.3
customer ['kʌstəmə] Kunde(-in) I/6.1
cycling ['saɪklɪŋ] Radfahren *II/G2*

D

dad [dæd] Vati I/2.3
dancing ['dɑːnsɪŋ] Tanzen *II/G2*
daughter ['dɔːtə] Tochter I/2.1: **daughter-in-law** Schwiegertochter II/6.1
day [deɪ] Tag I/2.2: **all day** den ganzen Tag I/5.R; **one day** eines Tages *II/6.3*; **the other day** kürzlich, neulich *II/G1*; **the day after tomorrow** übermorgen II/6.2; **the day before yesterday** vorgestern II/6.2
daytime ['deɪtaɪm]: **in the daytime** tagsüber, bei Tag *II/6.3P*
dead [ded] tot I/2.1
dear [dɪə] Liebe(r) … (*in Briefen*) I/2.3: **oh dear** oje!, meine Güte II/1.1
December [dɪ'sembə] Dezember I/2.2

decide [dɪ'saɪd] beschließen II/2.1
demonstrate ['demənstreɪt] zeigen, demonstrieren, vorführen *II/6.3P*
Denmark ['denmɑːk] Dänemark I/5.3
dentist ['dentɪst] Zahnarzt *II/3.1*, II/3.2
department [dɪ'pɑːtmənt] Abteilung II/5.3: **department store** Kaufhaus, Warenhaus II/5.2
describe [dɪ'skraɪb] beschreiben *II/2.3*
description [dɪ'skrɪpʃn] Beschreibung *II/1.3P*
deserted [dɪ'zɜːtɪd] verlassen, ausgestorben *II/G3*
desk [desk] Schreibtisch II/2.2
dessert [dɪ'zɜːt] Dessert, Nachspeise I/6.1
detail ['diːteɪl] Detail, Einzelheit *II/6.3*
diabetic [ˌdaɪə'betɪk] diabetisch, zuckerkrank; Diabetiker(-in) *II/3.3P*
diagnose ['daɪəgnəʊz] Diagnose *II/1.3P*
dial ['daɪəl] wählen *II/6.3P*: **dial telephone** Selbstanschlußtelefon, Wähltelefon *II/6.3P*
dialogue ['daɪəlɒg] Dialog *II/1.1*
dictionary ['dɪkʃənrɪ] Wörterbuch I/2.2
diet ['daɪət] Ernährung; Diät II/3.3
difference ['dɪfrəns] Unterschied *II/G1*
different ['dɪfrənt] andere(-r, -s); verschieden I/3.2
difficult ['dɪfɪkəlt] schwierig, schwer *II/2.3P*
dining room ['daɪnɪŋrʊm] Eßzimmer II/4.1
dinner ['dɪnə] warmes Abendessen, warmes Mittagessen I/1.3
directly [dɪ'rektlɪ] direkt *II/4.3P*
disagree [ˌdɪsə'griː] nicht übereinstimmen *II/6.1*
discuss [dɪ'skʌs] diskutieren *II/3.2*
distance ['dɪstəns] Distanz, Entfernung *II/6.3P*
do (did, done) [duː, dɪd, dʌn] tun (tat, getan), machen I/1.3, I/4.1, II/2.1: **does** (*Hilfsverb* do) I/2.3; **don't (= do not)** (*Hilfsverb* do, *Verneinung*) I/2.1; **do well** *hier*: gut daran sein *II/G1*
doctor ['dɒktə] Arzt I/5.R: **family doctor** Hausarzt, Hausärztin II/3.1
document ['dɒkjʊmənt] Dokument, Schriftstück *II/6.3P*
dog [dɒg] Hund I/2.2
dollar ['dɒlə] Dollar I/5.2
door [dɔː] Tür, Tor *II/G1*, II/4.1
dose [dəʊs] Dosis *II/3.3P*
double ['dʌbl] Doppel- I/1.2
down [daʊn] *hier*: senkrecht *II/2.R*
downstairs [ˌdaʊn'steəz] unten, (die Treppe) hinunter/herunter II/4.1
dozen ['dʌzn] Dutzend I/3.3
Dr ['dɒktə] (*Abkürzung für Doktor*) II/3.1
draw [drɔː] zeichnen *II/1.3P*
dream [driːm] Traum *II/6.3*
dress [dres] Kleid II/5.1: **get dressed** sich anziehen, sich ankleiden II/5.1
drink [drɪŋk] Getränk, Drink; *hier*: Trinken I/6.I
drink (drank, drunk) [drɪŋk, dræŋk, drʌŋk] trinken (trank, getrunken) I/2.2, I/5.2, II/1.2
drive (drove, driven) [draɪv, drəʊv, 'drɪvn] fahren (fuhr, gefahren) I/2.3, II/1.2, II/5.2
driver ['draɪvə] Fahrer(-in) II/2.1

E

each [iːtʃ] jede(-r, -s) I/5.1: **30 pence each** je 30 Pence I/5.1
ear [ɪə] Ohr II/3.1
early ['ɜːlɪ] früh II/2.1
earn [ɜːn] (*Geld*) verdienen I/5.2
earth [ɜːθ] Erde *II/2.3P*
east [iːst] Ost-, Osten I/3.1
eat (ate, eaten) [iːt, eɪt, 'iːtn] essen (aß, gegessen) I/4.2, I/5.2, II/1.2
editor ['edɪtə] Herausgeber(-in), Redakteur(-in) *II/G1*
education [ˌedʒʊ'keɪʃn] Bildung, Erziehung, Ausbildung *II/1.3P*
effective [ɪ'fektɪv] effektiv, wirkungsvoll *II/G2*
egg [eg] Ei *II/2.3P*
electricity [ˌɪlek'trɪsətɪ] Elektrizität *II/2.3P*
elephant ['elɪfənt] Elefant II/5.3
elevator ['elɪveɪtə] Lift, Fahrstuhl (*amerik.*) II/5.1
else [els] *hier*: andere(-r, -s) *II/2.3P*: **anything else?** noch etwas? (*in Fragen*) I/5.1
employer [ɪm'plɔɪə] Arbeitgeber II/2.3
empty ['emptɪ] leer II/5.3
end [end] Ende *II/1.R*
energy ['enədʒɪ] Energie *II/G3*
engineer [ˌendʒɪ'nɪə] Ingenieur(-in), Techniker(-in) II/2.1
English ['ɪŋglɪʃ] englisch(-e, -er, -es); Engländer(-in) I/1.1
enjoy [ɪn'dʒɔɪ] genießen, Gefallen finden; gern tun II/1.1
enjoyable [ɪn'dʒɔɪəbl] vergnüglich, erfreulich *II/1.3P*
enough [ɪ'nʌf] genug I/5.3
enter ['entə] betreten, eintreten *II/5.3P*
enthusiast [ɪn'θjuːzɪæst] Enthusiast(-in), Schwärmer(-in) *II/6.3P*
entrance ['entrəns] Eingang II/4.1: **entrance hall** Eingangshalle, Hausflur II/4.1
er [ɜː] *etwa*: äh, eh *II/G1*
escalator ['eskəleɪtə] Rolltreppe *II/5.3P*
etc. (= et cetera) [ɪt 'setərə] und so weiter *II/G1*
Europe ['jʊərəp] Europa I/5.1
European [ˌjʊərə'piːən] europäisch(-e, -er, -es); Europäer(-in) *II/2.3P*
even ['iːvn] selbst, sogar *II/2.R*, II/5.3
evening ['iːvnɪŋ] Abend I/1.3
ever ['evə] jemals, schon einmal II/1.1
every ['evrɪ] jede(-r, -s) I/2.2
everyday ['evrɪdeɪ] alltäglich, Alltags- *II/6.3P*
exactly [ɪg'zæktlɪ] genau *II/G3*
examination [ɪgˌzæmɪ'neɪʃn] Examen, Prüfung II/6.1: **take**

an examination eine Prüfung machen, sich einer Prüfung unterziehen II/6.1
example [ɪg'zɑ:mpl] Beispiel II/1.1: **for example** zum Beispiel II/1.1
excellent ['eksələnt] ausgezeichnet I/4.3
exchange [ɪks'tʃeɪndʒ] (aus)tauschen *II/2.1*
exclusive [ɪk'sklu:sɪv] exklusiv II/5.3
excuse me [ɪk'skju:z mi:] entschuldigen Sie, entschuldige, entschuldigt bitte I/3.1
exercise ['eksəsaɪz] Übung I/2.2: **get exercise** Sport treiben, Übungen machen II/3.I
expensive [ɪk'spensɪv] teuer I/4.1
experience [ɪk'spɪərɪəns] Erlebnis I/6.3
explain [ɪk'spleɪn] erklären *II/3.3P*
explanation [ˌeksplə'neɪʃn] Erklärung II/3.1
export ['ekspɔ:t] Export-, Ausfuhr- *II/5.3P*
express [ɪk'spres] ausdrücken *II/2.1*
expression [ɪk'spreʃn] Ausdruck *II/1.2*
extra cost ['ekstrə kɒst] Aufpreis II/1.1
eye [aɪ] Auge II/2.3: **up to (my) eyes in work** bis zum Hals in Arbeit, bis über beide Ohren in Arbeit *II/G2*

F

face [feɪs] schauen, blicken, liegen II/4.1
fact [fækt] Faktum, Tatsache *II/G1*: **in fact** in der Tat, tatsächlich *II/4.3P*
fair [feə] Messe, Ausstellung I/1.1
fall [fɔ:l] Herbst (*amerik.*) II/5.1
false [fɔ:ls] falsch I/3.1
family ['fæməlɪ] Familie I/2.1: **family doctor** Hausarzt, Hausärztin II/3.1
famous ['feɪməs] berühmt I/4.3
far [fɑ:] fern, weit I/2.I: **far from** weit von I/3.1
farm [fɑ:m] Bauernhof, Farm II/2.1: **farm worker** Landarbeiter(-in) II/2.1
fast [fɑ:st] schnell I/6.2: **fast-food** Fast Food I/6.2
father ['fɑ:ðə] Vater I/2.1: **father-in-law** Schwiegervater II/6.1
fault [fɔ:lt] Fehler, Mangel *II/1.3P*
favourite ['feɪvrɪt] Lieblings- *II/G1*
February ['februərɪ] Februar I/2.2
feel (felt) [fi:l, felt] (sich) fühlen (fühlte, gefühlt) II/3.I: **feel sick** übel, schlecht sein II/3.2
few [fju:]: **a few** einige *II/4.3P*
figure ['fɪgə] Zahl *II/G1*
fill (in) ['fɪl (ɪn)] (aus)füllen I/4.1
film [fɪlm] Film I/1.3: **go to see a film** ins Kino gehen I/1.3; **film star** Filmstar II/1.2
find (found) [faɪnd, faʊnd] finden (fand, gefunden) I/2.3, II/5.3P: **find out** herausfinden *II/1.1*
fine [faɪn] gut I/2.1; dünn, fein *II/3.3P*: **I'm fine, thanks** danke, mir geht's gut I/2.1
finger ['fɪŋgə] Finger II/3.1: **first finger** Zeigefinger *II/3.3P*
finish ['fɪnɪʃ] (be)enden I/4.R
first [fɜ:st] erste(-r, -s) I/1.3; zuerst I/6.1: **at first** zuerst *II/2.3P*; **first class** erste(-r) Klasse II/4.2; **first finger** Zeigefinger *II/3.3P*; **first floor** Erdgeschoß (*amerik.*) II/5.1; **first name** Vorname I/1.3
fish [fɪʃ] Fisch I/6.1
fit [fɪt] fit, in guter Form *II/1.3P*, II/3.1
fitness ['fɪtnəs] Fitneß II/3.I
flag [flæg] Fahne I/5.2
flat [flæt] Wohnung II/3.1: **two-roomed flat** 2-Zimmer-Wohnung II/4.1
flat [flæt] flach *II/2.3P*
flexi-time (= flexible time) ['fleksɪ taɪm] Gleitzeit, flexible Arbeitszeit II/2.1
flexibility [ˌfleksə'bɪlətɪ] Flexibilität; *hier*: Gelenkigkeit *II/1.3P*
flight [flaɪt] Flug II/1.1
floor [flɔ:] Fußboden; Etage I/4.1: **on the … floor** in der … Etage I/4.1; **ground floor** Erdgeschoß I/4.1; **first floor** Erdgeschoß (*amerik.*) II/5.1
florist's ['flɒrɪsts] Blumenladen, Blumengeschäft II/5.2
fog [fɒg] Nebel II/1.2
foggy ['fɒgɪ] neblig II/1.2
follow ['fɒləʊ] folgen *II/5.R*
food [fu:d] Essen I/1.3: **fast-food** Fast Food I/6.2
foot (feet) [fʊt, fi:t] Fuß I/4.2; (*Maßeinheit*) *II/G3*: **on foot** zu Fuß I/4.2; **put (your) foot in it** ins Fettnäpfchen treten *II/G2*
football ['fʊtbɔ:l] Fußball I/5.2
for [fɔ:, fə] für I/1.2; … lang (*zeitlich*) II/1.1: **for example** zum Beispiel II/1.1; **for weeks and weeks** wochenlang *II/4.3P*
forget [fə'get] vergessen *II/1.R*, II/5.R
form [fɔ:m] Formular I/4.1; Form *II/1.3P*
fossil ['fɒsl] Fossil, Versteinerung *II/5.3P*
France [frɑ:ns] Frankreich I/5.3
free [fri:] frei I/6.2; gratis, kostenlos *II/5.3P*: **free time** Freizeit II/1.I
freezing ['fri:zɪŋ] eisig *II/4.3P*
French [frentʃ] französisch(-e, -er, -es); Franzose, Französin I/1.1: **French fries** Pommes frites (*amerik.*) II/5.1
fresh [freʃ] frisch *II/4.3P*
Friday ['fraɪdɪ] Freitag I/2.1
fridge (= refrigerator) [frɪdʒ, rɪ'frɪdʒəreɪtə] Kühlschrank II/4.2
friend [frend] Freund(-in), Bekannte(-r) I/1.3: **a friend of hers** eine(-r) ihrer Freunde (Freundinnen), ein(-e) Freund(-in) von ihr *II/6.1*; **make friends** Freundschaft schließen, anfreunden *II/2.3P*, II/3.1
from [frɒm, frəm] aus I/1.I; von I/2.3: **from … to** von … bis I/2.R
front [frʌnt]: **in front of** vor I/3.1

fruit [fru:t] Frucht, Obst I/6.1
full [fʊl] voll I/4.1; *hier*: ganz *II/6.R*: **full-time** ganztägig II/2.3
furnished ['fɜ:nɪʃt] möbliert II/4.1
future ['fju:tʃə] Zukunft *II/1.3P*; Futur II/6.I

G

gallery ['gæləri] Galerie I/4.3
gallon ['gælən] Gallone (*Maßeinheit*) *II/G3*
game [geɪm] Spiel *II/3.2*
garage ['gærɑ:dʒ] Garage; Tankstelle, (Auto)Werkstatt II/4.1
garden ['gɑ:dn] Garten II/3.2
garden ['gɑ:dn] gärtnern, Gartenbau betreiben *II/G1*
gardener ['gɑ:dnə] Gärtner(-in) II/3.3
gazette [gə'zet] Zeitung, Zeitschrift *II/G1*
general ['dʒenrəl] allgemein *II/1.3P*: **in general** im allgemeinen *II/3.3*
gentleman (gentlemen) ['dʒentlmən, 'dʒentlmən] Gentleman, Herr (Herren) *II/G2*
Gents (= gentlemen) [dʒents] *hier*: Herrentoilette *II/G2*
German ['dʒɜ:mən] deutsch(-e, -er, -es); Deutsche(-r) I/1.I
Germany ['dʒɜ:mənɪ] Deutschland I/1.1
get (got) [get, gɒt] bekommen (bekam) I/4.R, I/5.2; *hier*: werden *II/1.2*; holen *II/4.3P*: **get around** herumlaufen in, seinen Weg finden in/durch *II/1.3P*; **get dressed** sich anziehen, sich ankleiden II/5.1; **get exercise** Sport treiben, Übungen machen II/3.I; **get home** zuhause ankommen I/4.R; heimgehen, -fahren, -kommen *II/G3*; **get married** heiraten, sich verheiraten II/6.1; **get on** einsteigen, aufsteigen *II/G3*; **get on well with** gut auskommen mit II/6.1; **get to** ankommen in/bei I/4.R; **get up** aufstehen I/5.2
girl [gɜ:l] Mädchen *II/2.3P*
give (gave, given) [gɪv, geɪv, 'gɪvn] geben (gab, gegeben) I/3.R, II/3.R, II/5.2: **give out** ausgeben, austeilen *II/3.R*; **give up** aufgeben I/6.2
glass [glɑ:s] Glas I/6.1
go (went) [gəʊ, went] gehen (ging) I/1.3, I/5.2: **go for** sich bemühen um, mitmachen bei *II/2.3P*; **go for a walk** spazierengehen I/5.R; **go jogging** joggen I/1.3; **go on** fortfahren, mitmachen *II/1.1*; **go out** ausgehen I/2.R; **go shopping** einkaufen gehen I/1.3; **go to** gehen in, fahren nach I/1.3; **go up** hinaufgehen *II/4.3P*
going to ['gəʊɪŋ tə] werden (*Form der Zukunft*) II/6.1
goldfish ['gəʊldfɪʃ] Goldfisch II/1.R
golf [gɒlf] Golf I/2.3
good [gʊd] der (die, das) Gute, Gutes II/5.R: **good at** gut in I/2.3; **what good does that do?** wozu soll das gut sein? *II/5.R*
goodbye [ˌgʊd'baɪ] auf Wiedersehen I/2.1
gram [græm] Gramm I/6.3
grammar ['græmə] Grammatik *II/1.2*
grammar table ['græmə teɪbl] Grammatiktafel *II/1.2*
gran (= grandmother) [græn, 'grænˌmʌðə] Großmutter, Oma II/6.2
grandmother ['grænˌmʌðə] Großmutter, Oma II/6.1
great [greɪt] großartig I/1.1
Greece [gri:s] Griechenland I/5.3
Greek [gri:k] griechisch(-e, -er, -es); Grieche, Griechin II/1.1
green [gri:n] grün I/5.1
grey [greɪ] grau I/2.3
grilled [grɪld] gegrillt I/6.2
ground [graʊnd] Boden I/4.1: **ground floor** Erdgeschoß I/4.1
group [gru:p] Gruppe I/4.2
guide [gaɪd] Führer *II/1.3P*
gun [gʌn] Gewehr, Pistole II/5.2
gymnastics [dʒɪm'næstɪks] Gymnastik, Turnen *II/G2*

H

hair [heə] Haar(e) II/6.3
half [hɑ:f] halb, Hälfte I/4.1: **half past six** halb sieben I/4.1
hall [hɔ:l] Halle; Flur II/4.1: **entrance hall** Eingangshalle, Hausflur II/4.1
ham [hæm] Schinken I/6.1
hamburger ['hæmbɜ:gə] Hamburger I/6.2
hand [hænd] Hand II/3.1
handkerchief ['hæŋkətʃɪf] Taschentuch *II/5.3P*
handsome ['hænsəm] schön (*bei Männern*) II/6.3
happen ['hæpən] passieren, geschehen, sich ereignen II/5.1
happy ['hæpɪ] glücklich I/6.2
hard [hɑ:d] hart, schwer, fleißig II/2.2
hate [heɪt] hassen I/6.2
have [hæv] haben I/2.2; *hier*: essen, zu sich nehmen I/4.R: **I'll have** ich nehme I/6.1; **have a nice day** einen schönen Tag noch I/5.1
have got [hæv 'gɒt] haben, besitzen: **I've got (= I have got)** ich habe I/2.1; **I haven't got (= I have not got)** ich habe kein(-e, -en) I/2.1
have to [hæv tə] müssen *II/2.3P*, II/4.1: **don't have to** nicht müssen II/3.2
he [hi:] er I/1.1
head [hed] Kopf II/3.1
headache ['hedeɪk] Kopfschmerzen II/3.2
health [helθ] Gesundheit I/4.3
healthy ['helθɪ] gesund II/3.3
hear (heard) [hɪə, hɜ:d] hören (hörte, gehört) II/1.3
heating ['hi:tɪŋ] Heizung II/4.1
heavy ['hevɪ] schwer, stark *II/3.3P*
hello [hə'ləʊ] Hallo. Guten Tag. Grüß' Gott. Grüezi. I/1.I
help [help] Hilfe I/4.1
help [help] helfen I/4.1
her [hɜ:] ihr(-e) I/2.1; sie, ihr (*Einzahl*) I/2.1
here [hɪə] hier I/2.1: **here you are** hier, bitte (*wenn man etwas überreicht*) I/5.1

hers [hɜ:z] ihre(-r, -s), der (die, das) ihre II/5.1
hi [haɪ] hallo! I/1.1
high [haɪ] hoch II/4.1
him [hɪm] ihn, ihm I/2.1
Hindu ['hɪndu:] hinduistisch(-e, -er, -es); Hindu; Hindu- *II/G2*
his [hɪz] seine(-r, -s), der (die, das) sein(ig)e II/5.2
history ['hɪstrɪ] Geschichte *II/5.3P*
hobby ['hɒbɪ] Hobby II/1.1
hold on [həʊld ɒn] *hier*: dranbleiben, am Apparat bleiben, warten II/2.1
holiday ['hɒlədeɪ] Urlaub, Ferien I/1.3
home [həʊm] Heim, Zuhause I/1.2: **at home** zuhause I/1.2; **get home** zuhause ankommen I/4.R
homeopath ['həʊmjəʊpæθ] Homöopath *II/3.3P*
homeopathy [ˌhəʊmɪ'ɒpəθɪ] Homöopathie *II/3.3P*
homesick ['həʊmsɪk]: **be homesick** Heimweh haben *II/2.3P*
homework ['həʊmwɜ:k] Hausaufgaben I/2.2
hope [həʊp] Hoffnung I/5.3
hope [həʊp] hoffen I/5.3
horse [hɔ:s] Pferd II/6.3
hospital ['hɒspɪtl] Krankenhaus I/2.3
hostel ['hɒstl] Herberge, Heim *II/4.3P*
hot [hɒt] heiß II/1.2
hotel [ˌhəʊ'tel] Hotel I/1.3
hour ['aʊə] Stunde I/4.1
house [haʊs] Haus I/4.2
household ['haʊshəʊld] Haushalt *II/G3*
how [haʊ] wie I/2.1: **how about ...?** wie wäre es mit ...? wie wäre es, wenn ...? II/3.1; **how are you?** wie geht es dir/Ihnen/euch? I/2.1; **how do you do?** wie geht es Ihnen? angenehm! *(höfliche Begrüßungsformel)* I/2.1; **how long** wie lange I/5.1; **how many** wie viele I/2.1; **how much** wieviel I/4.1; **how much is ...?** was kostet ...? I/4.1
husband ['hʌzbənd] Ehemann I/2.1
hut [hʌt] Hütte *II/2.3P*

I

I [aɪ] ich I/1.1: **I see** ach so *(Ausruf)* I/3.1
ice [aɪs] Eis I/6.1: **ice cream** Eiskrem I/6.1
idea [aɪ'dɪə] Idee I/5.1
ideal [aɪ'dɪəl] ideal *II/4.R*
if [ɪf] wenn, falls; ob *II/1.2*, II/3.1
ill [ɪl] krank II/3.1
illness ['ɪlnɪs] Krankheit *II/3.3*
immediate [ɪ'mi:djət] sofortig, unmittelbar *II/5.3P*: **immediately** sofort I/6.1
imperative [ɪm'perətɪv] Imperativ, Befehlssatz *II/2.2*
important [ɪm'pɔ:tnt] wichtig I/6.3
impossible [ɪm'pɒsəbl] unmöglich II/6.1
in [ɪn] in I/1.I: **in black and white** schwarz auf weiß II/5.R; **in fact** in der Tat, tatsächlich *II/4.3P*; **in front of** vor I/3.1; **in German** auf deutsch I/1.I; **in there** da drinnen *II/G1*
in-laws ['ɪnlɔ:z] angeheiratete Verwandte *II/6.1*
inch [ɪntʃ] Zoll *(Maßeinheit)* *II/G3*
include [ɪn'klu:d] einschließen, beinhalten I/4.1
including [ɪn'klu:dɪŋ] einschließlich I/4.1
India ['ɪndɪə] Indien I/5.3
Indian ['ɪndjən] indisch(-e, -er, -es); Inder(-in) I/3.3
individual [ˌɪndɪ'vɪdʒʊəl] Individuum, Einzelne(-r) *II/5.2*
industrial [ɪn'dʌstrɪəl] Industrie-, industriell I/3.1
information [ˌɪnfə'meɪʃn] Information, Auskunft I/3.1
inside [ˌɪn'saɪd] (der, die, das) Innere *II/G1*
inside [ˌɪn'saɪd] innerhalb, drinnen II/2.3; (der, die, das) Innere *II/G1*
instead [ɪn'sted] statt dessen II/3.2
instruction [ɪn'strʌkʃn] Instruktion, Anweisung *II/3.2*
interest ['ɪntrəst] Interesse *II/G1*
interested in ['ɪntrəstɪd ɪn] interessiert an II/1.3
interesting ['ɪntrəstɪŋ] interessant I/3.3
international [ˌɪntə'næʃnl] international I/1.1
interview ['ɪntəvju:] Interview, Vorstellungsgespräch II/2.1
interview ['ɪntəvju:] befragen, interviewen *II/6.R*
into ['ɪntʊ] in, in ... hinein *II/3.3P*
intonation [ˌɪntəʊ'neɪʃn] Intonation, Betonung *II/1.1*
introduce [ˌɪntrə'dju:s] einführen *II/5.3P*: **introduce ... to ...** vorstellen I/1.1
invent [ɪn'vent] erfinden *II/3.3P*
inventor [ɪn'ventə] Erfinder(-in) *II/6.3P*
invitation [ˌɪnvɪ'teɪʃn] Einladung *II/1.R*
invite [ɪn'vaɪt] einladen I/5.3
irregular [ɪ'regjʊlə] unregelmäßig II/1.I
is [ɪz] ist I/1.I: **isn't (= is not)** ist nicht I/1.1
island ['aɪlənd] Insel II/1.1
it [ɪt] es I/1.1
Italian [ɪ'tæljən] italienisch (-e, -er, -es); Italiener(-in) I/1.I
Italy ['ɪtəlɪ] Italien I/2.R
item ['aɪtəm] Gegenstand, Artikel *II/G3*
itself [ɪt'self] (sich) selbst *II/5.3P*

J

jacket ['dʒækɪt] Jacke, Jakett II/5.1
January ['dʒænjʊərɪ] Januar I/2.2
Japanese [ˌdʒæpə'ni:z] japanisch(-e, -er, -es); Japaner(-in) I/2.3
jeans [dʒi:nz] Jeans II/2.2
job [dʒɒb] Arbeit, Stelle I/5.2
jogging ['dʒɒgɪŋ] Jogging II/3.I: **go jogging** joggen I/1.3
journey ['dʒɜ:nɪ] Fahrt, Reise I/4.1
judo ['dʒu:dəʊ] Judo *II/G2*
juice [dʒu:s] Saft I/6.1
July [dʒʊ'laɪ] Juli I/2.2

June [dʒuːn] Juni I/2.2
just [dʒʌst] nur I/1.1

K

keen on [kiːn ɒn]: **(be) not too keen on** nicht allzu gern mögen I/6.1
keep [kiːp] *hier*: bleiben *II/G2*
key [kiː] Schlüssel I/4.1
kill [kɪl] töten *II/2.3P*
kilo ['kiːləʊ] Kilo I/6.3
kilometre ['kɪləˌmiːtə] Kilometer I/3.1
kind [kaɪnd] Art, Weise *II/2.3P*
kind [kaɪnd] nett, freundlich I/4.1
kitchen ['kɪtʃɪn] Küche II/4.1
knee [niː] Knie II/3.1
know (knew, known) [nəʊ, njuː, nəʊn] kennen (kannte, gekannt) I/3.1; wissen I/3.3, II/3.3P: **well-known** berühmt, wohlbekannt II/5.3

L

label ['leɪbl] beschriften *II/4.1*
Ladies ['leɪdɪz] *hier*: Damentoilette *II/G2*
lady ['leɪdɪ] Frau, Dame, Lady *II/3.3*, II/5.1
lamp [læmp] Lampe II/4.2
land [lænd] landen I/5.2
lane [leɪn] Gasse I/3.3
language ['læŋgwɪdʒ] Sprache, Sprach- I/6.R
large [lɑːdʒ] groß I/6.3
last [lɑːst] letzte(-r, -s) I/4.2; das letzte Mal I/5.2
late [leɪt] spät, verspätet I/4.1: **be in the late forties** Ende vierzig sein *II/6.1*
later ['leɪtə] später *II/2.3P*
learn [lɜːn] lernen I/3.1
learner ['lɜːnə] Lerner(-in) II/2.2
leave (left) [liːv, left] verlassen (verließ, verlassen), zurücklassen; (weg)gehen, (weg)fahren II/2.1
left [left] linke(-r, -s); (nach) links I/3.1: **on the left** links, auf der linken Seite I/3.1; **on your left** links von Ihnen/dir/euch, zu Ihrer/deiner/eurer Linken I/3.2
leg [leg] Bein II/3.1
legend ['ledʒənd] Legende *II/5.3P*
lemon ['lemən] Zitrone I/6.1
less [les] weniger *II/3.3P*
lesson ['lesn] Unterrichtsstunde I/2.2
let [let] *hier*: vermieten II/4.3: **let's (= let us)** laß' uns (+ *Vorschlag*) II/1.1
letter ['letə] Brief I/2.3; Buchstabe *II/1.R*: **capital letter** Großbuchstabe *II/G3*
library ['laɪbrərɪ] Bibliothek, Bücherei *II/1.3P*
life (lives) [laɪf, laɪvz] Leben *II/1.3*, II/3.2
lift [lɪft] Lift, Aufzug II/4.1
light [laɪt] Licht I/3.1: **traffic lights** Ampel I/3.1
light [laɪt] leicht *II/3.3P*
like [laɪk] gern haben I/1.1: **I'd like (= I would like)** ich möchte I/4.1; **like doing** gern tun II/1.1
like this [laɪk ðɪs] wie dies(-e, -es, -er) *II/1.1*: **what is he like?** wie sieht er aus? *II/G3*
line [laɪn] Linie, Zeile, Strich *II/4.2*
linear measure ['lɪnɪə 'meʒə] Längenmaß *II/G3*
liquid measure ['lɪkwɪd 'meʒə] Flüssigkeitsmaß *II/G3*
list [lɪst] Liste *II/1.R*
listen to ['lɪsn tə] (zu)hören I/2.2
listener ['lɪsnə] Hörer, Zuhörer, Horcher *II/5.1*
litre ['liːtə] Liter *II/G3*
live [lɪv] wohnen, leben I/1.3: **live on** leben von *II/2.3P*
lively ['laɪvlɪ] lebhaft, lebendig *II/1.3P*
living room ['lɪvɪŋrʊm] Wohnzimmer II/4.1
long [lɒŋ] lang I/5.2: **how long** wie lange I/5.1
loo [luː] Toilette, Klo *II/G2*
look [lʊk] Blick II/5.1: **have a look** (sich) etw. ansehen II/5.1
look [lʊk]: **look after** sich kümmern um, sorgen für II/6.2; **look (at)** (an)sehen I/2.1
Lord [lɔːd] Herr *II/G2*
lose [luːz] verlieren II/4.2
lot [lɒt]: **a lot of** viele I/2.1; **lots of** viele I/3.3
love [lʌv] lieben I/6.1
lovely ['lʌvlɪ] wunderschön, reizend *II/1.3P*, II/4.1
lunch [lʌntʃ] Mittagessen I/4.R
lunchtime ['lʌntʃˌtaɪm] Mittagszeit, -pause II/2.R

M

machine [mə'ʃiːn] Maschine *II/G1*
madam ['mædəm] (*höfliche Anrede für eine Kundin*) I/6.1
magazine [ˌmægə'ziːn] Zeitschrift I/5.1
main [meɪn] Haupt- I/3.2: **main course** Hauptgericht I/6.1
make (made) [meɪk, meɪd] machen (machte, gemacht), bilden I/2.2, II/6.3P: **make an appointment** eine Verabredung treffen, einen Termin ausmachen II/3.1; **make friends** Freundschaft schließen, anfreunden *II/2.3P*, II/3.1
man (men) [mæn, men] Mann (Männer) I/3.1
manage ['mænɪdʒ] (es) schaffen, klarkommen I/4.1
many ['menɪ] viele I/2.1: **how many** wie viele I/2.1; **many more** viele andere *II/2.3P*
map [mæp] (Land)karte, Stadtplan I/5.1
March [mɑːtʃ] März I/2.2
market ['mɑːkɪt] Markt *II/2.3P*, II/5.2
married ['mærɪd] verheiratet I/2.1: **get married** heiraten, sich verheiraten II/6.1
marry ['mærɪ] heiraten II/2.2
match [mætʃ] Spiel (*Sport*) II/6.R
match [mætʃ] *hier*: zuordnen *II/1.1*
matter ['mætə] Sache, Angelegenheit II/5.1: **it doesn't matter** es macht nichts II/5.1; **what's the matter** worum geht es? was ist los? II/5.1
May [meɪ] Mai I/2.2
may [meɪ] dürfen II/4.1: **may do sth.** vielleicht etwas tun II/2.1

me [miː] mich, mir, *auch*: ich I/1.2
meal [miːl] Essen, Mahlzeit *II/1.3P*
mean [miːn] bedeuten *II/1.1*
meaning [ˈmiːnɪŋ] Bedeutung *II/3.1*
measure [ˈmeʒə] Maß, Maßeinheit *II/G3*
meat [miːt] Fleisch I/6.1
medicine [ˈmedsɪn] Medizin *II/3.3P*
medium-sized [ˈmiːdɪəmˈsaɪzd] mittelgroß I/3.1
meet (met, met) [miːt, met, met] kennenlernen, treffen (traf, getroffen) I/1.I, I/5.2, II/1.2: **pleased to meet you** angenehm; nett, Sie/dich/euch kennenzulernen I/1.1
meeting [ˈmiːtɪŋ] Treffen, Versammlung, Konferenz *II/G2*
melon [ˈmelən] Melone I/6.1
member [ˈmembə] Mitglied *II/6.R*
menu [ˈmenjuː] Speisekarte I/6.1
message [ˈmesɪdʒ] Mitteilung, Botschaft I/6.3
method [ˈmeθəd] Methode *II/3.3P*
metre [ˈmiːtə] Meter *II/4.3P*
middle [ˈmɪdl]: **in the middle** in der Mitte, mitten *II/G3*
midnight [ˈmɪdnaɪt] Mitternacht II/5.2
midnight [ˈmɪdnaɪt] mitternächtlich, Mitternachts- *II/5.3P*
might [maɪt]: **might do sth.** vielleicht etwas tun II/2.1
migraine [ˈmiːgreɪn] Migräne II/3.2
mile [maɪl] Meile *II/G3*
milk [mɪlk] Milch I/6.1: **powdered milk** Trockenmilch *II/2.3P*
million [ˈmɪljən] Million I/6.3
millionaire [ˌmɪljəˈneə] Millionär(-in) I/5.2
mind [maɪnd] etwas gegen etwas haben I/5.1
mine [maɪn] mein(-e, -er, -es), der (die, das) mein(ig)e II/5.1
minus [ˈmaɪnəs] minus I/1.2
minute [ˈmɪnɪt] Minute I/3.1
miss [mɪs] verpassen I/3.1; vermissen *II/2.3P*: **missing** fehlend *II/1.1*
Miss [mɪs] Fräulein (*Anrede*) *II/G1*
mistake [mɪˈsteɪk] Fehler *II/3.3P*, II/5.1
mixed [mɪkst] gemischt *II/1.2*
modern [ˈmɒdən] modern I/4.3
moment [ˈməʊmənt] Augenblick I/6.1
Monday [ˈmʌndɪ] Montag I/2.1
money [ˈmʌnɪ] Geld I/5.I
month [mʌnθ] Monat I/2.3: **monthly** monatlich, Monats- *II/4.3P*
moon [muːn] Mond II/4.2
more [mɔː] mehr I/6.2: **more again** noch(mals) mehr II/2.3
morning [ˈmɔːnɪŋ] Morgen, Vormittag I/2.2: **this morning** heute morgen I/4.R; **in the mornings** vormittags I/2.2
most [məʊst] meiste(-r, -s) *II/1.1*, II/1.2
mother [ˈmʌðə] Mutter I/2.1: **mother-in-law** Schwiegermutter II/6.1
motor-bike [ˈməʊtəbaɪk] Motorrad, Kraftrad *II/G3*
motto [ˈmɒtəʊ] Motto, Wahlspruch *II/5.3P*
mountain [ˈmaʊntɪn] Berg I/3.1
mouth [maʊθ] Mund II/3.1
move [muːv] (sich) bewegen *II/5.3P*
movie [ˈmuːvɪ] Film (*amerik.*) II/5.1: **movie theater** Kino (*amerik.*) II/5.1
Mr [ˈmɪstə] Herr (*Anrede*) *II/G1*, II/5.1
Mrs [mɪsɪz] Frau (*Anrede für eine verheiratete Frau*) I/2.1
Ms [mɪz] Frau (*Anrede*) *II/2.1*
much [mʌtʃ] viel I/2.3: **how much** wieviel I/4.1; **how much is ...?** was kostet ...? I/4.1
Mum [mʌm] Mutti I/2.3
muscle [ˈmʌsl] Muskel *II/1.3P*
museum [mjuːˈzɪəm] Museum I/3.2
mushroom [ˈmʌʃrʊm] Pilz I/6.1
music [ˈmjuːzɪk] Musik I/3.R
musician [mjuːˈzɪʃn] Musiker (-in), Musikant(-in) II/5.3
must [mʌst] müssen II/2.3: **mustn't (= must not)** nicht dürfen II/3.2
my [maɪ] mein(-e) I/1.1

N

name [neɪm] Name I/1.1: **first name** Vorname I/1.3; **my name's** ich heiße I/1.1; **what's your name?** wie heißen Sie?, wie heißt du/ihr? I/1.1
nationality, -ies [ˌnæʃəˈnælətɪ] Nationalität, -en I/1.1
near [nɪə] in der Nähe von I/1.1: **nearly** fast, beinahe *II/4.3P*
necessary [ˈnesəsərɪ] nötig, notwendig II/3.2
need [niːd] Bedürfnis, Bedarf *II/4.1*
need [niːd] benötigen I/5.1
needle [ˈniːdl] Nadel *II/3.3P*
negative [ˈnegətɪv] negativ *II/1.2*
neighbour [ˈneɪbə] Nachbar(-in) II/4.3
nervous [ˈnɜːvəs] nervös *II/5.3P*
Netherlands [ˈneðələndz]: **The Netherlands** die Niederlande I/5.3
never [ˈnevə] nie I/2.2
new [njuː] neu I/2.3
New Zealand [njuː ˈziːlənd] Neuseeland I/2.1
news [njuːz] Nachrichten I/5.2
newsagent's [ˈnjuːzˌeɪdʒənts] Zeitungsladen, Zeitungsgeschäft II/5.2
newspaper [ˈnjuːsˌpeɪpə] Zeitung I/1.3
next [nekst] nächste(-r, -s) I/2.2: **next to** neben I/5.1
nice [naɪs] nett, schön I/1.1: **nice to meet you** angenehm; nett, Sie/dich/euch kennenzulernen I/1.1
Nigerian [naɪˈdʒɪərɪən] nigerianisch(-e, -er, -es); Nigerianer(-in) *II/2.3P*
night [naɪt] Nacht I/4.1: **one night** eines Nachts *II/5.3P*
no [nəʊ] nein I/1.1
nobody [ˈnəʊbədɪ] niemand *II/1.R*
normal [ˈnɔːml] normal II/2.3
north [nɔːθ] Nord-, Norden I/2.R

nose [nəʊz] Nase II/3.1
not [nɒt] nicht I/1.1: **not ... anymore** nicht mehr, nicht länger *II/5.R*; **not at all** bitte, nichts zu danken I/3.1
note [nəʊt] Note, Notiz I/5.I: **bank note** Banknote I/5.I
nothing ['nʌθɪŋ] nichts II/3.1
November [nəʊ'vembə] November I/2.2
now [naʊ] jetzt I/1.3
number ['nʌmbə] Zahl, Nummer I/1.2
number ['nʌmbə] (durch)numerieren, zählen *II/2.1*
nurse [nɜ:s] Krankenschwester II/6.1

O

object ['ɒbdʒɪkt] Gegenstand *II/2.3*
October [ɒk'təʊbə] Oktober I/2.2
of [ɒv, əv] von I/1.3: **of course** selbstverständlich I/5.1
offer ['ɒfə] Angebot I/4.1
offer ['ɒfə] anbieten *II/3.1*
office ['ɒfɪs] Büro I/4.2: **office assistant** Bürogehilfe, Bürogehilfin II/2.1
official [ə'fɪʃl] offiziell, amtlich *II/G1*
often ['ɒfn] oft I/1.3
oh [əʊ] Null *(in Telefonnummern)* I/1.2
oh dear [əʊ dɪə] oje!, meine Güte II/1.1
okay [ˌəʊ'keɪ] in Ordnung, *hier*: mir geht's gut I/2.1
old [əʊld] alt I/3.1
omelette ['ɒmlət] Omelett I/1.2
on [ɒn] auf I/1.3; an I/3.1: **and so on** usw. *II/2.R*; **on a train** im Zug, in der Bahn I/4.2; **on foot** zu Fuß I/4.2; **on offer** im Angebot *II/1.3P*; **on Saturdays** samstags I/1.3; **on television** im Fernsehen I/5.1; **on the ... floor** in der ... Etage I/4.1; **on your left** links von Ihnen, zu Ihrer Linken I/3.2; **on your right** rechts, auf der rechten Seite I/3.2
once [wʌns] einmal, einst II/3.2
one [wʌn]: **one day** eines Tages *II/6.3*; **one night** eines Nachts *II/5.3P*; **a Japanese one** *(Stützwort)* ein(-e) japanische(-r, -s) I/2.3
onion ['ʌnjən] Zwiebel I/6.3
only ['əʊnlɪ] nur *II/2.3P*: **only child** Einzelkind I/2.1
open ['əʊpən] öffnen I/4.R
open ['əʊpən] offen I/3.3
operation [ˌɒpə'reɪʃn] Operation *II/3.3P*
operator ['ɒpəreɪtə] *hier*: Vermittlung *II/6.3P*
opposite ['ɒpəzɪt] gegenüber I/5.1
or [ɔ:] oder I/1.3
orange ['ɒrɪndʒ] Apfelsine I/6.1
orange ['ɒrɪndʒ] orange I/5.1
order ['ɔ:də] Reihenfolge, Ordnung *II/1.2*; Befehl, Anordnung II/3.2; Bestellung *II/5.3P*
order ['ɔ:də] bestellen I/6.1
originally [ə'rɪdʒənəlɪ] ursprünglich I/1.1
other ['ʌðə] andere(-r, -s) I/2.1: **the other day** kürzlich, neulich *II/G1*
ouch [aʊtʃ] *etwa*: au, aua *II/3.1*
ounce [aʊns] Unze *II/G3*
our ['aʊə] unser(-e) I/1.3
ours ['aʊəz] unsere(-r, -s), der (die, das) unsere II/5.2
ourselves [aʊə'selvz] uns (selbst) *II/2.3P*
out [aʊt]: **out of** aus, heraus I/3.2; **be out** *hier*: ausgegangen sein II/2.1; *hier*: ausscheiden *II/3.2*
outside [ˌaʊt'saɪd] außerhalb II/2.I, II/2.3; hinaus, nach draußen *II/4.3P*
over ['əʊvə] über I/3.2; mehr als I/3.3: **be over** vorbei sein *II/2.3*; **over there** da drüben I/5.1
overseas [ˌəʊvə'si:z] nach/in Übersee *II/2.3P*

P

packet ['pækɪt] Paket, Päckchen I/6.3
page [peɪdʒ] Seite II/1.1
pain [peɪn] Schmerz *II/3.3P*
painful ['peɪnfʊl] schmerzhaft *II/3.3P*
paint [peɪnt] malen *II/1.3P*
pair [peə] Paar *II/2.2*, II/5.1: **in pairs** paarweise, zu zweit *II/2.2*
palace ['pælɪs] Palast, Schloß *II/1.1*
pants [pænts] (lange) Hose(n) *(amerik.)* II/5.1
paper ['peɪpə] Papier, Blatt *II/2.1*
paradise ['pærədaɪs] Paradies *II/1.1*
paragraph ['pærəgrɑ:f] Absatz, Abschnitt, Paragraph *II/2.3*
pardon? ['pɑ:dn] wie bitte? I/3.1
parents ['peərənts] Eltern I/2.1
park [pɑ:k] Park I/3.2
park [pɑ:k] parken II/2.2
part [pɑ:t] Teil I/3.1: **part-time** Teilzeit- II/1.1
participle ['pɑ:tɪsɪpl] Partizip, Mittelwort *II/1.2*
partner ['pɑ:tnə] Partner(-in) I/2.1
party ['pɑ:tɪ] Party II/4.3
passport ['pɑ:spɔ:t] (Reise)Paß II/1.2
past [pɑ:st] Imperfekt, Vergangenheit *II/1.2*: **past progressive** Verlaufsform der Vergangenheit *II/5.2*
past [pɑ:st] an ... vorbei I/3.2; nach I/4.1; vergangen *II/1.3*: **half past six** halb sieben I/4.1
patient ['peɪʃnt] Patient *II/3.3P*
pay [peɪ] Bezahlung, Gehalt II/2.1
pay for (paid) ['peɪ fə, peɪd] bezahlen (bezahlte) I/5.2, I/6.1
pea [pi:] Erbse I/6.1
pen [pen] Feder(halter), Füller II/2.2
pence [pens] *(Mehrzahl von* penny) I/5.1: **30 pence each** je 30 Pence I/5.1
pencil ['pensl] (Blei)Stift II/2.2
people ['pi:pl] Leute, Menschen I/1.I
per [pɜ:] pro I/4.1
perfect ['pɜ:fɪkt] perfekt, vollkommen, genau richtig II/4.1
perhaps [pə'hæps] vielleicht I/6.1
permission [pə'mɪʃn] Erlaubnis *II/4.1*
Persian ['pɜ:ʃn] persisch(-e, -er, -es); Perser(-in) *II/5.3P*

person [ˈpɜːsn] Person I/4.1
personal [ˈpɜːsənəl] persönlich I/1.3
petrol [ˈpetrəl] Benzin *II/G3*
phone [fəʊn] (*Kurzform für*) Telefon I/1.2: **picture phone** Bildtelefon *II/6.3P*
phone [fəʊn] anrufen I/5.1
photo [ˈfəʊtəʊ] Foto I/5.2: **take a photo** ein Foto machen I/5.2
photocopier [ˈfəʊtəʊˌkɒpɪə] Fotokopiergerät II/2.2
photocopy [ˈfəʊtəʊˌkɒpɪ] (Foto)Kopie II/2.2
photographer [fəˈtɒgrəfə] Fotograf(-in) *II/4.3P*
photography [fəˈtɒgrəfɪ] Fotografie II/6.R
piano [pɪˈænəʊ] Klavier I/1.2
picture [ˈpɪktʃə] Bild *II/1.1*: **picture phone** Bildtelefon *II/6.3P*
piece [piːs] Stück *II/3.R*
pilot [ˈpaɪlət] Pilot, Flieger II/6.2
pint [paɪnt] (*engl. Maßeinheit*) *II/G3*
place [pleɪs] Ort I/1.1; Platz, Stelle; Haus, Wohnung I/6.R
plan [plæn] Plan II/1.1
plane [pleɪn] Flugzeug I/4.I
play [pleɪ] Bühnenstück I/5.2
play [pleɪ] spielen I/1.2
please [pliːz] bitte I/1.2
pleased [pliːzd] erfreut I/1.1: **pleased to meet you** angenehm; nett, Sie/dich/euch kennenzulernen I/1.1
poem [ˈpəʊɪm] Gedicht *II/6.2*
point [pɔɪnt] Punkt, Stelle *II/3.3P*
Poland [ˈpəʊlənd] Polen I/5.3
police [pəˈliːs] Polizei II/2.2: **police station** Polizeiwache I/3.1
policeman [pəˈliːsmən] Polizist II/2.1
poor [pɔː] (der, die, das) Arme, (die) Armen *II/4.3P*
popular [ˈpɒpjʊlə] beliebt, populär *II/G1*
positive [ˈpɒzətɪv] positiv *II/1.2*
possessive pronoun [pəˈzesɪv ˈprəʊnaʊn] Possessivpronomen, besitzanzeigendes Fürwort *II/5.2*
possibility [ˌpɒsəˈbɪlətɪ] Möglichkeit *II/2.1*
possible [ˈpɒsəbl] möglich *II/1.1*, II/3.1
possibly [ˈpɒsəblɪ] vielleicht, möglicherweise II/3.1
post [pəʊst] Post I/3.1: **post office** Postamt I/3.1
postcard [ˈpəʊstkɑːd] Postkarte I/3.3
potato [pəˈteɪtəʊ] Kartoffel I/6.1
pound [paʊnd] Pfund (*englische Währung*) I/5.1; (*Maßeinheit*) *II/G3*
powdered milk [ˈpaʊdəd mɪlk] Trockenmilch *II/2.3P*
practical [ˈpræktɪkl] praktisch *II/1.3P*
practise [ˈpræktɪs] üben *II/1.1*
prefer [prɪˈfɜː] vorziehen I/6.1: **I'd prefer** ich würde vorziehen, ich nehme lieber … I/6.1
present [ˈpreznt] Geschenk II/5.I; Gegenwart *II/6.2*: **present perfect** Perfekt, vollendete Gegenwart *II/1.2*; **present progressive** Verlaufsform der Gegenwart *II/3.2*
present [ˈpreznt] gegenwärtig, momentan *II/2.3*
president [ˈprezɪdənt] Präsident *II/5.3P*
price [praɪs] Preis I/5.1
prince [prɪns] Prinz II/4.2
princess [prɪnˈses] Prinzessin II/4.2
private [ˈpraɪvɪt] privat *II/G2*
prize [praɪz] (Sieger)Preis II/1.3
probably [ˈprɒbəblɪ] wahrscheinlich II/2.1
problem [ˈprɒbləm] Problem II/2.3
produce [prəˈdjuːs] produzieren, herstellen *II/3.3P*
professor [prəˈfesə] Professor(-in) *II/G1*
profile [ˈprəʊfaɪl] Profil I/1.3
promise [ˈprɒmɪs] Versprechen I/6.1
proud (of) [praʊd (əv)] stolz (auf) II/6.2
pub [pʌb] Gasthof, Kneipe I/4.2
public [ˈpʌblɪk] öffentlich *II/1.3P*
publish [ˈpʌblɪʃ] veröffentlichen II/2.1
pullover [ˈpʊlˌəʊvə] Pullover II/5.1
put [pʊt] legen, stellen, setzen *II/1.R*, II/2.2; **put through** *hier*: durchstellen II/2.1: **put (your) foot in it** ins Fettnäpfchen treten *II/G2*
pyjama(s) [pəˈdʒɑːmə(z)] Schlafanzug, Pyjama *II/6.3P*

Q

quart [kwɔːt] Quart (*Maßeinheit*) *II/G3*
quarter [ˈkwɔːtə]: **a quarter** Viertel I/4.1
Queen [kwiːn] Königin (von England) II/6.3
question [ˈkwestʃən] Frage I/2.1: **question mark** Fragezeichen *II/1.1*; **question tag** Frageanhängsel *II/6.2*
quick [kwɪk] schnell II/2.2: **quickly** schnell II/2.1
quite [kwaɪt] ganz, völlig, ziemlich II/6.1

R

rain [reɪn] Regen II/1.3
rain [reɪn] regnen II/1.2
re-export [ˈriːˌɪkspɔːt] wieder ausführen *II/5.3P*
react [rɪˈækt] reagieren *II/5.1*
reaction [rɪˈækʃn] Reaktion *II/1.1*
read (read, read) [riːd, red, red] lesen (las, gelesen) I/1.3, II/1.2: **read out** vorlesen *II/4.R*
reader [ˈriːdə] Leser(-in) *II/G1*
realistic [ˌrɪəˈlɪstɪk] realistisch *II/4.R*
really [ˈrɪəlɪ] wirklich, eigentlich I/3.1
receipt [rɪˈsiːt] Quittung I/6.1
reception [rɪˈsepʃn] Empfang, Rezeption I/4.1
receptionist [rɪˈsepʃənɪst] Person am Empfang I/4.1
red [red] rot I/5.1
regular [ˈregjʊlə] regelmäßig II/2.3
remember [rɪˈmembə] sich erinnern an *II/1.3*
rent [rent] Miete II/4.1
rent [rent] mieten II/4.1
repair [rɪˈpeə] reparieren *II/1.3P*

repeat [rɪ'pi:t] wiederholen *II/1.1*
replace [rɪ'pleɪs] ersetzen *II/6.1*
report [rɪ'pɔ:t] Bericht *II/4.3P*
report [rɪ'pɔ:t] berichten, melden *II/1.2*
research [rɪ'sɜ:tʃ] Forschungs- *II/G1*
reserve [rɪ'zɜ:v] reservieren *II/2.R*
restaurant ['restərɔ̃, 'restərɒnt] Restaurant I/1.3
retire [rɪ'taɪə] in Pension gehen, in den Ruhestand treten II/6.1: **retired** pensioniert, im Ruhestand II/2.I
return [rɪ'tɜ:n] Rück- *II/4.3P*
return [rɪ'tɜ:n] zurückkehren *II/1.3P*
revision [rɪ'vɪʒn] Revision, Überarbeitung *II/1.R*
rice [raɪs] Reis I/6.1
rich [rɪtʃ] reich II/3.1
ride [raɪd] reiten; fahren II/1.R
right [raɪt] richtig I/1.1: **all right** in Ordnung I/3.1; **be right** recht haben *II/G2*, II/6.1; **that's all right** bitte, ist schon in Ordnung I/3.1
right [raɪt] (nach) rechts I/3.1: **on the right** rechts, auf der rechten Seite I/3.2
ring (rang, rung) [rɪŋ, ræŋ, rʌŋ] klingeln, läuten (läutete, geläutet) I/4.1, II/5.2; anrufen II/2.1
river ['rɪvə] Fluß I/3.1
road [rəʊd] Straße, Fahrbahn I/3.1
robber ['rɒbə] Räuber II/5.2
robot ['rəʊbɒt] Roboter II/4.2
role [rəʊl] Rolle *II/5.R*
room [ru:m] Zimmer, Raum I/3.2: **two-roomed flat** 2-Zimmer-Wohnung II/4.1
round [raʊnd] (rund) um, um ... (herum) II/6.1
rowing ['rəʊɪŋ] Rudern *II/G2*
rule [ru:l] Regel, Vorschrift *II/2.2*
Russian ['rʌʃən] russisch(-e, -er, -es); Russe, Russin *II/1.3P*, II/1.R

S

salad ['sæləd] Salat I/6.1
salary ['sælərɪ] Lohn, Gehalt II/2.3
sale [seɪl] Verkauf II/4.3: **for sale** verkäuflich, zum Verkauf II/4.3
same [seɪm] der- (die-, das-)selbe; gleich I/3.2: **and the same to you** gleichfalls I/5.1
sandwich ['sænwɪdʒ] Butterbrot I/5.2
sardine [sɑ:'di:n] Sardine *II/2.3P*
Saturday ['sætədɪ] Samstag I/1.3: **on Saturdays** samstags I/1.3
sauce [sɔ:s] Soße I/6.3
save [seɪv] sparen I/5.2
say (said) [seɪ, sed] sagen (sagte, gesagt) I/6.1, II/3.1
school [sku:l] Schule I/2.3: **secondary school** weiterführende Schule *II/2.3P*
Scotland ['skɒtlənd] Schottland I/1.1
Scottish ['skɒtɪʃ] schottisch(-e, -er, -es); Schotte, Schottin I/1.1
screen [skri:n] Bildschirm *II/6.3P*
sea [si:] Meer I/3.1
season ['si:zn] Jahreszeit I/2.3
second ['sekənd] zweite(-r, -s) I/3.1: **secondary school** weiterführende Schule *II/2.3P*
secret ['si:krɪt] Geheimnis II/3.3
section ['sekʃn] Abschnitt, Ausschnitt *II/1.3P*
see (saw, seen) [si:, sɔ:, si:n] sehen (sah, gesehen) I/1.3, I/5.2, II/1.2: **I see** ach so (*Ausruf*) I/3.1
seldom ['seldəm] selten II/3.I
self-service [ˌself 'sɜ:vɪs] Selbstbedienung, Selbstbedienungs- I/6.2
sell (sold) [sel, səʊld] verkaufen (verkaufte, verkauft) I/5.1, II/1.1
send [send] senden, schicken *II/1.3*, II/3.1
sentence ['sentəns] Satz I/2.1
September [sep'tembə] September I/2.2
serious ['sɪərɪəs] ernst(haft) *II/1.R*, II/3.1
service ['sɜ:vɪs] Bedienung I/4.3; Dienst *II/2.3P*: **self-service** Selbstbedienung, Selbstbedienungs- I/6.2
set lunch ['set 'lʌntʃ] (Mittags-)Menü I/6.1
shall I ...? ['ʃæl aɪ] kann ich ...? (*Vorschlag, Angebot*) I/4.1: **shall we ...?** sollen wir II/1.1
share [ʃeə] teilen II/4.3
she [ʃi:] sie I/1.1
shine [ʃaɪn] scheinen II/3.2
shirt [ʃɜ:t] Hemd II/5.1
shock [ʃɒk] schockieren *II/4.3P*: **shocked** schockiert I/5.3
shoe [ʃu:] Schuh II/1.1: **beach shoe** Strandschuh, Badeschuh II/1.1
shop [ʃɒp] Geschäft, Laden I/2.R: **shop assistant** Verkäufer(-in), Ladengehilfe, Ladengehilfin II/2.1
shopper ['ʃɒpə] (Ein)Käufer(-in) *II/5.3P*
shopping ['ʃɒpɪŋ] Einkauf, Einkaufen *II/4.3P*: **do the shopping** Einkäufe machen *II/4.3P*; **go shopping** einkaufen gehen I/1.3
short [ʃɔ:t] kurz *II/2.1*: **shorthand** Kurzschrift *II/1.3P*
should [ʃʊd] sollen *II/1.2*; sollte(-st, -t, -n) II/3.1
shoulder ['ʃəʊldə] Schulter II/3.1
show [ʃəʊ] zeigen *II/G2*
shower ['ʃaʊə] Dusche I/4.1: **have/take a shower** (sich) duschen, eine Dusche nehmen II/5.1
sick [sɪk] krank II/3.2: **feel sick** übel, schlecht sein II/3.2
side [saɪd] Seite *II/G1*: **side-effect** Nebenwirkung *II/3.3P*
sight seeing ['saɪt ˌsi:ɪŋ] Besichtigung von Sehenswürdigkeiten II/5.3
sign [saɪn] Zeichen, Schild II/3.2
sincerely [sɪn'sɪəlɪ]: **yours sincerely** mit freundlichen Grüßen (*am Briefschluß*) *II/G1*
sing [sɪŋ] singen II/2.2
singer ['sɪŋə] Sänger(-in) II/2.2
single ['sɪŋgl] unverheiratet I/2.1; Einzel- I/4.1
sir [sɜ:] (mein) Herr (*höfliche Anrede*) II/5.1
sister ['sɪstə] Schwester I/2.1: **sister-in-law** Schwägerin II/6.1
sit [sɪt] sitzen *II/1.2*; setzen II/2.2
situation [ˌsɪtjʊ'eɪʃn] Situation II/2.I

size [saɪz] Größe II/5.1
skirt [skɜːt] Rock II/5.1
sleep [sliːp] schlafen II/3.1
slow [sləʊ] langsam II/2.2
small [smɔːl] klein I/3.1
smoke [sməʊk] Rauch II/2.2
smoke [sməʊk] rauchen II/2.2
smoker ['sməʊkə] Raucher *II/3.3P*
snack bar ['snæk bɑː] Schnellimbiß I/6.2
snow [snəʊ] Schnee II/1.3
snow [snəʊ] schneien II/1.2
so [səʊ] so I/6.1: **and so** also I/2.3
sock [sɒk] Socke, Strumpf II/5.1
sofa ['səʊfə] Sofa II/4.2
some [sʌm] einige, etwas I/3.1
someone ['sʌmwʌn] jemand(-em, -en) *II/1.1*, II/3.1
something ['sʌmθɪŋ] etwas II/1.1
sometimes ['sʌmtaɪmz] manchmal I/1.3
son [sʌn] Sohn I/2.1: **son-in-law** Schwiegersohn II/6.1
song [sɒŋ] Lied II/3.2
soon [suːn] bald *II/2.3P*, II/3.1
sore [sɔː] weh, wund, entzündet II/3.2: **sore throat** Halsentzündung II/3.2
sorry ['sɒrɪ]: **I'm sorry** es tut mir leid I/3.1
sort [sɔːt] Sorte, Art I/1.3: **what sort of** was für I/1.3
sort into [sɔːt 'ɪntʊ] sortieren in *II/1.2*
soup [suːp] Suppe I/6.1
south [saʊθ] Süd-, Süden I/3.1
spaghetti [spə'getɪ] Spaghetti I/3.2
Spanish ['spænɪʃ] spanisch(-e, -er, -es); Spanier(-in) I/1.I
speak (spoke) [spiːk, spəʊk] sprechen (sprach) I/1.1, I/5.2: **speaking practice** Sprachpraxis *II/1.1*
special ['speʃl] Sonder-, speziell I/4.1
specialist ['speʃəlɪst] Fach-, Spezial- II/5.3
speech bubble ['spiːtʃ ˌbʌbl] Sprechblase *II/6.R*
spell [spel] buchstabieren I/1.2
spelling ['spelɪŋ] Schreibweise, Rechtschreibung, Buchstabierung *II/5.1*
spend [spend] ausgeben I/5.2; verbringen *II/4.3P*, II/6.1
sport [spɔːt] Sport I/3.1
spring [sprɪŋ] Frühling I/2.2
square [skweə] Quadrat, Viereck *II/3.3*
squash [skwɒʃ] Squash *II/G2*
stairs [steəz] Treppe, Treppenhaus II/4.1
stamina ['stæmɪnə] Lebenskraft; *hier*: Ausdauer *II/1.3P*
stamp [stæmp] Briefmarke I/5.1
stand [stænd] stehen *II/4.3P*; stellen *II/6.3P*: **can't stand** nicht ausstehen können I/6.1
star [stɑː] Stern I/4.3: **film star** Filmstar II/1.2
start [stɑːt] Anfang I/5.R
start [stɑːt] beginnen, anfangen I/3.2; *hier*: losfahren *II/G3*
starter ['stɑːtə] Vorspeise I/6.1; *hier*: Einstieg *II/1.2*
statement ['steɪtmənt] Aussage, Behauptung *II/6.1*
station ['steɪʃn] Bahnhof I/3.1: **police station** Polizeiwache I/3.1
statistics [stə'tɪstɪks] Statistik *II/G1*
stay [steɪ] bleiben I/1.3; *hier*: übernachten I/5.2
steak [steɪk] Steak I/6.1
step [step] Schritt *II/1.1*
stereo ['sterɪəʊ] Stereo(anlage) II/4.2
still [stɪl] noch (immer) *II/G1*
stone [stəʊn] Stein (*Maßeinheit*) *II/G3*
stop [stɒp] Haltestelle I/5.2; Aufenthalt, Pause *II/4.3P*: **bus stop** Bushaltestelle I/5.2
stop [stɒp] anhalten, aufhören II/2.2
store [stɔː] Laden, Geschäft (*amerik.*) II/5.1: **department store** Kaufhaus, Warenhaus II/5.2
story ['stɔːrɪ] Geschichte *II/2.3P*
straight on ['streɪt 'ɒn] geradeaus I/3.1
strange [streɪndʒ] seltsam, komisch *II/5.3P*
stranger ['streɪndʒə] Fremde(-r) I/3.1
street [striːt] Straße (*in der Stadt, mit Häusern*) I/3.2
stressed [strest] gestreßt, unter Druck II/3.I
strudel ['struːdl] Strudel I/6.1
student ['stjuːdnt] Student(-in), *auch*: Kursteilnehmer(-in) II/1.2
study ['stʌdɪ] Studium *II/1.3P*
stupid ['stjuːpɪd] dumm, töricht II/5.1
suburb ['sʌbɜːb] Vorort I/3.1
successful [sək'sesfʊl] erfolgreich *II/3.3P*
such as [sʌtʃ əz] *hier*: wie (zum Beispiel) *II/2.3P*
sugar ['ʃʊgə] Zucker II/3.3
suggestion [sə'dʒestʃən] Vorschlag *II/1.1*
suitcase ['suːtkeɪs] Koffer II/5.3
summer ['sʌmə] Sommer I/2.2
sun [sʌn] Sonne II/1.3
Sunday ['sʌndɪ] Sonntag I/1.3
sunglasses ['sʌnglɑːsɪz] Sonnenbrille II/1.1
sunny ['sʌnɪ] sonnig II/1.2
suntan ['sʌntæn] (Sonnen)Bräune II/1.1: **suntan cream** Bräunungscreme II/1.1
super ['suːpə] herrlich, prima, super II/4.1
superlative [suː'pɜːlətɪv] Superlativ (*2. Steigerungsstufe*) *II/1.2*
supermarket ['suːpəˌmɑːkɪt] Supermarkt I/3.1
sure [ʃɔː] sicher I/5.3
surname ['sɜːneɪm] Familienname I/1.3
survival [sə'vaɪvl] Überleben *II/1.3P*
swim [swɪm] schwimmen I/1.2
swimming costume ['swɪmɪŋ ˌkɒstjuːm] Badeanzug II/1.1
swimming pool ['swɪmɪŋ puːl] Schwimmbad I/4.3
Swiss [swɪs] schweizerisch(-e, -er, -es); Schweizer(-in) I/1.1
switch off [swɪtʃ 'ɒf] ausschalten, abstellen *II/6.3P*
Switzerland ['swɪtsələnd] die Schweiz I/1.1
swop [swɒp] tauschen, austauschen II/6.1
symptom ['sɪmptəm] Symptom *II/3.3P*

T

table ['teɪbl] Tisch I/5.2
take (took, taken) [teɪk, tʊk, 'teɪkən] nehmen (nahm,

genommen) I/3.1, I/5.2, II/1.2: **take a photo** ein Foto machen I/5.2; **take up** aufnehmen, beginnen II/1.1
takeaway ['teɪkəˌweɪ] „zum Mitnehmen" I/6.2
talent ['tælənt] Talent, Begabung *II/1.3P*
talk [tɔ:k] reden I/6.2
taxi ['tæksɪ] Taxi I/5.2
tea [ti:] Tee I/2.2
teach [ti:tʃ] unterrichten, lehren *II/2.3P*
teacher ['ti:tʃə] Lehrer(-in), Kursleiter(-in) II/1.R
technique [tek'ni:k] Technik *II/1.3P*
technology [ˌtek'nɒlədʒɪ] Technologie, Technik *II/2.3P*
teeline ['ti:laɪn] (*moderne Form der Kurzschrift*) *II/1.3P*
telephone ['telɪfəʊn] Telefon I/1.2: **dial telephone** Selbstanschlußtelefon, Wähltelefon *II/6.3P*; **telephone answering machine** Telefonanrufbeantworter *II/6.3P*
telephone ['telɪfəʊn] telefonieren I/5.2
telephonist [tɪ'lefənɪst] Telefonist(-in) II/2.1
television ['telɪˌvɪʒn] Fernsehen, Fernseher I/1.3: **watch television** fernsehen I/1.3; **on television** im Fernsehen I/5.1
tell (told) [tel, təʊld] erzählen, sagen (sagte, gesagt) I/2.1, II/3.3
temperature ['temprətʃə] Temperatur II/3.2: **have a temperature** Temperatur/Fieber haben II/3.2
tennis ['tenɪs] Tennis I/1.2
terrible ['terəbl] schrecklich II/3.1
Texan ['teksən] texanisch(-e, -er, -es); Texaner(-in) *II/5.3P*
text [tekst] Text *II/1.1*
than [ðæn, ðən] als (*Vergleich*) II/1.1
thank you very much [θæŋk jʊ verɪ 'mʌtʃ] vielen herzlichen Dank I/3.1
thanks [θæŋks] danke I/1.2: **thanks a lot** danke vielmals I/3.1; **with thanks** dankend, mit Dank *II/G2*
that [ðæt, ðət] das I/1.1; jene(-r, -s) I/5.1; der, die, das; welche(-r, -s) II/4.1
the [ðə, ði:] der, die, das I/1.I
theatre ['θɪətə] Theater I/3.1
their [ðeə] ihr(-e) (*Mehrzahl*) I/1.3
theirs [ðeəz] ihre(-r, -s) der (die, das) ihr(ig)e II/5.2
them [ðem, ðəm] sie, ihnen (*Mehrzahl*) I/2.1
then [ðen] dann I/1.3
there [ðeə] dort I/2.3: **there is** es gibt, da ist I/3.1; **in there** da drinnen *II/G1*
these [ði:z] diese (*Mehrzahl*) I/5.I
they [ðeɪ] sie (*Mehrzahl*) I/1.2: **they say** man sagt II/5.3
thing [θɪŋ] Ding, Sache I/3.3
think (thought) [θɪŋk, θɔ:t] denken (dachte, gedacht), glauben, meinen I/3.3, II/5.1
this [ðɪs] dies(-e, -er, -es) I/1.1: **this morning** heute morgen I/4.R; **this time** dieses Mal II/1.1
those [ðəʊz] jene (*Mehrzahl*) I/5.1
thousand ['θaʊznd] Tausend *II/4.3P*
throat [θrəʊt] Hals, Kehle II/3.2: **sore throat** Halsentzündung II/3.2
through [θru:] durch *II/G3*
thumb [θʌm] Daumen *II/3.3P*
Thursday ['θɜ:zdɪ] Donnerstag I/2.1
ticket ['tɪkɪt] Ticket, Fahrkarte *II/4.3P*, II/5.2
tie [taɪ] Krawatte II/5.1
tights [taɪts] Strumpfhose II/5.1
time [taɪm] Zeit I/4.1; *hier*: Mal II/5.R: **a long time ago** vor längerer Zeit I/5.2; **this time** dieses Mal II/1.1; **what time?** (um) wieviel Uhr? I/4.R; **what's the time?** wieviel Uhr ist es? I/4.1
tin [tɪn] Blech, Dose *II/2.3P*
tired ['taɪəd] müde I/2.1
to [tʊ, tə] zu I/3.2; vor I/4.1
today [tə'deɪ] heute I/4.1
together [tə'geðə] zusammen *II/5.R*
toilet ['tɔɪlɪt] Toilette, WC II/4.1
tomato [tə'mɑ:təʊ] Tomate I/6.1
tomorrow [tə'mɒrəʊ] morgen I/6.1: **this time tomorrow** morgen um diese Zeit I/6.1; **the day after tomorrow** übermorgen II/6.2
tone [təʊn] *hier*: Spannung, Spannkraft *II/1.3P*
tonight [tə'naɪt] heute abend, heute nacht II/4.2
too [tu:] auch I/1.2; (*vorangestellt*) zu, allzu I/6.1
tooth (teeth) [tu:θ, ti:θ] Zahn (Zähne) II/1.1
toothache ['tu:θeɪk] Zahnschmerzen II/3.2
toothbrush ['tu:θbrʌʃ] Zahnbürste II/1.1
toothpaste ['tu:θpeɪst] Zahnpasta II/1.1
top [tɒp] Ober-, oberste(-r, -s) I/4.1: **at the top** oben *II/5.3P*; **on top of** (oben) auf II/3.1; **on top of the world** obenauf, rundum glücklich II/3.1
topic ['tɒpɪk] Thema, Gegenstand *II/1.R*
tourist ['tʊərɪst] Tourist I/3.1
towel ['taʊəl] Handtuch II/1.1
town [taʊn] Stadt I/3.1
traditional [trə'dɪʃnl] traditionell, herkömmlich *II/3.3P*, II/5.3
traffic ['træfɪk] Verkehr I/3.1: **traffic lights** Ampel I/3.1
train [treɪn] Zug I/4.I: **catch a train** einen Zug erreichen *II/4.3P*; **on a train** im Zug, in der Bahn I/4.2
train [treɪn] (sich) ausbilden, trainieren, eine Ausbildung machen II/2.1
training ['treɪnɪŋ] Ausbildung, Training II/6.1
translator [træns'leɪtə] Übersetzer *II/1.3P*
transport ['trænspɔ:t] Transport, Verkehr *II/G3*
travel ['trævl] Reise-, Reisen I/3.2: **travel agent** Reisebürokaufmann II/1.1
travel ['trævl] reisen I/4.I
traveller ['trævlə] Reisende(-r) *II/G2*
traveller's cheque [ˌtrævləz 'tʃek] Reisescheck I/5.2
treat [tri:t] behandeln *II/3.3P*
trip [trɪp] Ausflug, Reise *II/1.3P*

trousers ['traʊzəz] (lange) Hose(n) II/5.1: **a pair of trousers** eine lange Hose II/5.1
trout [traʊt] Forelle I/6.1
true [tru:] wahr I/3.1: **come true** wahr werden, sich verwirklichen II/6.3
try [traɪ] versuchen, probieren II/2.1: **try on** anprobieren II/5.1
Tuesday ['tju:zdɪ] Dienstag I/2.1
tunnel ['tʌnl] Tunnel *II/G3*
Turkish ['tɜ:kɪʃ] türkisch(-e, -er, -es) *II/G2*
turn [tɜ:n] drehen, wenden, abbiegen; ein-, ausschalten I/3.1
twice [twaɪs] zweimal *II/4.3P*
two-roomed flat ['tu:ru:md 'flæt] 2-Zimmer-Wohnung II/4.1
type [taɪp] tippen, mit der Maschine schreiben II/2.2
typewriter ['taɪpˌraɪtə] Schreibmaschine II/2.2
typical ['tɪpɪkl] typisch *II/G1*

U

uncle ['ʌŋkl] Onkel I/2.1
under ['ʌndə] unter II/3.1: **feel under the weather** nicht in Form sein II/3.1
underground garage ['ʌndəgraʊnd 'gærɑ:dʒ] Tiefgarage *II/4.3P*
underground station ['ʌndəgraʊnd 'steɪʃn] U-Bahn-Station, U-Bahn-Haltestelle *II/4.3P*
underline ['ʌndəlaɪn] unterstreichen *II/2.3*
understand [ʌndə'stænd] verstehen II/2.3
uninteresting [ˌʌn'ɪntrəstɪŋ] uninteressant *II/2.3P*
unique [ju:'ni:k] einzigartig *II/5.3P*
unit ['ju:nɪt] Einheit, Lektion I/1.I
university [ˌju:nɪ'vɜ:sətɪ] Universität *II/2.3P*, II/6.1
until [ʌn'tɪl] bis I/3.2
unusual [ʌn'ju:ʒl] ungewöhnlich II/5.3
up [ʌp]: **go up** hinaufgehen *II/4.3P*; **up to (my) eyes in work** bis zum Hals in Arbeit, bis über beide Ohren in Arbeit *II/G2*
upstairs [ˌʌp'steəz] oben, (die Treppe) hinauf/herauf II/4.1
us [ʌs, əs] uns I/2.1
USA (= United States of America) [ˌju: es 'eɪ] USA I/5.3
use [ju:s] Gebrauch *II/1.1*
use [ju:z] benutzen *II/1.2*, II/2.1: **used to** früher (etw. [regelmäßig] getan haben); pflegte(-n, -st, -t) zu II/2.1
usually ['ju:ʒəlɪ] gewöhnlich I/2.2

V

vacation [və'keɪʃn] Urlaub *II/G1*
value ['vælju:] Wert *II/5.3P*
various ['veərɪəs] verschieden *II/1.3P*
VAT (= Value Added Tax) [ˌvi: eɪ 'ti:, vælju: 'ædɪd tæks] Mehrwertsteuer I/4.1
vegetable ['vedʒtəbl] Gemüse(art) I/6.1
vegetarian [ˌvedʒɪ'teərɪən] vegetarisch(-e, -er, -es); Vegetarier(-in) I/6.1
veranda [və'rændə] Veranda *II/G2*
verb [vɜ:b] Verb, Zeitwort *II/1.2*
very ['verɪ] sehr I/2.1
video ['vɪdɪəʊ] Video I/3.2
view of ['vju: əv] Aussicht auf I/4.1
village ['vɪlɪdʒ] Dorf I/3.1
visit ['vɪzɪt] besuchen I/3.R
vocabulary [vəʊ'kæbjʊlərɪ] Wortschatz *II/1.1*
voluntary ['vɒləntrɪ] freiwillig *II/2.3P*
volunteer [ˌvɒlən'tɪə] Freiwillige(-r) *II/2.3P*

W

waiter ['weɪtə] Kellner I/6.1
waitress ['weɪtrɪs] Kellnerin II/2.1
walk [wɔ:k] Spaziergang I/5.R: **go for a walk** spazierengehen I/5.R
walk [wɔ:k] (zu Fuß) gehen I/3.2
want [wɒnt] wollen I/3.2
warm [wɔ:m] warm *II/4.3P*
wash [wɒʃ]: **have a wash** sich waschen *II/4.3P*
wash basin ['wɔ:ʃ ˌbeɪsn] Waschbecken *II/4.3P*
washing machine ['wɒʃɪŋ məˌʃi:n] Waschmaschine II/4.2
watch [wɒtʃ] zuschauen I/1.3
water ['wɔ:tə] Wasser I/6.1
way [weɪ] Weg I/3.1; Art, Weise *II/1.R*: **by the way** übrigens II/5.1; **way of life** Lebensweise, Lebensstil *II/2.3P*
we [wi:] wir I/1.2
weather ['weðə] Wetter II/1.1: **feel under the weather** nicht in Form sein II/3.1
Wednesday ['wenzdɪ] Mittwoch I/2.1
week [wi:k] Woche I/2.2
weekend [ˌwi:k'end] Wochenende I/4.1
weight [weɪt] Gewicht *II/G3*
welcome ['welkəm]: **you're welcome** bitte (sehr), gern geschehen I/3.1; **welcome to** willkommen in I/4.1
well [wel] gut I/2.1; *etwa*: nun ja I/3.1; *hier*: gesund *II/1.3P*: **get on well with** gut auskommen mit II/6.1; **well-known** berühmt, wohlbekannt II/5.3
Welsh [welʃ] walisisch(-e, -er, -es); Waliser(-in) I/3.1
were [wɜ:] wäre(-st, -t, -n) II/3.1
west [west] West-, Westen I/3.1
what [wɒt] was I/1.I; welche(-r, -s) I/1.1: **what about …?** wie ist es mit …? I/2.1; **what is he like?** wie sieht er aus? *II/G3*; **what time?** (um) wieviel Uhr? I/4.R; **what's the time?** wieviel Uhr ist es? I/4.1
when [wen] wenn I/2.3; wann I/2.2; als I/5.2
where [weə] wo(-hin, -her) I/1.I: **where are the people from?** woher sind die Menschen? I/1.I
which [wɪtʃ] welche(-r, -s) I/2.3
while [waɪl] Weile II/6.1: **for a while** eine Zeitlang, einige Zeit II/6.1
while [waɪl] während II/4.1

whisky ['wɪskɪ] Whisky II/3.3
whistle ['wɪsl] pfeifen I/1.2
white [waɪt] weiß I/5.1: **in black and white** schwarz auf weiß II/5.R
who [hu:] wer, wem, wen I/5.2
whose [hu:z] wessen II/5.2
why [waɪ] warum I/5.1
wide [waɪd] breit, weit *II/4.3P*
wife (wives) [waɪf, waɪvz] Ehefrau(-en) I/1.3
will [wɪl] (*Hilfsverb, Zukunft*) I/6.1
win (won) [wɪn, wʌn] gewinnen (gewann, gewonnen) II/1.3
window ['wɪndəʊ] Fenster II/4.1
windy ['wɪndɪ] windig II/1.2
wine [waɪn] Wein I/1.3
winter ['wɪntə] Winter I/2.2
wish [wɪʃ] (Glück)Wunsch *II/G1, II/4.1*
with [wɪð] mit I/1.1
without [wɪ'ðaʊt] ohne *II/1.3P*
woman (women) ['wʊmən, 'wɪmɪn] Frau (Frauen) I/3.1
won't (= will not) [wəʊnt] (*Hilfsverb, Zukunft*) I/6.2
wonder ['wʌndə] sich fragen *II/6.3P*
wonderful ['wʌndəfʊl] wunderbar I/1.2
word [w3:d] Wort I/2.I
wordfield ['w3:dfi:ld] Wortgruppe, Wortfeld *II/1.R*
work [w3:k] Arbeit I/1.2: **at work** bei der Arbeit I/1.2
work [w3:k] arbeiten I/1.3: **work for** arbeiten bei I/1.3
worker ['w3:kə] Arbeiter(-in) II/2.1
working hours ['w3:kɪŋ 'aʊəz] Arbeitszeit, -stunden II/2.3
workplace ['w3:kpleɪs] Arbeitsplatz *II/4.3P*
world [w3:ld] Welt I/5.1
worry ['wʌrɪ] sich sorgen, sich Sorgen machen II/3.3: **worried** besorgt, beunruhigt *II/G3*
worse [w3:s] schlechter, schlimmer II/1.2
worst [w3:st] schlechteste(-r, -s), schlimmste(-r, -s) II/1.2
would [wʊd]: **I would like** ich möchte I/4.1; **would you mind ...?** würden Sie/würdest du/würdet ihr so freundlich sein ...? I/5.1
write [raɪt]: **write (down)** (auf)schreiben I/2.1; **write in** einsetzen *II/1.1*
writer ['raɪtə] Autor, Schriftsteller, Verfasser *II/6.2*
wrong [rɒŋ] falsch, verkehrt *II/G2*

Y

yard [jɑ:d] Yard, Elle (*Maßeinheit*) *II/G3*
year [jɪə] Jahr I/2.3
yellow ['jeləʊ] gelb I/5.1
yes [jes] ja I/1.1
yesterday ['jestədɪ] gestern I/4.2: **the day before yesterday** vorgestern II/6.2
yet [jet] schon II/6.1: **not yet** noch nicht II/6.1
you [ju:] Sie, dich, euch; Ihnen, dir I/1.1; du, ihr I/1.1
young [jʌŋ] jung II/2.2
your [jɔ:] Ihr(-e), dein(-e), euer(eure) I/1.1
yours [jɔ:z] Ihre/eure/deine(-r, -s), der (die, das) Ihr/euer/dein(ig)e II/5.2: **yours sincerely** mit freundlichen Grüßen (*am Briefschluß*) *II/G1*
yourself [jɔ:'self] (du, ihr, Sie) selbst *II/1.3P*

Z

zero ['zɪərəʊ] Null I/1.2

Fact finder

Armstrong, Neil [niːl ˈɑːmstrɒŋ]	amerikanischer Astronaut (*1930); betrat 1969 als erster Mensch den Mond
Bell, Alexander Graham [ælɪgˈzɑːndə ˈgreɪəm bel]	(1847-1922), Erfinder des Telefons
Bhutan [buːˈtɑːn]	Bhutan (Königreich im Himalaja)
Bristol [ˈbrɪstl]	Stadt in Westengland
British Airways [ˌbrɪtɪʃ ˈeəweɪz]	britische Fluggesellschaft
Cambridge [ˈkeɪmbrɪdʒ]	Universitätsstadt in England
Canada [ˈkænədə]	Kanada
Canterbury [ˈkæntəbrɪ]	Stadt im Südosten Englands
China [ˈtʃaɪnə]	China
Corfu [kɔːˈfuː]	griechische Adriainsel
Covent Garden [ˌkɒvənt ˈgɑːdn]	Platz und Opernhaus im Zentrum von London
Denmark [ˈdenmɑːk]	Dänemark
England [ˈɪŋglənd]	England
Greece [griːs]	Griechenland
Hahnemann, Samuel [ˈsæmjʊəl ˈhɑːnəmæn]	Begründer der Homöopathie
Harrod, Henry Charles [ˈhenrɪ tʃɑːlz ˈhærəd]	Begründer des Kaufhauses Harrods
Harrods [ˈhærədz]	Kaufhaus in London
Hillary, Edmund [ˈedmənd ˈhɪlərɪ]	neuseeländischer Bergsteiger und Polarforscher (*1917)
Hilton Hotel [ˈhɪltən həʊˈtel]	Name eines Hotels
Hotel Apollo Beach [həʊˈtel əˈpɒləʊ biːtʃ]	Name eines Hotels
Hotel Lido [həʊˈtel ˈliːdəʊ]	Name eines Hotels
Hotel Palace [həʊˈtel ˈpælɪs]	Name eines Hotels
Hotel Paradise [həʊˈtel ˈpærədaɪs]	Name eines Hotels
Hyde Park [ˈhaɪd ˈpɑːk]	Park in London
Indonesia [ˌɪndəˈniːzjə]	Indonesien
Istanbul [ˌɪstænˈbʊl]	Stadt in der Türkei
Japan [dʒəˈpæn]	Japan
Knightsbridge [ˈnaɪtsbrɪdʒ]	Stadtteil von London
Kumbaya [kʊmbaɪˈjɑː]	Name eines traditionellen amerik. Liedes
Lincoln [ˈlɪŋkən]	Stadt in Ostengland
Liverpool [ˈlɪvəpuːl]	Hafenstadt im Nordwesten Englands
Los Angeles [lɒs ˈændʒɪliːz]	Großstadt an der amerik. Westküste im Bundesstaat Kalifornien
McDonald's [məkˈdɒnəldz]	Restaurantkette
Madrid [məˈdrɪd]	Hauptstadt von Spanien
Manchester [ˈmæntʃɪstə]	Stadt im Nordwesten Englands
Mega Magazines [ˈmegə ˌmægəˈziːnz]	Name eines Zeitschriftenverlags
Mega Mags (= Mega Magazines) [ˈmegə mægz]	Name eines Zeitschriftenverlags
Monaco [ˈmɒnəkəʊ]	Monaco
Morocco [məˈrɒkəʊ]	Marokko
Moscow [ˈmɒskəʊ]	Moskau
Mount Everest [maʊnt ˈevərɪst]	höchster Berg der Erde in Nepal (8872 m)
Nepal [nɪˈpɔːl]	Nepal (Staat im Himalaja)
New York [ˌnjuː ˈjɔːk]	Großstadt an der Ostküste der USA
Nigeria [naɪˈdʒɪərɪə]	Nigeria (Staat in Afrika)
Oxford Street [ˈɒksfəd ˌstriːt]	große Einkaufsstraße in London
Pakistan [ˌpɑːkɪˈstɑːn]	Pakistan
Persia [ˈpɜːʃə]	Persien
Prince Charles [prɪns ˈtʃɑːlz]	britischer Thronfolger (*1948)
Princess Diana [ˈprɪnses daɪˈænə]	Ehefrau von Prinz Charles (*1961)
Reagan, Ronald [ˌrɒnld ˈreɪgən]	ehemaliger Präsident der USA (*1911)
Rhine [raɪn]	Rhein (*dt. Fluß*)
Rolls Royce [ˌrəʊlz ˈrɔɪs]	Automarke
Rome [rəʊm]	Rom (Hauptstadt von Italien)
Russia [ˈrʌʃə]	Rußland
Savona [səˈvəʊnə]	Stadt in Italien
Sweden [ˈswiːdn]	Schweden
Texas [ˈteksəs]	Stadt in den USA
Thailand [ˈtaɪlænd]	Thailand (Land in Asien)
Thames [temz]	Themse (*Fluß durch London*)
Times, The ~ [ðə taɪmz]	englische Tageszeitung
Tinos [ˈtiːnɒs]	griechische Insel (im Ägäischen Meer)

Tokyo ['təʊkjəʊ]	Tokio (Hauptstadt von Japan)
Toronto [tə'rɒntəʊ]	Stadt in Kanada
Turin [tjʊ'rɪn]	Stadt in Norditalien
Voluntary Service Overseas (VSO) ['vɒləntrɪ 'sɜ:vɪs ˌəʊvə'si:z]	Überseedienst für Freiwillige (eine Institution der Entwicklungshilfe)
Waizoona [waɪ'zu:nə]	Ortsname (fiktiv)
Westminster Abbey ['wesˌmɪnstə 'æbɪ]	Kirche in London
Wimbledon ['wɪmbldən]	Ortsteil von Merton bei London; Austragungsort der internationalen englischen Tennismeisterschaften
Wukari [wʊ'kɑ:rɪ]	Ort in Nigeria
York [jɔ:k]	Stadt in Ostengland

People's names

Women

Angela ['ændʒələ]
Ann [æn]
Anne [æn]
Barbara ['bɑ:bəra]
Betty ['betɪ]
Caroline ['kærəlaɪn]
Christine [krɪ'sti:n]
Diana [daɪ'ænə]
Doreen [dɔ:'ri:n]
Doris ['dɒrɪs]
Dorothy ['dɒrəθɪ]
Emma ['emə]
Erica ['erɪkə]
Eve [i:v]
Janet ['dʒænɪt]
Karin ['kærɪn]
Kath [kæθ]
Lena ['li:nə]
Linda ['lɪndə]
Lynn [lɪn]
Marge [mɑ:dʒ]
Mary ['meərɪ]
Nancy ['nænsɪ]
Pamela ['pæmələ]
Paula ['pɔ:lə]
Sarah ['seərə]
Sharon ['ʃærən]
Sue [su:]
Susan ['su:zn]
Vanessa [və'nesa]

Men

Al [æl]
Albert ['ælbət]
Andrew ['ændru:]
Bob [bɒb]]
Charles [tʃɑ:lz]
Edgar ['edgə]
Fred [fred]
George [dʒɔ:dʒ]
John [dʒɒn]
Mark [mɑ:k]
Paul [pɔ:l]
Peter ['pi:tə]
Philip ['fɪlɪp]
Samuel ['sæmjʊəl]
Simon ['saɪmən]
Steve [sti:v]
Thomas ['tɒməs]
Tim [tɪm]
Tom [tɒm]

Families

Bagley ['bæglɪ]
Brown [braʊn]
Bryant ['braɪənt]
Day [deɪ]
Drake [dreɪk]
Garrard ['gærɑ:d]
Hamilton ['hæmɪltən]
Hogan ['həʊgən]
Jones [dʒəʊnz]
Lamb [læm]
Lloyd [lɔɪd]
Marshall ['mɑ:ʃl]
Newton ['nju:tn]
Partington ['pɑ:tɪŋtən]
Pelman ['pelmən]
Peter ['pi:tə]
Reach [ri:tʃ]
Read [ri:d]
Riley ['raɪlɪ]
Ryan ['raɪən]
Selby ['selbɪ]
Selwood ['selwʊd]
Simpson ['sɪmpsn]
Smith [smɪθ]
Stafford ['stæfəd]
Walsh [wɔ:lʃ]
Williams ['wɪljəmz]
Wilson ['wɪlsn]

Bitte geben Sie die Bestellkarte(n) an Ihre Buchhandlung oder senden Sie sie an unseren Verlag.

Absender:

Name/Vorname

Straße/Nr.

PLZ/Ort

Bitte liefern Sie die angekreuzten Titel über die Buchhandlung

Name/Straße

PLZ/Ort

(Sollte keine Buchhandlung genannt sein, erfolgt die Lieferung über eine Buchhandlung nach Wahl des Verlags.)

Antwort

An den Verlag
Langenscheidt-Longman
Postfach 40 11 20

80711 München

Absender:

Name/Vorname

Straße/Nr.

PLZ/Ort

Bitte liefern Sie die angekreuzten Titel über die Buchhandlung

Name/Straße

PLZ/Ort

(Sollte keine Buchhandlung genannt sein, erfolgt die Lieferung über eine Buchhandlung nach Wahl des Verlags.)

Antwort

An den Verlag
Langenscheidt-Longman
Postfach 40 11 20

80711 München

Mit unseren Begleitmaterialien zu English Network zu optimalen Lernerfolgen

Unsere Lernercassetten bzw. -CDs enthalten alle mit **weißem** Cassettensymbol gekennzeichneten Dialoge (mit Nachsprechpausen!) sowie Ausspracheübungen aus den jeweiligen Lektionsteilen.
Unsere Textcassetten bzw. -CDs enthalten Hörtexte, die für den Gruppenunterricht mit Kursleiter/in gedacht sind; ein **schwarzes** Cassettensymbol weist auf solche Texte hin. Wenn Sie diese Texte zu Hause nacharbeiten möchten, dann empfiehlt sich die Anschaffung.
Unsere Nachschlagegrammatik unterstützt Ihren Lernweg sinnvoll durch alle Network-Bände. Vergessene Grammatik kann so jederzeit nachgeschlagen werden. Das Workbook stellt zusätzlich Übungsmaterial bereit.
Unser Wiederholungsheft Break 2 frischt erworbene Kenntnisse im Schnelldurchgang in der unterrichtsfreien Zeit wieder auf – Sie sind für den neuen Kursbeginn dann bestens gerüstet.

Ich bestelle hiermit:

English Network 2

O **Lernercassette 1 (Units 1–3)**
(Best.-Nr. 3-526-57 **567-3** / DM 18,90* / öS 140,–* / sFr. 18,–*)

O **Lernercassette 2 (Units 4–6)**
(Best.-Nr. 3-526-57 **568-1** / DM 18,90* / öS 140,–* / sFr. 18,–*)

O **3 Lerner-CDs (Units 1–6)**
(Best.-Nr. 3-526-57 **525-8** / DM 36,90* / öS 273,–* / sFr. 34,–*)

O **2 Textcassetten (Units 1–6) – Institutsversion –**
(Best.-Nr. 3-526-57 **566-5** / DM 39,80* / öS 295,–* / sFr. 37,–*)

O **2 Text-CDs (Units 1–6) – Institutsversion –**
(Best.-Nr. 3-526-57 **521-5** / DM 39,80* / öS 295,–* / sFr. 37,–*)

O **Break 2 (Wiederholungsheft)**
(Best.-Nr. 3-526-**50 410-5** / DM 11,20* / öS 82,–* / sFr. 10,50*)

O **Nachschlagegrammatik**
(begleitet alle Network-Bände)
(Best.-Nr. 3-526-**50 412-1** / DM 22,90* / öS 167,–* / sFr. 21,–*)

O **Workbook 1 zur Nachschlagegrammatik**
(begleitet Network 1–3)
(Best.-Nr. 3-526-**50 413-X** / DM 11,20* / öS 82,–* / sFr. 10,50*)

Unterschrift/Datum (Absender auf Vorderseite ---->)

* Preisänderung vorbehalten
- Zutreffendes ist angekreuzt -

Ich bestelle hiermit:

English Network 2

O **Lernercassette 1 (Units 1–3)**
(Best.-Nr. 3-526-57 **567-3** / DM 18,90* / öS 140,–* / sFr. 18,–*)

O **Lernercassette 2 (Units 4–6)**
(Best.-Nr. 3-526-57 **568-1** / DM 18,90* / öS 140,–* / sFr. 18,–*)

O **3 Lerner-CDs (Units 1–6)**
(Best.-Nr. 3-526-57 **525-8** / DM 36,90* / öS 273,–* / sFr. 34,–*)

O **2 Textcassetten (Units 1–6) – Institutsversion –**
(Best.-Nr. 3-526-57 **566-5** / DM 39,80* / öS 295,–* / sFr. 37,–*)

O **2 Text-CDs (Units 1–6) – Institutsversion –**
(Best.-Nr. 3-526-57 **521-5** / DM 39,80* / öS 295,–* / sFr. 37,–*)

O **Break 2 (Wiederholungsheft)**
(Best.-Nr. 3-526-**50 410-5** / DM 11,20* / öS 82,–* / sFr. 10,50*)

O **Nachschlagegrammatik**
(begleitet alle Network-Bände)
(Best.-Nr. 3-526-**50 412-1** / DM 22,90* / öS 167,–* / sFr. 21,–*)

O **Workbook 1 zur Nachschlagegrammatik**
(begleitet Network 1–3)
(Best.-Nr. 3-526-**50 413-X** / DM 11,20* / öS 82,–* / sFr. 10,50*)

Unterschrift/Datum (Absender auf Vorderseite ---->)

* Preisänderung vorbehalten
- Zutreffendes ist angekreuzt -

Übungsanweisungen

Diese Wörter und Wendungen kommen im Lehrbuch häufiger vor. Sie brauchen sie nur zu verstehen, aber nicht selbst anwenden zu können. Damit Sie die gängigen Wendungen schnell nachschlagen können, haben wir sie für Sie hier gesammelt aufgeführt.

A five-minute conversation	Eine fünfminütige Unterhaltung
Answer the questions.	Beantworten Sie die Fragen.
Ask a partner.	Fragen Sie einen Partner / eine Partnerin.
Ask the(se) questions.	Stellen Sie die(se) Fragen.
Before you go on ...	Ehe Sie weitermachen ...
Complete. (Please ...)	Ergänzen Sie. (Bitte ...)
Comprehension	Verständnis(übung)
Correct. (Please ...)	Berichtigen Sie. (Bitte ...)
Dialogue	Dialog
Grammar	Grammatik
Grammar in action	Grammatik in Aktion
Homestudy	Arbeit für zuhause
How to say it: ... Practise the intonation first.	So sagen Sie es richtig: ... Üben Sie zuerst die Satzbetonung.
Language in use	Sprache im Gebrauch
Language and life	Sprache und Leben
Listen. Are the sentences about ... true or false?	Hören Sie. Sind die Sätze über ... richtig oder falsch?
Listen and check your answers.	Hören Sie und überprüfen Sie Ihre Antworten.
Look at page	Schlagen Sie Seite ... auf.
Make sentences / groups of four.	Bilden Sie Sätze / Vierergruppen.
Match. (Please ...)	Ordnen Sie zu. (Bitte ...)
Personal dictionary You want to .... What words do you need?	Persönliches Wörterbuch Sie möchten .... Welche Wörter benötigen Sie dazu?
Repeat the words / sentences / questions / expressions.	Wiederholen Sie die Wörter / Sätze / Fragen / Wendungen.
Revision activities	Wiederholungsübungen
Speaking practice. Listen and do the exercises on the cassette.	Sprechübung. Hören und machen Sie die Übungen auf der Cassette.
Starter	Einstieg
Step	Schritt
Vocabulary	Wortschatz
Write about ... / down the answer.	Schreiben Sie über ... / die Antwort auf.

Acknowledgements

We are grateful to the following for permission to reproduce/use copyright material:

Illustrations

Jürgen Bartz, München: pp. **IV**, **2**, **4** (top), **7**, **8**, **14**, **22** (top), **23** (middle left), **26** (top left), **30**, **31** (middle right)
NAS/Distr. Bulls: pp. **114**, **122**
S.I./NAS/Distr. Bulls: p. **118**
John Fraser, Long Sutton, Somerset: pp. **3** (bottom), **4** (bottom), **5**, **11** (bottom), **12**, **13**, **14**, **21** (bottom), **22** (bottom), **23** (middle, bottom right), **26** (top right), **31** (middle left, bottom), **35**, **39** (bottom), **41** (bottom), **47** (bottom), **55**, **57**, **65** (top), **70**, **71**, **73**, **75**, **77**, **78**, **80**, **83**, **85**, **90**, **91**, **94**, **95**, **96**, **97**, **99**
Kathrin Hälbich, München: p. **72**
Bettina Koenig, München: pp. **18**, **69**, **74**, **98**
Kunstkonzern Werner Lüning, Lübeck (Punch): pp. **65** (bottom), **92**, **116**, **119**
Chris Ryley, Pulborough, Sussex: pp. **3** (top), **6**, **10**, **11** (top), **17**, **21** (top), **28**, **29**, **36**, **38**, **39** (top), **46**, **47** (top), **54**
Heribert Schulmeyer, Köln: pp. **41** (middle), **44**, **48**

Photographs

Adidas AG, PR & Presse Deutschland, Herzogenaurach: p. **30** (bottom middle)
Beate Andler-Teufel, München: pp. **VI** (4th from top), **19** (bottom)
Archiv für Kunst und Geschichte, Berlin: pp. **VII** (4th from bottom; 2nd from bottom; bottom), **25** (left), **45** (top; 2nd from bottom, bottom),
British Consulate-General, München: p. **30** (middle right)
British Tourist Authority, London: pp. **VII** (2nd from top), **37** (2nd from top)
Deutsche Lufthansa AG, München: pp. **V** (3rd from bottom), **9** (2nd from top)
Deutsche Presse-Agentur GmbH, Frankfurt: pp. **33** (right), **51** (Lehtikuva Oy)
EWA Elizabeth Whiting & Associates, London: p. **32** (top middle)
Focus Photo- und Presseagentur, Hamburg: p. **25** (right)
Mohamed Ali Fayed, Chairman of Harrods Ltd., London: p. **43** (middle left & right)
Kate Goldrick, London/Beate Andler-Teufel, München: p. **15**
IBM Deutschland GmbH, Stuttgart: pp. **V** (bottom), **9** (bottom)
Günther Knopp, München: pp. **V** (2nd from top), **1** (2nd from top)
Longman Group UK Ltd., Harlow Essex, Trevor Clifford: p. **32** (top left & right)
Bildagentur Mauritius GmbH, Mittenwald: pp. **V** (3rd from top: Messerschmidt; 4th from top: Superstock; 4th from bottom: Rosenfeld), VI (2nd from top: Rawi), **1** (2nd from bottom: Messerschmidt; bottom: Superstock), **9** (top: Rosenfeld), **19** (2nd from top: Rawi), **20** (Grasser)
Österreichische Fremdenverkehrswerbung, München: p. **30** (bottom left)
Gaynor Ramsey, Zürich: pp. **VII** (4th from top), **33** (top left), **37** (bottom)
Petra Spiola Pressefotografin, Wien: pp. **VI** (4th from bottom; 3rd from bottom; bottom), **27** (top; middle; bottom: from "Hundertwasserhaus", Verlag ORAC)
Süddeutscher Verlag Bilderdienst, München: pp. **VII** (3rd from bottom), **30** (middle left), **45** (2nd from top)
Transglobe Agency, Hamburg: p. **33** (middle left: Gera Dillon)
TSW Tony Stone Worldwide Bildagentur, München: pp. **V** (top: Alan Kearney), **VI** (top: Jon Gray; 3rd from top: Oliver Benn), **VII** (3rd from top: Jean Marc Truchet), **1** (top: A. Kearney), **19** (top: J. Gray; 2nd from bottom: O. Benn), **37** (2nd from bottom: J. M. Truchet), **43** (top left: John Freeman)
U.S. Information Service, Bonn: p. **30** (bottom right)
Angelika Wagner, München: pp. VII (top), **2**, **37** (top)
Ernst Wagner sen., Schwabmünchen: p. **24**
John Walmsley Photo-Library, Epsom, Surrey: pp. **V** (2nd from bottom), **9** (2nd from bottom)
Farbbildarchiv Wolfsberger, Wien: pp. **VI** (bottom), **27** (2nd from bottom)

Cover photograph by V.K.Guy Photography Ltd., Windermere, Cumbria

We should be very grateful for any information which might assist us in tracing the copyright owners of sources which we have been unable to acknowledge.

*Wir führen auch die bekannten **Penguin Readers** in unserem Programm. Mit den folgenden Lektüren, die auf Ihre Lernstufe abgestimmt sind, können Sie Unterhaltsames und Spannendes in der Originalsprache lesen und so »ganz nebenbei« Ihren Wortschatz erweitern und Ihr Englisch verbessern.*

The Black Cat and Other Stories
Edgar Allan Poe
Vier mysteriöse Kurzgeschichten in bewährter Edgar A. Poe-Manier.
Bestellnr. 3-526-**41774**-1
DM 10,50 / öS 77,- / sFr. 10,50

Braveheart
Randall Wallace
Die Geschichte von William Wallace, der die Schotten im Freiheitskampf gegen England führte.
Bestellnr. 3-526-**41680**-X
DM 10,50 / öS 77,- / sFr. 10,50

Forrest Gump
Winston Groom
Der gutmütige und einfältige Forrest Gump aus Alabama erreicht in seinem Leben vieles, wovon manch patriotisch gesinnter US-Amerikaner träumt: z.B. einen Orden oder eine Audienz beim US-Präsidenten.
Bestellnr. 3-526-**41781**-4
DM 10,50 / öS 77,- / sFr. 10,50

The Fugitive
J. M. Dillard
Dr. Kimble ist auf der Flucht vor der Polizei, die ihn für den Mörder seiner Frau hält; er selbst sucht verzweifelt nach dem tatsächlichen Mörder.
Bestellnr. 3-526-**41793**-8
DM 10,50 / öS 77,- / sFr. 10,50

Psycho
Robert Bloch
Marions Aufenthalt im Bates Motel wird zum unerträglichen Alptraum. Das Buch zum berühmten Hitchcock-Thriller.
Bestellnr. 3-526-**41672**-9
DM 10,50 / öS 77,- / sFr. 10,50

Rain Man
Leonore Fleischer
Als Charlie Babbitt nach dem Tod seines Vaters seinen in einem Heim lebenden autistischen Bruder kennen lernt, beginnt für beide ein neues Leben voller Überraschungen.
Bestellnr. 3-526-**41785**-7
DM 10,50 / öS 77,- / sFr. 10,50

Fragen Sie Ihren Buchhändler nach diesen Titeln - oder bestellen Sie mit der Bestellkarte beim Verlag.

Ich bestelle hiermit die folgenden Lektüren:

- ○ **The Black Cat and Other Stories** (Best.-Nr. 3-526-**41774**-1 / DM 10,50* / öS 77,-* / sFr. 10,50*)
- ○ **Braveheart** (Best.-Nr. 3-526-**41680**-X / DM 10,50* / öS 77,-* / sFr. 10,50*)
- ○ **Forrest Gump** (Best.-Nr. 3-526-**41781**-4 / DM 10,50* / öS 77,-* / sFr. 10,50*)
- ○ **The Fugitive** (Best.-Nr. 3-526-**41793**-8 / DM 10,50* / öS 77,-* / sFr. 10,50*)
- ○ **Psycho** (Best.-Nr. 3-526-**41672**-9 / DM 10,50* / öS 77,-* / sFr. 10,50*)
- ○ **Rain Man** (Best.-Nr. 3-526-**41785**-7 / DM 10,50* / öS 77,-* / sFr. 10,50*)

- Zutreffendes ist angekreuzt - *Preisänderung vorbehalten

Unterschrift/Datum (Absender auf Vorderseite ---->)

Absender:

Name/Vorname

Straße/Nr.

PLZ/Ort

Bitte liefern Sie die angekreuzten Titel
über die Buchhandlung

Name/Straße

PLZ/Ort

(Sollte keine Buchhandlung genannt sein, erfolgt die Lieferung über eine Buchhandlung nach Wahl des Verlags.)

Antwort

An den Verlag
Langenscheidt-Longman
Postfach 40 11 20

80711 München